Professorial Pathways

Professorial Pathways

Academic Careers in a Global Perspective

EDITED BY

Martin J. Finkelstein

Glen A. Jones

Johns Hopkins University Press

Baltimore

© 2019 Johns Hopkins University Press
All rights reserved. Published 2019
Printed in the United States of America on acid-free paper
9 8 7 6 5 4 3 2 1

Johns Hopkins University Press
2715 North Charles Street
Baltimore, Maryland 21218-4363
www.press.jhu.edu

Library of Congress cataloging data is available.

ISBN-13: 978-1-4214-2873-4 (hc: alk. paper)
ISBN-10: 1-4214-2873-3 (hc: alk. paper)
ISBN-13: 978-1-4214-2874-1 (electronic)
ISBN-10: 1-4214-2874-1 (electronic)

A catalog record for this book is available from the British Library.

Special discounts are available for bulk purchases of this book.
For more information, please contact Special Sales at 410-516-6936
or specialsales@press.jhu.edu.

Johns Hopkins University Press uses environmentally friendly book
materials, including recycled text paper that is composed of at least
30 percent post-consumer waste, whenever possible.

Contents

Acknowledgments

This has been a collaborative project from the beginning, emerging from our preliminary conversations at conferences in Wuhan and Berlin, and then gaining momentum as we saw the opportunity to deepen the international conversation on academic work. Our early draft materials were widely circulated to our colleagues from the Changing Academic Professions project who provided valuable feedback. We are deeply indebted to the national experts who contributed outstanding chapters that were foundational to the project and to the many who also participated in project meetings in Rome and São Paulo and made significant contributions to the conceptual development of the study. The meeting at the University of São Paulo was expertly coordinated by Elizabeth Balbachevsky with financial support from FAPESP—the State of São Paulo Science Foundation—through the project no. 2015-13858-9. We also recognize the support given by the University of São Paulo's Research Centre for Public Policy Studies (NUPPs/USP) and the supportive role of Renato Hyuda Pedrosa, from the State University of Campinas (UNICAMP). Additional support for the meeting was provided by the Ontario Research Chair in Postsecondary Education Policy and Measurement.

Glen would like to acknowledge research funding from the Social Sciences and Humanities Research Council of Canada and the Ontario Ministry of Advanced Education and Skills Development (through the Ontario Human Capital Research and Innovation Fund). Marty would like to acknowledge travel assistance from the College of Education and Human Services at Seton Hall University.

Diane Barbaric, an outstanding University of Toronto PhD student, provided editorial assistance in the final stages of the project. She carefully reviewed every chapter and gave thoughtful, substantive suggestions. We are extremely grateful for her enormous contribution to strengthening the national chapters. On the US side of the border, Kinta Montilus, another outstanding doctoral student, at Seton Hall University, whipped the completed manuscript into "publisher-ready" shape. Finally, we are also grateful for the feedback on the concluding chapter that we received from Philip Altbach, Christine Musselin, Barbara Kehm, Akiyoshi Yonezawa, and Peter Scott. Their comments played an important role in strengthening this integrative chapter, while the abiding shortcomings remain our own.

1 | Introduction

The Academic Profession Enters
a New Global Era

MARTIN J. FINKELSTEIN and GLEN A. JONES

The first decade of the twenty-first century has focused increased attention on the academic profession in both the developed and developing countries worldwide. The academic staff of universities, those who offer instruction in degree programs and conduct research, is widely viewed as a—if not *the*—key driver of the knowledge economy and society in at least two analytically distinct ways. First, in many nations, university faculty have historically been the leaders and chief production workers in national research and development (R&D) systems, directly responsible for knowledge production and dissemination. Even in those nations that have historically separated the research and development function from the university sector (e.g., France and Russia) there is clear evidence of a developing convergence and integration across these sectors (Musselin, 2010). Second, beyond stewardship of the national R&D system, academic staff are universally the stewards of the national training and human capital development system. They train the next generation of scientists and skilled workers for the knowledge economy. The current historical moment reflects the unique confluence of this growing recognition of the academic profession's key position in national economic futures with the realization that the strength and stature of academic professions have been strained—perhaps to the breaking point—in many countries over the past generation by the pressures of massification. Indeed, the imperative to accommodate demands for increased access globally has placed enormous pressures on the national higher education systems to economize, to do more with less. This has effectively translated into placing greater workloads on individual faculty, allowing the working environment and conditions to deteriorate, and, in many countries, precipitating a wholesale reconfiguration of the profession to include a growing army of contingent workers to handle the workload increase at lower cost. This in turn has raised the question of whether academic careers continue to be attractive to the ablest students and young researchers as well as whether top academics can be retained within the national system. Moreover, in systems that have been historically dominated by the public sector, privatization as a strategy to accommodate increased demand has meant, among other things, the de-regulation of academic work and careers in what is increasingly a for-profit enterprise, dominated globally by multinational education corporations (e.g., Apollo Group and Corinthian) (Wildavsky, 2010).

These converging perceptions of the rising criticality of the academic profession amid risks to its future has spawned, over the past decade, a growing spate of national and international studies of the academic profession, the scientific workforce, and R&D labor force. These include a major international survey, the Changing Academic Profession (CAP), in 2007–8 involving 18 developed and developing countries in Asia, Europe, the Americas, and Africa, as well as a follow up in 2017–18, the Academic Profession in the Knowledge Society (APIKS), involving more than 30 countries. These studies built, and build on, the pioneering 1992 International Survey of the Academic Profession led by Philip G. Altbach and sponsored by the Carnegie Foundation for the Advancement of Teaching in the United States (Altbach, 1996). The CAP survey generated more than a dozen research volumes between 2010 and 2015 as well as hundreds of journal articles and reports (Teichler, Arimoto & Cummings, 2013). At about the same time, the European Commission sponsored the MORE (Mobility of Academic Researchers in Europe) project, followed in 2012–13 by the MOREII study. While these latter studies focused more broadly on scientific and research workers outside as well as inside the academy, they explicitly recognized the central role of the academic system in the national science and innovation systems of Europe. In Asia, led by the Institute of Higher Education at Hiroshima University, national surveys of the academic profession were conducted in a number of countries in the region in 2011–12 (Huang, 2015). In the Americas, national surveys have been undertaken in Mexico, Brazil, and Argentina.

This global burst of research on the academic profession has been a welcome boon by providing data on this key subpopulation for human capital policy and planning purposes. But it has also raised several troubling conundrums and research challenges, which have served directly as inspiration for this volume. The new availability of vast reservoirs of data for comparison thus forces us to confront the question: How do we compare academies across national boundaries that are so fundamentally different in their organization and dynamics? How do we allow for salient features of national context to enter into our data analysis in ways that ensure we provide appropriate nuance in our analysis of quantitative data? How, for example, do we comparatively assess the career markers of academic staff who in one national setting are civil servants governed by national labor regulations with academic staff in another national setting who are "at will" employees of autonomous corporate entities such as universities in North America? How do we compare doctorally trained academic staff in university systems with a mission that centers predominantly on research, as in Europe or East Asia, with university systems devoted to undergraduate pre-professional education, as in Latin America? What does it mean to speak about professorial attitudes toward their work activities and career progression without contextualizing the discussion of those comparisons with the major structural differences between national systems? Most fundamentally, how do we find common metrics to describe and compare the different kinds of work activities and career trajectories of academic staff embedded in institutions with different missions and expectations and in national systems differently organized? What, in short, are the common building blocks of academic work and academic careers that can serve as the framework for this cross-national conversation? And what are the basic features of national systems that can provide a framework within which to discuss certain basic components of academic work and careers?

To date, the international surveys have reported basic country characteristics such as size, level of economic development or wealth, national linguistic tradition (role of English in the system), and cultural tradition (Western vs. Eastern), but these provide only the grossest sorts of contextual indicators and largely ignore the pervasive influence of how the higher education system and the academic marketplace are differentially organized across national boundaries (Jones, 2013). Of course, the pioneering work of sociologists such as Joseph Ben-David (1977), Burton Clark (1983), and Christine Musselin (2010) has demonstrated the extraordinary extent to which higher education systems are creatures of nation-states, designed to achieve national purposes and structured to reflect national traditions and values. How can we capture the variation in these national contexts of the higher education system as they impinge on and shape academic work and careers in reasonably parsimonious but meaningful ways, and enter them into our newly emerging quantitative analyses of cross-national data sets?

The current historical moment with its growing perception of the academic profession's centrality in ensuring national prosperity amid the concomitant acknowledgment of threats posed to the profession by contemporary massification pressures, is further complicated by the revolution in information and communications technology over the past decade that is pushing higher education—for the past 400 years a largely "localized" institution bounded by national interests—into a globalized industry. Thus, we see the emergence of the concept of the delocalized or global university in which institutional markets have expanded beyond the traditional student catchment area, indeed beyond national borders. In the United States, former New York University (NYU) President John Sexton has argued that in this globalized environment a major research university such as NYU is as much obliged to offer its brand of undergraduate education in Shanghai or Abu Dhabi as in New York as well as to bring students in those cities to New York (Wildavsky, 2010). It self-consciously seeks to join a fraternity of "world-class" universities competing for an ever-growing corps of students worldwide who are actively seeking the "best" education money will buy, wherever it may be (Altbach & Salmi, 2011). On the for-profit side, this idea has spawned the rapid growth of global education and training corporations whose certificate and degree programs are increasingly dominating tertiary enrollments in Latin America, South Asia, and China (Wildavsky, 2010). In Europe, the so-called Bologna Process has removed barriers to student and faculty mobility and is beginning to open up a new brand of European or continent-wide higher education.[1]

Insofar as nations are now seeking to compete in a globalized higher education market, they have begun reshaping aspects of their national systems to accommodate global standards and metrics. In an effort to balance their historic traditions with global standards, many nations have designated an elite sector of institutions within the national system as the locus of global competition, while the rest of the system continues to function—at least theoretically—with localized institutions playing by national rules. That strategy yields a stratified national system with a predominantly traditional localized system functioning alongside an elite, globally competitive subsystem—for example, universities supported under China's 985 and 211 funding programs. Depending on the scale of the national system, there are bound to be pressures both on the elite global sector to maintain national tradition and on the localized traditional sector to adapt aspects of the global standard of academic quality. The tension between growing global isomorphism and maintaining traditional national structures greatly complicates the kinds of analyses required to make sense of developments in academic professions at the national level. In some sense, then, this volume is focused not only on identifying the basic dimensions of academic work and careers—and aspects of national context that shape those dimensions in the local setting—but also on developing a framework for disentangling the localized from the globalized contexts that shape the academic professions worldwide.

Cast broadly in terms of the field of comparative higher education, the purpose of this project is to explicitly build on the work of pioneering scholars such as Joseph Ben-David, Burton Clark, and Christine Musselin with a view to identifying the major structural features of national higher education systems and academic markets in 2017 that directly shape academic work and careers. Our analysis has also been influenced by the recent work by Cantwell, Marginson, and Smolentseva (2018) on high participation systems of higher education. While it is clear that the national context continues to be extremely important, there has been little research on the implications of system differences and globalization pressures as reflected in seemingly parallel recent national reforms on academic careers. This volume makes an important contribution to the literature by addressing and comparing academic career pathways and their increasingly complex relationships with national systems in the midst of adapting to global pressures.

We use the phrase "academic work" as a broad, inclusive term for the wide range of activities (tasks) that academics perform, including research, teaching, administration, and internal governance as well as service to the profession and the surrounding community. While these activities are associated with the professoriate, we also recognize that academic work in our sense is frequently undertaken by others both inside and outside institutions of higher education, for instance, postdoctoral researchers, sessional/adjunct instructional staff who teach a single course but are employed full-time outside the academic sector, researchers at public and private research institutes, and so on. The work *roles* may also vary; some academic workers will undertake relatively specialized activities, that is, will be only teachers or researchers, while others will have responsibilities that include some combination of research, teaching, and service activities. The term "academic careers" refers to the occupational journey of academic professionals—individually and collectively—over time. Finally, we use the term "academic career pathways" to refer to the stepping-stones of professorial careers, including points of entrance into the profession, and opportunities and mechanisms for progression or advancement within these career structures. The academic career may be an individual journey, but these careers are structured or influenced by formal or informal rules that map out the direction and opportunities within this career—for example, in the United States, the pathway from initial appointment as an assistant professor through promotion to full professor. An academic career in the United States may be shortened by the failure to obtain tenure, or for some it may mean spending an entire career without obtaining the highest rank. Academic work and work roles are the content and scope of substantive tasks (narrow/specialized vs. broad), respectively, in which academic professionals engage, while academic career pathways are the structural arrangements embedded in a national context that shape and influence how academic professionals navigate individual careers within these systems.

The Broader Context of Contemporary Higher Education Reform

We have already alluded to the common challenges posed by globalization and massification as they make their way through developed and developing economies of the world. Chief among those challenges have been the twin imperatives to expand access to the system substantially while lowering unit costs and increasing "quality" (or, at least, not compromising quality) to allow it to compete in the newly globalized knowledge and education market. The extent to which very different national systems across the world are demonstrating, to a greater or lesser degree, a surprisingly common set of responses to these challenges is unusual. National governments are reducing per capita levels of university support in the public sector and encouraging entrepreneurial behavior by universities, variously referred to as the advent of the entrepreneurial university (Clark, 1998), of academic capitalism (Slaughter & Rhoades, 2004), marketization (Bok, 2013), or privatization (Marginson, 1997). This includes incentivizing the external support of research by industry and government, and monetizing research by supporting technology transfer processes; uncapping tuition to allow for competitive student recruitment and generation of tuition revenues; privatizing university functions such as student residential life, food service, and educational supplies; and allowing greater freedom to the development of private sector institutions—frequently for-profits—to meet excess student demand. Governments have extended greater autonomy to individual institutions and universities have taken steps to increase their internal capacity for strategic decision making. This has largely occurred through empowering a new cadre of appointed (rather than elected) administrative leaders to strategically position or reposition institutions to increase their prestige (usually through publications in leading refereed journals and citation indexes), to generate revenue through successful competition for research grants, and to successfully transfer research findings into marketable products. That has typically meant a valorization of those academic fields and research areas with the greatest revenue-generating potential (e.g., life and earth/environmental sciences, business, political economy, and public policy) and devaluing others (e.g., the humanities and the arts).

In some jurisdictions universities that were once considered component parts of government, such as the public universities in Japan, have been repositioned as relatively autonomous entities. Governance structures have increasingly taken on the characteristics of business corporations, with governing boards, strong central administrative authority, and related accountability mechanisms, a transition that frequently has been referred to as corporatization. The view that universities should be "managed" organizations has taken hold within some national contexts, such as in England, and this ideology of managerialism has important implications for the professional autonomy of academic workers, and has transformed the role of academic administrators such as deans and chairs, once viewed as peer leaders within collegial decision processes, into academic managers directing and overseeing the performance of academic workers (Austin & Jones, 2015).

At the same time, governments have put into place much more elaborate accountability frameworks, including versions of performance funding for institutions based on student graduation rates, and research funding based on indicators in national assessments of research performance (as in the United Kingdom). They have also recalibrated the balance between teaching and research in the faculty role by the development of new kinds of faculty appointments, typically involving teaching-only or research-only duties—and, in the United States, administration-only positions. This has resulted in a more fragmented academic staff stratified by function but also by prestige value of their academic field (Jones, 2013).

Looking outward, national systems and institutions have sought to project a more global presence beyond national borders both physically, in terms of establishing outposts in other countries and by supporting student and faculty mobility, and symbolically, by improving their position in global knowledge production and in the global university rankings that reflect their contribution. Beyond national systems, supranational associations and agencies have assumed an increasing role in steering the newly globalized industry. Most visibly, the European Union, through its Research Commission, has taken the lead in supporting competitive European social science research. We have already alluded to the Bologna Process, which has standardized degree structures across most of the European Higher Education Area, thus creating, in effect, a European version of higher education, and through the Erasmus Programme, which has promoted the mobility of faculty and students across Europe. Similar, if less fully developed and visible, efforts are afoot in Southeast Asia, through ASEAN (the Association of Southeast Asian Nations), in North America, through CONAHEC (the Consortium for North American Higher Education Collaboration), and in Latin America through Mercosur. Beyond these regional collaboration efforts, international organizations such as the OECD (Organisation for Economic Co-operation and Development) and the World Bank are increasingly involved in driving policy debates and practices in higher education. Accrediting organizations originally established within a single country or region are now extending their purviews to include academic programs in countries halfway around the world and organizations such as the Paris-based International Association of Universities are assuming a leading role in disseminating information on developments and policies in the internationalization of higher education.

All of these developments have put into play what it means to be an academic staff or faculty member and the nature of academic work and careers. Faculty are increasingly navigating more specialized academic work roles (teaching vs. research) and less clearly defined career pathways. Their employment status is moving from civil servant or other protected status to organizational employee. They are increasingly subject to accountability for performance amid declining availability of, and increasing competition for, resources. In several respects, their historical professional autonomy and even their academic freedom (in terms of choice of research topics and approaches) is subject to increasing institutional and external encroachments. Their role in steering their academic units and their institutions is increasingly circumscribed by the rise and proliferation of managerialism and new corporatist forms of university governance. Thus, academic work roles and careers in many nations are becoming a moving target—just as we seek to get a conceptual handle on their common essential building blocks.

The Key Characteristics of National Systems

Just as academic work and careers are in flux, so are the basic structural features of national systems. In *The Higher Education System* (1983), Burton Clark argues that national systems differ systematically in how they structure *academic work* and *authority* within institutions, disciplines, and within institutional systems in the form of guilds and government bureaucracies; how systems institutionalize *belief systems* about core values, such as access to higher education and the relation of university education to the labor market (e.g., government service careers and the professions); and in the mix of *mechanisms they employ for system integration/coordination* (state authority, academic oligarchy, and markets). In terms of the division of academic labor, for example, Clark identified systematic national variation in the fineness of disciplinary subdivisions *within* institutions (perhaps 50 academic departments in 10 faculties or schools in North America; perhaps 200 chairs and institutes in Germany), in the degree of interdependence among such units (from virtual independence to identified spheres for required cooperation, as in general education programs in North America), and in the relationship of general to specialized education. He also identified systematic variation in the differentiation of systems and institutional types within systems (e.g., a single public system or multiple public systems at different levels of government) and within those systems he pointed out the diversity of types of institutions with different roles/functions.

Clark also used the concept of *level of authority* to illuminate important differences in the types of authority and responsibility found at various levels of higher education systems; for example, there may be important differences between systems at the superstructure level in establishing national conditions for all employment or specifically regulating the academic profession, just as there may be important differences in authority in relation to academic work at the institutional or subunit levels of the system. In terms of belief systems, Clark identified beliefs about access (restricted, differentiated, or unrestricted) and about the relationship of the system to the labor market, especially the civil service and the professions. In terms of authority, Clark differentiated between forms of disciplinary authority (personal authority of faculty oligarchs in a chair system, or peer group collegiality in a departmentalized organization) and institutional and system-based authority (bureaucratic, governmental, oligarchic), thus identifying systematic national differences in the relative influence mix between academic guildlike and personal authority, institutional administrators, and state bureaucracy. Finally, in terms of overall system integration, Clark identified the basic alternatives of bureaucratic coordination via state authority, professional coordination via academic oligarchy, and political coordination via the use of market mechanisms. Indeed, with the depiction of the "Triangle of Coordination," Clark shows how each of eight major national systems could be located within a three-dimensional space defined by the three sources of coordination: state, academic oligarchy, and market.

Within the framework of Clark's complex taxonomy, we have identified a more parsimonious set of dimensions that are increasingly defining substantive differences across national systems. Perhaps the most basic of such distinctions is between what we have termed "unitary" versus "federated" systems. France and Russia would serve as the prototypical unitary system where a single national ministry of education establishes a single set of regulations and manages the system centrally—although as the chapters on France and Russia will show, that is beginning to change. At the other extreme, the United States and Canada represent the classic federated system where the national government plays a more limited role in favor of the state or provincial governments. Germany represents a "mixed" model with roles for both central and state (Länder) governments in higher education policy.

A second structural aspect of the national system is its functional institutional differentiation, that is, the extent to which it supports a single type of institution versus a highly differentiated set of institutions reflecting a diversity of missions, degree levels, and programming. Italy would represent a unified system where each university unit looks much like every other university unit, that is, a university is a university is a university. At the other extreme, the United States represents a system that supports many types of institutions that differ markedly in mission, degree levels, and programs. In between are many European nations that support basically binary systems—academic and vocational. Added to the mix are the existence, size, and nature of a private sector. Does it exist? How large is it? Is it primarily demand-absorbing? How is it regulated?

A third structural characteristic of national systems is the degree of autonomy experienced by institutions in terms of selecting students and staff, determining the mix of academic programs, setting tuition and fees, and the raising and expenditure of resources. National systems differ systematically—and are currently in flux—in terms of who sets these policies.

The final structural characteristic is, generally, the extent to which a national system is authoritarian versus democratic and, more specifically, the status of, and meaning it ascribes to, academic freedom. At one extreme, China represents an authoritarian system with a fairly circumscribed notion of academic freedom. At the other extreme, Canada and the United States in North America, Germany in Europe, and Japan in Asia represent relatively absolute notions of academic freedom. All of these, as we shall see in the following chapters, constitute moving targets that are in flux as we write.

Academic Career Pathways in National Systems

Many of the characteristics of a higher education system have direct or indirect implications for academic careers. A number of concepts and ideas can be used to explore and analyze the relationships between the higher education system and the academic career pathways within that system, and these concepts played a fundamental role in the development of the national case studies included in this volume and the comparative analysis of these case studies presented in the concluding chapter.

Control of Academic Careers: Who Is the Employer and Who Has Jurisdiction?

The relationship between the national system and the prototypical academic career can be framed as the answer to the question "Who employs the academic worker?" In many systems, professors work at universities but are technically employed by the state and are categorized as civil servants. In federal systems, the employer could be government at either the national or local level (state, canton, or province). In other systems, professors are employed by individual universities. The employer may shift at different stages in an academic career, with junior academic contract workers employed, for example, by the university, but professors employed as senior civil servants, as is the case in Germany.

Beyond the employer's identity, a related but independent dimension of the control over academic career pathways is the distinction between system-level institutional and mixed or hybrid levels/loci of control. Using Clark's (1983) notion of "levels of authority," we can observe that the control over the pathways that structure academic careers can be located at different levels in different systems, and that these differences can be quite important in comparative analyses of academic work. In some jurisdictions, this academic career pathway is prescribed or regulated at the system level. *System-level academic career pathways* are largely shaped by government legislation or system-level regulations, which establish the fundamental rules and procedures associated with the structure of academic careers.

In other jurisdictions it is the institution, rather than the system, that plays the major role in determining the structure of academic career pathways. An *institutional academic career pathway* means that each university has the discretion and autonomy to determine the specific processes and criteria associated with appointments, career advancement, and salary structures. There may be national traditions and commonalities, but the authority for determining academic career

Table 1.1.   Employer and Level of Authority over Academic Career Framework

Academic Career Framework	Employer	
	Government	University
System-level	System-level authority over career framework; government is employer	System-level authority over career framework; university is employer
Hybrid	Career framework determined by system and institution; government is employer	Career framework determined by system and institution; university is employer
Institution	Institution has authority over career framework and government is employer	Institution has authority over career framework and university is employer

pathways is at the institutional level and is frequently operationalized by detailed policy documents that regulate decision processes.

One can also imagine national systems where only some elements of academic career structures are regulated at the system or national level of authority and where the remaining decisions or elements are left in the hands of individual universities. Under a mixed or *hybrid academic career pathway* neither the system nor the institution plays the dominant role in determining the structure of academic careers; decisions at both levels of authority shape the structure of academic career pathways.

Table 1.1 illustrates the multiple relationships associated with issues of authority over academic career pathways in different systems. The table's top left example describes a context where professors are employed by government and where decisions about the structure of the academic career are made centrally at the system level. The professor works within a university, but the professor is employed by government within a career structure that is determined at the system level. At the other extreme, in the bottom right corner of the table, the professor is employed by the university, and the rules governing academic careers are determined at the institutional level. Between these extremes is a range of possible employment relationships with different decisions being made at various levels of authority within the higher education system.

INSTITUTIONAL DIVERSITY AND ACADEMIC CAREERS

The term "diversity" is frequently used to refer to horizontal differences among institutional types within a higher education system. Indeed, this is what Birnbaum

(1983) refers to as systemic diversity (differences in institutional type). Horizontal diversity refers to the number of entities or institutional types or categories within a higher education system (Van Vught, 2008).

Does the existence of multiple institutional types within a higher education system mean that there are also differences in academic career pathways depending upon the type of institution? One can certainly imagine a higher education system where the academic careers of professors working at one type of institution (e.g., an institution that focuses on undergraduate teaching) might be quite different than the careers of professors working at a very different type of institution (such as a university focusing on research and graduate education). On the other hand, one can also imagine a situation where a system has different types of institutions, but where academic careers vary little by institutional type. In other words, there are common career frameworks for all professors in the system, even though they work in institutions with quite different characteristics, roles, or legal foundations.

Vertical Stratification and Academic Careers

One can also observe differences in status or prestige between institutions of the same type (see Cantwell, Marginson & Smolentseva, 2018). This vertical stratification has received increasing attention as a function of national and international rankings. The level of vertical stratification within a higher education system can have an important impact on academic careers and career pathways. In some systems, such as in Germany, the level of vertical stratification within the university sector may be modest, and institutional status may have only a modest impact on academic careers. In other systems, such as in the United States and China, there may be a very high level of vertical stratification; the status of the institution in which the professor works may have huge implications for the availability of resources, academic work roles, and career pathways.

In considering vertical stratification and academic career pathways, it is may be necessary to consider the "world-class university" as a special institutional category or phenomenon. The desire on the part of some governments to create world-class universities, frequently defined as those that are in the top echelon of international rankings, has led to new policy initiatives and major investments associated with a small subset of institutions within these systems (Altbach & Salmi, 2011; Hazelkorn, 2015). This phenomenon may have special implications for the academic careers of those who work in these world-class aspiring institutions, especially given the distinctive ways these institutions are regulated and resourced within some systems.

LABOR MARKETS AND THE ACADEMIC PROFESSION

A number of very useful concepts emerge from labor economics and from the study of professions as a distinct type or category of occupation. Labor economists, for example, have noted an important distinction between *internal* and *external* labor markets (Doeringer & Piore, 1971). With an internal labor market, a firm promotes employees from within the organization. An individual is hired into a junior position at the firm. As the individual develops skills and expertise within the organization, they may move up the career ladder to more senior positions. The assumption is that employees will advance as they learn on the job through some combination of work experience and professional development or occupational training. The labor market is internal to the firm and the allocation of labor and salary arrangements are governed by administrative procedures and rules.

With an external labor market, a firm will frequently fill positions by considering candidates who are not currently employed by the firm. An external labor market involves a more traditional economic market where economic variables influence or control the allocation of labor, salaries and benefits (price structure), and decisions on investments in training.

As Christine Musselin notes in her foundational comparative analyses of academic markets (2003, 2010), the concepts of internal and external labor markets can be usefully applied to the study of academic career pathways. In the context of higher education, an *internal labor market* describes an academic career framework where a professor can move up the career ladder from a junior position while employed at the same university. Although there may be exceptions, the appointment of a senior academic normally involves a promotion from within the university. At the extreme, the doctoral graduates of a university can be viewed as the labor pool for junior professorial appointments, and an entire career, a pathway from graduate studies through senior academic appointment, could take place at the same university.

In contrast, an *external labor market* refers to a situation where individuals from outside the university are frequently appointed to fill academic positions. In an extreme form, there may be regulations that require that only qualified individuals from outside the university can be appointed to a position, or that an individual can only reach the next step in the career ladder by taking a higher-ranked position at another university. A less-extreme form would be a situation where there is competition for a senior appointment, and where the most qualified individual is chosen from a pool that includes both external and internal candidates.

In some systems, the external labor market is essentially a national labor market because government policies make it difficult or impossible to employ foreign candidates, or because position requirements are defined in such a way that they favor applicants from within the national system. In others, the external labor market is international in that the university will look for the best candidate to fill a position regardless of nationality.

A range of useful concepts emerges from the study of professions as distinct occupational categories. Unlike more traditional forms of work, a profession presumes that specialized knowledge is required as a prerequisite to practice, and considerable emphasis is placed on self-regulation of the profession, autonomy, and ethics. In some systems, requirements for entry to practice in the academic profession (the entry credentials) may be quite flexible and essentially left in the hands of the employer. A PhD may be the common standard, but there are no formal minimum qualifications required of a junior professor. In other systems, the standards associated with entry are highly regulated and may require the completion of a major academic study following the PhD (such as the *habilitation* in Germany) or passing a national examination (such as in India). Regulating entry to practice is a form of professional closure in which entrance to the academic profession is restricted to those who are suitably qualified. Entry to practice requirements may specify different requirements for different categories within the profession (e.g., licensure may focus on a certain field of scholarship) or different functions within the profession (e.g., research funding may only be available to PhD-trained professors).

Other concepts from the literature relate to the profession's organization and self-regulation. In some systems, the academic profession has considerable influence over the its career pathways; in others these decisions are left in the hands of the government or institutions, while in still others professors are members of trade unions and decisions on salaries and working conditions emerge through some form of collective bargaining. The practice of the profession may be guided by notions of professional standards or ethics.

National Social Policy

National social policy may also have major implications for academic careers. Many jurisdictions have antidiscrimination policies that address issues of gender, age, religion, or caste that influence selection and appointment processes. In some jurisdictions, such as India, governments have attempted to address issues of equity by establishing hiring quotas or accountability requirements that impact hiring or promotion decisions. Immigration policies may make it difficult or impossible to hire a professor who is not a national citizen, or limit the career progress of foreign professors employed within the system.

NATIONAL SCIENCE AND INNOVATION POLICY

While much of our emphasis is on the relationship between the characteristics of national higher education systems and academic career pathways, we also acknowledge that national science and innovation policies may be playing an increasing role in influencing academic work within these national systems. Science and innovation are increasingly viewed as core elements in the development of knowledge economies. Government policies that steer the direction of science and innovation toward areas viewed as strategically important can have major implications for academic work. Major research investments in specific fields can lead to differences in status and prestige relationships among fields of study. Policies that encourage new linkages between universities and industry can lead to new academic career pathways, sometimes blurring the career boundaries between professors employed by universities and researchers employed by industry or government laboratories.

All of these concepts and ideas can be usefully applied to the comparative analysis of academic careers within the context of national systems of higher education.

The Design of the Project

The idea for this project emerged from our discussions of the limitations and possibilities of international comparative studies of the academic profession. We had both participated in the Changing Academic Profession project and shared an interest in furthering the conceptual foundation for comparative work in this important field. Our objective was to focus on four broad questions:

1. What are the basic dimensions of academic work roles (the scope and content of what professors do) that can usefully be compared across national systems?
2. What are the basic structural components or dimensions of academic career pathways (recruitment and advancement) that are required to understand them in comparative perspective?
3. What are the internal dynamics of academic career pathways—within and across countries? How are the pieces mutually dependent and reciprocal?

4. What are the key aspects of national context that shape the various key components of academic career pathways?

In 2013 we carefully reviewed the literature on national systems and developed a template or questionnaire of issues and topics that we believed might be fundamental to understanding how the characteristics of national higher education systems impact and relate to academic careers and career pathways. We circulated the template to many of our colleagues within the CAP project to obtain feedback and advice. The revised template and project description invited national experts to write draft papers that would describe and analyze academic career pathways within the context of their national systems using the initial template as a resource.

We paid considerable attention to determining which national systems to include and decided upon a number of European systems (England, France, Germany) that have had significant historical influence (in some cases through colonization) on the developments of higher education in other jurisdictions, including influencing the structure of academic career pathways. Previous studies that are directly relevant to this work have noted the historical distinctiveness of these three systems (Clark, 1983; Musselin, 2010). We then selected a sample of additional systems in an attempt to balance regional/geographic representation and levels of national economic development. The United States, Canada, and Japan were chosen as highly developed, research-intensive higher education systems within mature, developed economies. The United States and Canada are both former British colonies and were influenced by English university models, although they have both evolved into unique systems. The research university that emerged in the United States is frequently positioned as the model of the global or world-class university, and it has influenced developments in many other systems, including Japan. Brazil, Russia, India, and China are four of the five BRICS countries, and they are large, uniquely structured, rapidly changing higher education systems. Russia represents yet another distinctive European system, and it influenced the development of the Chinese system as well as systems of Eastern Europe. Brazil, India, and China are the largest higher education systems in their respective regions, and China is now the largest higher education system in the world in terms of student enrollment.

Once the national systems were chosen, we invited a leading national scholar in this field to participate. We had originally planned to include a collaborator from South Africa, but the scholars that we approached were unable to take part, and the absence of a contribution from Africa is an important limitation. Recognizing that no 10 countries can represent an entire world of higher education systems, the chapters in this volume provide a very useful international collection of different national systems and a firm foundation for our exploratory comparative analysis.

The first drafts of most chapters were prepared in 2014, and a team meeting and preliminary presentation of our work took place at the annual meeting of the Consortium of Higher Education Researchers (CHER) in Rome in September of that year. Elizabeth Balbachevsky organized a project workshop at the University of São Paulo in October 2015, and this meeting provided an important forum for discussing the national chapters and reviewing the key concepts and ideas underscoring our work. The inductive approach underscoring our São Paulo discussions played a major role in strengthening the conceptual foundation of the project. National chapters were revised in light of these discussions to ensure that common issues were addressed in every case study. These national chapters then provided the foundation for the cross-case analysis and conceptual developments described in the concluding chapter.

We decided to present the chapters by geographic region, beginning with the four quite distinct European systems (German, France, United Kingdom, and Russia). This is followed by Brazil (Latin America) and India, China, and Japan (Asia, though obviously Russia also has a very large footprint in this region). The last two chapters are from North America (the United States and Canada). The final chapter of the book presents our cross-case analysis of the national chapters, discusses core concepts and findings emerging from this analysis that make important contributions to the comparative study of the academic profession, and provides suggestions for further study.

Conclusion

Universities have come to assume a central role in human resource and economic development, and they have been positioned as key institutions in the transition toward knowledge economies and societies. The transformation of higher education systems and university reforms have had major implications for the academic profession, and have led to a renewed interest in understanding academic careers within national systems and through a comparative lens. However, while the number of international studies of the academic profession has grown, there has been little emphasis on understanding academic career pathways within the context of national systems or on contextualizing comparative analyses by highlighting key differences in the structure of systems and academic career pathways.

Our objective in this volume is to address this gap through an exploratory study of ten national systems using the key concepts and frameworks described above, and, through cross-case analysis, developing analytic tools to advance research in this critical area. This project makes an important contribution to the study of academic work, and perhaps even more so to the methodological foundation for the comparative analysis of the academic profession and professorial pathways in the context of national higher education systems.

NOTE

1. The Bologna Process represents an initiative of European ministers of education to align degree levels and programs across national boundaries to facilitate student mobility. This integration process has expanded to include a wide range of reforms (see, e.g., Maassen & Olsen, 2007).

REFERENCES

Altbach, P. G., ed. 1996. *The international academic profession: Portraits of fourteen countries.* San Francisco: Jossey-Bass.

Altbach, P. G., and J. Salmi, eds. 2011. *The road to academic excellence: The making of world-class research universities.* Washington, D.C.: World Bank.

Austin, I., and G. A. Jones. 2015. *Governance of higher education: Global perspectives, theories and practices.* New York: Routledge.

Ben-David, J. 1977. *Center of learning: Britain, France, Germany, United States.* New York: McGraw-Hill.

Birnbaum, R. 1983. *Maintaining diversity in higher education.* San Francisco: Jossey-Bass.

Bok, D. 2013. *Higher education in America.* Princeton, NJ: Princeton University Press.

Cantwell, B., S. Marginson, and A. Smolentseva, eds. 2018. *High participation systems of higher education.* Oxford: Oxford University Press.

Clark, B. L. 1983. *The higher education system: Academic organization in cross-national perspective.* Berkeley: University of California Press.

——— 1998. *Creating entrepreneurial universities: Organizational pathways of transformation.* Oxford: IAU Press, Pergamum.

Doeringer, P. B., and M. J. Piore. 1971. *Internal labor markets and manpower analysis.* Lexington, KY: Heath Lexington Books.

Hazelkorn, E. 2015. *Ranking and the reshaping of higher education: The battle for world-class excellence.* 2nd ed. New York: Palgrave Macmillan.

Huang, F. 2015. The internationalization of the academy in Asia: Major findings from the international survey. In *The changing academic profession in Asia: The formation, work, academic productivity and internationalization of the academy,* 55–68. Hiroshima: Research Institute for Higher Education.

Jones, G. A. 2013. The horizontal and vertical fragmentation of academic work and the challenge for academic governance and leadership. *Asia Pacific Education Review* 14 (1): 75–83.

Maassen, P., and J. P. Olsen, eds. 2007. *University dynamics and European integration.* Dordrecht, Netherlands: Springer.

Marginson, S. 1997. Imagining Ivy: Pitfalls in the privatization of higher education in Australia. *Comparative Education Review* 41 (4): 460–80.

Musselin, C. 2003. Internal versus external labor markets. *Higher Education Management and Policy* 15 (3): 9–23.

———. 2010. *The market for academics.* New York: Routledge.

Slaughter, S., and G. Rhoades. 2004. *Academic capitalism and the new economy: Markets, state, and higher education.* Baltimore: Johns Hopkins University Press.

Teichler, U., A. Arimoto, and W. Cummings. 2013. *The changing academic profession: Major findings of a comparative survey.* Dordrecht, Netherlands: Springer.

Van Vught, F. 2008. Mission diversity and reputation in higher education. *Higher Education Policy* 21:151–74.

Wildavsky, B. 2010. *The great brain race: How global universities are reshaping the world.* Princeton, NJ: Princeton University Press.

2 | Germany

Unpredictable Career Progression but Security at the Top

BARBARA M. KEHM

A s a prelude to an analysis of the structure of academic careers and academic work in Germany, I provide an overview of the basic organization of the German system of higher education, recent changes in the roles of the federal and state governments, as well as trends in institutional autonomy and equity issues. While initially treating teaching and research, I address as well the role of academic staff in institutional governance and, more broadly, in influencing national educational policy. I conclude with an examination of compensation and employment contracts.

The German Higher Education System
A BINARY SYSTEM WITH EMERGING "VERTICAL"
DIFFERENTIATION (WITHIN TYPES)

German higher education is essentially a binary system consisting of 121 universities and 245 universities of applied sciences (UASs), the latter of which include 30 institutions for public administration. Universities and universities of applied sciences each have a distinct mission, namely, that universities offer an academic education and carry out teaching and research while universities of applied sciences offer professional education but have no explicit research tasks. The distinction between "academic" and "professional" is not quite as clear-cut as it perhaps once was because universities offer professional programs as well (e.g., engineering, business administration, law, or teacher training). Moreover, many universities of applied sciences have developed into quite research active institutions, typically in cooperation with industry; however, they do not have a proper research infrastructure as universities have and they are not allowed to award doctoral degrees.[1] Students who want to enroll at universities of applied sciences can do so with one year less of upper secondary schooling than students wanting to enroll at a university, but many of the former have undergone vocational education and training before taking up studies at a university of applied sciences. Some of the most research-active universities of applied sciences are involved in doctoral training, but they need a cooperation agreement with a university to award the degree and appoint a cosupervisor from that university. In addition, universities of applied sciences have a smaller range of subjects, mainly engineering, business administration, and social work, and offer only a limited number of master's degree programs.

In addition to these two distinct institutional types, there are 6 separate teacher-training colleges (which remain following the integration of most teacher-training colleges into universities in the framework of reforms in the 1970s) and 52 colleges for fine arts and music. All of these are public institutions. There is a sizeable sector of 163 private higher education institutions, among them 38 church-related institutions. In 2013, private higher education institutions enrolled about 7.5 percent of all students in Germany (Buschle & Haider, 2016). The majority of the mostly small private higher education institutions offer business administration programs. There are only a handful of private, but state-recognized, institutions that have university status and offer a broader range of subjects and programs.

In 2015, there were roughly 2.76 million students enrolled in German higher education institutions: about 63 percent of all students in the public system were enrolled in universities and almost 34 percent in universities of applied sciences.[2] The remaining 3 percent study at one of the other public higher education institutions mentioned above. The proportion of new entrant students among the relevant age group of the overall cohort, that is, the gross enrollment ratio, or GER, was 59 percent in the same year (Statistisches Bundesamt [Federal Statistical Office], 2016).[3]

Historically there had been a high degree of legal "homogeneity" in the sectors of German higher education. All institutions of one type were treated equally by the states and degrees were officially regarded as having the same value on the labor market. Of course, there were employers who preferred graduates from a particular institution, and there were differences in institutional reputation, but this was more tacit though common knowledge. This particular German type of legal homogeneity changed with the introduction of the excellence initiative in

2006 (cf. Kehm & Pasternack, 2009). After the disappointing outcomes for German universities in several of the newer global rankings of universities, the Federal Ministry of Education and Research and the ministries of the 16 German states responsible for higher education decided to implement a competition among universities (universities of applied sciences were excluded) for considerable extra funding in three areas: graduate schools, research clusters, and institutional development. In contrast to the first two funding areas, the third one was not geared toward research and research training but awarded grants for managerial strategies and mission specification geared toward the future. Universities that managed to win funding for their institutional development concepts were considered to be or to become the (future) German elite institutions. As in many other continental European countries, German policy makers suffered from the "Harvard here" syndrome, which means that they wanted to have at least one elite university like Harvard in their system. The results of this initiative led to a profound restructuring of the German higher education landscape, which traditionally had been diversified horizontally but was now being forced to accept a growing vertical stratification as well.

The additional funding and the resulting "Matthew effect"—"to those who have, more will be given"—enabled the winning universities to attract better students and even poach highly reputed research staff from other universities. This development created winners and losers in a system that had previously treated all institutions of the same type as equal, and institutions that had lost out in the competition highly resented this system.

Systems Governance and Institutional Autonomy

Since the expansion phase of higher education began in the 1960s in West Germany, the federal government had successively addressed a variety of approaches to system governance. All matters of education (from kindergarten to higher education) and culture originally were regulated by the responsible ministries of the states. In fact, a federal ministry for education and research was only established in 1969. With higher education expansion, it was increasingly harder for the states to shoulder the financial burden of funding their higher education institutions, and the issue of introducing tuition fees to help finance the system was not considered as opportune for the political agenda. Instead, education—including higher education—was regarded as a civic right for which the welfare state had to provide adequate funding. Thus, the federal government increasingly contributed funding to the maintenance of existing and establishment of new buildings, to research funding, to student assistance in terms of grants and loans, and began to play a more decisive role in educational planning. This "buy-in" culminated in the federal governments' framework law for higher education passed in 1976. One of the most important objectives of the framework law was to establish legal homogeneity between all institutions of one type (i.e., the recognition of degrees as being of equal value regardless of the institution which had awarded it) and a guarantee that students could move freely between universities (including moving from one state to another one) without having to suffer disadvantages. In addition, the framework law specified the areas of the higher education system in which the federal government was allowed to participate.

Another important issue in the framework law was the explicit prohibition of tuition fees. While the responsible state ministries opposed the idea of a federal framework law on higher education, they tolerated it because the federal government ministry was supporting the higher education system with considerable amounts of money. This kind of grudging truce ended in 2004 over a conflict between the federal government and the state governments about tuition fee reforms. The conflict eventually led to a "reform" of federalism, including a strict ban on cooperation between the federal government ministry and the states in all matters of (higher) education. The federal government withdrew most of its funding, which had until then flowed into the higher education system. In the ensuing decade, the original decision of noncooperation has been modified to some extent, but the states continue to anxiously guard their authority in all matters of education vis-à-vis the federal government. Still, the framework law on higher education was silently buried, though never officially abolished, and there is no new law to substitute for the old one or its functions. Furthermore, tuition fees were successively abolished in the ten states, which had introduced them whenever there was a change of government after elections. Lower Saxony was the last state to abolish tuition fees toward the end of 2014. Thus, the German higher education system is now a system free of tuition fees, and that includes not only domestic students but international students as well.

In the last ten to fifteen years, the 16 German states that are responsible for the higher education institutions located on their territory have successively introduced new forms of governance, for example, granting their institutions more autonomy in exchange for a higher degree of public accountability. However, the degree of autonomy varies considerably according to the state. For example, in the states located in the southern part of Germany, institutional autonomy is less advanced than in the northern and western parts. Higher education institutions in the state of North Rhine Westphalia had the highest degree of autonomy until recently, but the new higher education law that came into effect in autumn 2014 reduced that autonomy again to some extent owing to the state ministry wanting to reassert control over its institutions.

Reforms to grant higher education institutions more autonomy in Germany have gone less far than in many other European countries. Institutional autonomy is basically characterized by four main elements:

1. Lump sum budgets with the possibility to carry over funds from one year to the next (instead of earmarked funding and line item budgets).
2. Eleven universities being the employers of professors (instead of the state) by opting to become foundations.
3. Control over the number and structure of program offerings, which previously had to be sanctioned by the state.
4. Determining the number of students that newly enroll every year and selecting them.

These elements, however, are not equally present in all universities and some are also conditional. Basically, it is the responsible state ministry that determines the degree of autonomy. For example, new degree programs still need the approval of the state after accreditation in order to avoid overlap within the jurisdiction and enable economies of scale; and the number of students who can be accepted at the beginning of each academic year is dependent on resources (teaching staff and space), which are determined by a capacity law. The four elements listed above are regulated in different ways in each of the states.

Typically, universities need ministerial approval for the recruitment of professors as well as for the vice-chancellor position. Other academic staff can be recruited autonomously. However, the state budget prescribes how many positions are included in the regular budget of the institution. Additional staff, mostly on fixed-term contracts, can only be recruited when money is available in the framework of third-party funded research projects or if additional teaching staff is needed for the growing number of students.

EQUITY AND MARKETS IN GERMAN HIGHER EDUCATION

With a Gini index of 30.6 percent in 2010, Germany ranks globally among countries with a very high equity level. However, equity issues of a quite serious nature continue to persist. Migrants or families with an immigrant background are still disadvantaged in many respects—in particular, the level of schooling, access to higher education, and academic careers. Furthermore, Germany has made less progress than many other highly developed countries in terms of equal opportunities for women. Female incomes and salaries are typically one-third less than those of males in comparable jobs in the general economy, and women are not well represented in leadership positions.

Despite diversity management being currently popular in German higher education, diversity tends to cover adequate representation of all social groups among the student body rather than, for example, in academic and senior administrative or managerial positions. About 26 percent of German professors are female, but with large differences according to subject. Among institutional leadership, around 14 percent are women and in boards of governors, around 30 percent are women (Destatis, 2014). Several state governments have introduced quotas in order to rectify the situation. For example, the higher education ministry in the state of North Rhine Westphalia has recently decreed that at least 40 percent of members on boards of governors must be women.

Many higher education institutions have also been certified as "family friendly," according to an audit that is carried out by an independent agency but supported by the Federal Ministry for Education and Research. The audit covers eight dimensions of family-friendly study and work conditions: time, organization, location, information and communication about available support, leadership, human resource development, salaries and funding, and family services. At the end of a successful auditing process, the university will receive a certificate stating that it is providing a study and work environment that is family friendly, that is, conducive to a good work-life or study-life balance if one has children or responsibilities of caring for an elderly family member.

Universities are neither more nor less equitable than the rest of the German society and its public and private sectors of the economy. In principle, the professoriate tends to be a more conservative force and women continue to be underrepresented in the upper echelons. However, as mentioned earlier, this varies considerably according to subject. Typically, the humanities have more female professors than, for example, the STEM subjects. But veterinary medicine in Germany is almost exclusively female.

As Germany has no tuition fees—neither for domestic nor for international students—competition for students is different compared to countries that have tuition fees because more students, including international students, do not generate any kind of income for the institution from fees. In addition, many universities, especially in the western German states, have more applications than they have places available. This has led to the widespread introduction of a *numerus clausus*, a grade-point-average threshold in the school graduation certificate, for most subjects. The threshold varies according to subject and institution. It is highest in highly reputed universities and in subjects that are in high demand (e.g., medicine, psychology, law). However, as every university nowadays claims to want to attract only the best talent (including international students) for reasons of reputation, institutions can't afford to disregard the *numerus clausus* because they would otherwise become known for attracting students who have been rejected elsewhere, that is, only mediocre or low talent.

Still, differences in terms of competition for students are clearly observable. Such competition was also manifest in the failed introduction of tuition fees. In 2005, the Federal Constitutional Court acceded to the petition of those states governed by the conservative party to abolish the ban on tuition fees in the Higher Education Framework Law. Immediately 10 out of 16 states introduced tuition fees. Those states that did not were mostly located in East Germany. With the decision not to introduce tuition fees, East German universities hoped to attract more students from the western parts of Germany, who would migrate to avoid having to pay tuition fees. Many East German universities continue to have the capacity to accept more students and fear being forced to merge with other institutions or having to close down departments and lose staff. Those states that *had* introduced tuition fees began to abolish them again with every change of government after state elections. The issue of tuition fees was simply too controversial to achieve a sustainable implementation. In 2014, Lower Saxony was the last state to abolish tuition fees. The universities negotiated with the state governments and the federal ministry to be compensated for the loss of income from fee abolishment and came to an agreement. In the framework of a "quality pact," universities now receive financial compensation but can only spend it on quality assurance and improvement measures related to teaching. In addition, the states stipulated that students had to be involved in decisions on how the money from the pact was going to be spent.

Academic Careers within the German Higher Education System
Entry into an Academic Career
and Early Career Trajectory

In the German higher education system, entry to an academic career begins with enrollment in doctoral study. The majority of doctoral candidates (who are not considered students in Germany but rather junior academic staff) are employed by their university as junior research (and teaching) assistants or as junior contract researchers (about 60 percent). Both junior staff categories have contracts for 50 to 60 percent of the regular working hours, and do their thesis work partially during paid working hours and partially during their remaining (unpaid) time. Junior research (and teaching) assistants support a chair holder or professor in his or her teaching duties, and contract researchers are involved as junior researchers in third-party funded projects. Only the first group is considered junior faculty. The other 40 percent of doctoral candidates are either scholarship holders or they are externals, meaning they work to support themselves and pursue their doctorate in their spare time. Both of these latter types have no status vis-à-vis the university, apart from having a supervisor, and are neither counted as academic staff nor have to be registered with the university in any way.[4]

The European Bologna reform process has put considerable emphasis on structuring the phase of doctoral education and training and addressed it as a third cycle of studies (after bachelor's and master's degree studies). Although most continental European countries continue to regard this qualification phase as research training rather than studies, many European countries have made an effort to provide this phase with more structure and more systematic skills and competence training. This has resulted in an increasing number of doctoral programs or schools being established (Konsortium Bundesbericht Wissenschaftlicher Nachwuchs, 2017). Doctoral candidates who are members of such programs and schools or associated with them have the opportunity to participate in seminars, lectures, or workshops to enhance their skills and competences. However, apart from scholarship holders officially linked to these doctoral programs and schools, participation is mostly voluntary. Collecting experiences in (typically unpaid) teaching is also an option and mostly welcome by the departments.

The current regulations in Germany prescribe that a young researcher can be employed by the university for up to six years before and up to six years after completing the doctorate. At each of these thresholds, it is either "up or out." The years after the doctorate are meant as a time to gain reputation, acquire further qualifications (such as the *habilitation*), and apply for professorships. Due to the lack of tenure tracks, this always entails switching institutions, as a possible candidate cannot progress at his or her home institution. In the phase after the doctorate, many young researchers are employed as fixed-term contract researchers because academic staff positions within the regular institutional budget are few and competition for them is fierce.

There are currently reform discussions taking place in the German higher education policy sector concerning an overhaul of the traditional academic career structure (Konsortium Bundesbericht Wissenschaftlicher Nachwuchs, 2017). These discussions are focused on shaping and giving structure to the postdoctoral phase (postdoc) in order to enable more predictable career planning. This includes debates about whether or not to introduce a tenure-track model.

The Introduction of the Junior Professorship

A first reform of academic career structures in German higher education was the introduction in 2002 of junior professorships. Insofar as the German higher education system does not generally have a tenure track, achieving eligibility through successfully completing a habilitation did not always result in actually getting a professorship and—as previously mentioned—a change of institution was always required because career progression could not be achieved at the same institution. In many subjects or disciplines, the habilitation remains the entrance ticket to a professorship. The junior professor position was introduced to support young and highly talented postdoctoral students toward earlier independence (from a professor or chair holder) and faster achievement of a regular professorship without having to earn a habilitation first. With its six-year term, the junior professorship can be compared to the American assistant professorship, although, in Germany, only a small proportion of junior professorships offers a true probationary period with prospects for promotion within the same institution. Altogether, about 1,000 junior professorships were established and filled between 2002 and 2009 (about 4 percent of all professorships in German universities, but again without a tenure track in most cases). Interestingly, the junior professorships had a much higher proportion of women (37 percent) than could be found among associate and full professorships (22 percent) and among habilitations (24 percent). The original goal of the Federal Ministry for Education and Research, which initiated this reform, was to have 6,000 junior professorships. Habilitation and junior professorship are different routes to a professorship, but both are uncertain and only create an eligibility status. The Ludwig Maximilian University in Munich is one of the few universities in Germany that has introduced a tenure-track model for junior professors. All junior professors are evaluated after three years and only after a positive evaluation is the tenure-track option made available (Statistisches Bundesamt, 2009; Burkhardt & Nickel, 2015; Konsortium Bundesbericht Wissenschaftlicher Nachwuchs, 2017).

THE DISTRIBUTION OF ACADEMIC STAFF,
OR THE ACADEMIC PYRAMID

An overview of the different full-time positions at universities and their change in numbers between 2005 and 2014 is provided in table 2.1. The category "professors" includes all full-time professors.[5] Until about the mid-2000s, all professors (all categories) at German universities were civil servants appointed by the responsible Ministry of the respective State, upon proposal by the university that had recruited them.

With growing university autonomy, some of the German states introduced experimental clauses into their state higher education laws that enabled universities to become foundations under public law, if they so wished. Examples are University of Göttingen, University of Hildesheim, and Leuphana University of Lüneburg in Lower Saxony; Goethe University Frankfurt in Hesse; University of Lübeck in Schleswig-Holstein; and Viadrina European University in Brandenburg. These universities were then allowed to become employers of their professoriate (instead of the state) and independently recruit their professors without having to seek state approval. In turn, professors at these universities were no longer civil servants. Altogether 11 universities opted for this change.

In Germany, there are three levels of professorships: the junior professor position can be compared to the level of assistant professor (in Germany called W1, according to the level on the pay scale); the next level up can be compared to that of an associate professor (in Germany called W2); and finally, the highest professorial position, which is often linked to being a chair holder can be compared to a full professor (in Germany called W3). Full professors are normally civil servants with permanent contracts. Moving up on the career ladder from being a W1 professor to a W3 professor always entails applying for the higher position at another

Table 2.1.   Full-time Academic Staff Positions at German Universities
(2005 and 2014)

Categories of Academic Staff	2005	2014
Professors, including W1(Junior), W2, W3	37,865	45,749
Docents and postdoc assistants	9,874	3,431
Research and teaching assistants	111,343	177,528
Teaching staff for special tasks	6,655	9,656
Total	165,737	236,364

Source: Statistisches Bundesamt: Personal an Hochschulen, 2014, 23

university because there is no tenure track in German higher education and career progress cannot be achieved within the same institution. Applying elsewhere is also typical for W3 professors who can then negotiate a salary increase or better infrastructure for their research with their home university and with the new university.[6]

Docents have a habilitation but no professorship, and postdoc assistants are in the phase of getting their habilitation. Research and teaching assistants occupy budgeted positions (i.e., not third-party funded positions but positions that are part of the regular university budget for staff), and they are working on either their PhD or they are postdocs working on their habilitation. Finally, teaching staff for special tasks are teaching-only positions; they are often on fixed-term contracts but in some cases can be in permanent positions. As a rule, to which some exceptions exist, all positions below W2 professorships are fixed-term (for a maximum of six years). However, they are not considered to be casual labor.

When comparing the data for 2005 and 2014, some of the previously mentioned funding reforms as well as higher education expansion are reflected in the numbers. For example, the increase in professorships to some extent reflects the increase in the number of students enrolled in universities and the growth of the higher education sector in general. The steep decline in positions for docents and postdoc assistants reflects the reform of staff structures. Junior professorships are now included in the professorial category, the positions for postdocs (called assistants in Germany and designating the qualification phase during which the habilitation is produced) have been reduced considerably and postdocs now tend to be employed on full-time research and teaching positions below the previous assistant positions if they can't get a junior professorship.[7] The increase in teaching and research junior positions (doctoral candidates as well as postdocs) reflects the growth in professorial positions, as all university professors of the W2 and W3 categories usually have between one and four such positions attached to their chair or professorship as part of the research infrastructure. Furthermore, the excellence initiative with its considerable extra funding for doctoral schools and research clusters has led to an increase in positions below professorships.

An ideal-type academic career track would look as follows. A good student at graduate level (master's level studies) who has come to a professor's attention might be offered a student/junior research assistantship already at the master's degree level (up to 81 hours paid academic work per month). Upon successfully completing the degree, he or she would be offered a doctoral position as a junior researcher or a research and teaching assistant by the same professor. Upon successful completion of the doctoral degree—typically after four years—the traditional career track would entail the professor offering the graduate a research assistant position (postdoc) in order to qualify for a habilitation. All these positions are dependent on the professor, although the habilitation itself must be an independent piece of research work.

As is in many other countries, the decision to pursue an academic career has shifted from the doctoral stage to the postdoc stage. Nowadays, the postdoc phase is rather unstructured, with many possibilities to remain in the system but no guarantee of eventually getting a professorship. The most promising track is that of a junior professorship with early independence. Junior professorships are offered for six years with a performance evaluation after three years. Once a potential candidate believes that he or she has acquired sufficient qualifications, skills, competences, and networks, he or she will start applying for a professorship at the W2 or W3 level. All professorships in Germany must be publicly advertised. The candidate will typically have to apply several times until he or she is invited to a hearing by a search committee, makes it through the evaluation, and is eventually offered the position, which is normally at the W2 level. A first-time professorial position will often be offered for six years, followed in rare cases by the offer of tenure at the same institution or an application to the same or the highest level of professorship, again entailing a switch of institution.

Professors are contractually obliged to split their time more or less equally between research and teaching, with the more junior positions having a lower teaching load.[8] Due to high increases in student numbers in recent years, a special kind of academic position was created: teaching staff with special tasks. This is a teaching-only position with a teaching load of 14 to 16 hours per week during term time. Likewise, professors at universities of applied sciences who have no official research duties have teaching loads of 14 and up to 18 hours per week.

Other academic appointments can be found outside the higher education sector in the so-called extra-university research institutes of the Max Planck Society, the Fraunhofer Institutes, the Leibniz and the Humboldt Societies. These positions are typically research-only positions and neither academic staff nor directors have teaching obligations. However, directors often have a part-time teaching contract at a university because the institutes, especially those of the Max Planck Society, might have their own doctoral school but cannot award a doctoral degree because this is the sole responsibility (perhaps "privilege") of universities. No other institution in Germany is allowed to award doctoral degrees.

German Academic Staff at Work

TEACHING AND RESEARCH

In the German university sector, all professors have to carry out teaching and research. At the professorial level, there are hardly any teaching-only or research-only positions. The typical teaching load per semester week of a university professor is eight or, in some states, nine hours. In certain cases—for example, when taking over management positions as director of a centre or as a dean—a reduction of the regular teaching load can be negotiated for the duration of the term of office. The salary of a professor, which is part of the university budget, includes research support in the form of research assistant positions, secretarial support, and budgets for library book purchases and journal subscriptions, technical equipment, or laboratory expenses.

Workloads of other academic staff below a professorship are defined in terms of the number of teaching hours. The number of teaching hours depends on the type of position and typically ranges from two to six hours per week during the semester. For the remaining working time, staff are either expected to carry out research or work on their qualification, such as their doctoral thesis or their habilitation. There is no fixed number of hours per week during which academic staff are expected to do research or administration. There is one staff position that constitutes an exception to this: the teaching staff for particular tasks. These positions are mainly filled with doctorate holders on teaching-only contracts who have a teaching obligation of 12 hours or more per week and mostly teach in undergraduate programs.

Universities of applied sciences were originally conceived as professional education institutions without research. Therefore, most of these institutions do not have a proper research infrastructure in terms of more junior research staff. Furthermore, professors have to teach between 14 and 16 hours per week during term time. Nowadays, most universities of applied sciences do carry out research, but it is more applied and is often in cooperation with industry. However, they do not have access to funding from the German Research Council (German acronym: DFG, i.e., Deutsche Forschungsgemeinschaft) and they also cannot participate in the excellence initiative.

SUPPORT FOR RESEARCH

There are four main ways in which research is supported in the German university sector: as part of the regular and salaried duties of academic staff, in the form of competitive grants and third-party funding (DFG, private foundations, industry), in the form of targeted research programs of the federal and state ministries, and in the form of seed money or performance bonuses from the university budget. During the initial recruitment process, institutional research support is negotiated among the candidate for a professorship, the department, and the university leadership. Typically the objects of such negotiations will include the number of research assistants (doctoral researchers and postdocs) associated with the professorship (or chair), secretarial support, library, computer and laboratory budgets, travel expenses, and personal salary, although the latter tends to be capped by civil service regulations.

However, due to financial constraints and a stronger emphasis on performance-related salary components, there are an increasing number of professorships within universities (in particular, when a candidate is recruited to a professorship for the first time) that do not have the additional institutional research support described above. These are the so-called "naked" professorships, and it is expected that the candidate, once recruited, will acquire such infrastructure for research by successfully attracting third-party research funding.

Apart from the DFG, there is a wide range of private foundations that support research in universities. Grant applications are always peer reviewed and accepted (or rejected) on a competitive basis. Grants from the DFG are rather prestigious and often include the opportunity to fund one or more junior research assistants / doctoral candidates because a given research project is funded for between two and five years. Increasingly, in the last 10 years, the DFG has also been funding larger research clusters and doctoral schools. In the life sciences and engineering, industry also plays a vital role in terms of research funding.

Federal and state ministries also have a research budget, which is typically distributed on a competitive basis and in the framework of strategic funding programs. For example, the Federal Ministry of Education and Research established a research program in the field of higher education studies several years ago. Every two years there is a new call for tenders on a specified topic and between eight or ten larger research projects are funded for two to three years. State ministries responsible for higher education tend to spend their research budgets on initiatives promising outstanding and innovative results. Other ministries also have a research budget for which researchers and research groups in universities can compete. As a rule, research topics are determined by the portfolio of the respective ministry and are typically policy oriented and not considered to be basic research.

Finally, the universities themselves can earmark parts of their budgets to support research in a strategic and profile-building manner. This mostly takes the form of either seed money to support a research group in its beginning phase or is part of performance-related funding to reward successful researchers and research groups.

The main sources of external research funding in universities are:

- The German Research Foundation (DFG): 20 percent
- Industry: 26 percent
- Federal government: 19 percent
- Other (EU, private foundations, public sector): 26 percent

Current government policy encourages more cooperation between universities and extra-university research institutes. Frequently, directors of the Max Planck or Fraunhofer Institutes are also professors at universities based on joint appointments. This enables them to award doctoral degrees to junior staff who did their research work and thesis at an extra-university research institute since only universities have the right to award doctoral degrees. Currently, there is a debate in the German higher education and research system about abolishing the university monopoly to award doctoral degrees and allowing universities of applied sciences and extra-university research institutes to award doctoral degrees as well. No decision has been made yet, and such a decision is the responsibility of the state ministries.

Governance and Service

Despite organizational reforms emphasizing university autonomy with strengthened management, including the introduction of boards of governors, academics still play a rather influential role in all decisions concerning academic matters. Their strongest influence is on academic appointments and study programs. Their weakest influence is on the budget and its allocation, which is negotiated between the deans and the institutional leadership, and on the administration, which is headed centrally by a high-level position called *Kanzler* (chancellor). The senate, departmental committees, as well as search commissions usually include representatives from other groups in addition to professors—students, more junior academic staff, and, depending on the issues being discussed, nonacademic staff as well. However, in all major academic matters, professors are given a guaranteed majority of votes. At universities, the academic culture tends to be collegial, despite the fact that reforms over the last 15 years have strengthened hierarchies and introduced more managerial approaches. Deans nowadays have more responsibilities and more decision-making power, but they still tend to protect the department and their colleagues from too much managerial intervention. Deans serve for two or three years. They are normally elected from among the professors of a given department, and the decision has to be approved by the vice-chancellor. After their term of office, they return to the ranks of the professoriate.

Academic freedom is a constitutional right in Germany; academic freedom is enshrined in the federal constitution. Despite concerns that academic freedom is increasingly being threatened by managerial practices within universities and related accountability agendas, recent research (Schimank, Enders & Kehm, 2015) has shown that this is not really the case. Professors are held increasingly accountable for their output, impact, and success, but they continue to be free in their choice of topics for research and teaching. While the DFG and the federal ministry can introduce targeted research programs on specific topics or issues, most professors are able to formulate their research topics in such a way that they are compatible with funding priorities or themed programs of the national research council or other funders.

Beyond their formal role in decision making in the university organization proper, academic staff in Germany can exert more general influence on higher education policy making through their memberships in external organizations. The first way is to become a member of a professional organization, of which there are two: the German Higher Education Association (*Deutscher Hochschulverband*) and the Higher Education Teachers' Association Germany (*Hochschullehrerbund Deutschland*). The German Higher Education Association is open to university professors as well as academic staff at universities below the professorial level. It advises its members in legal, strategic, or tactical professional matters and frequently assumes advisory functions when professorial positions have to be filled. Its focus is on legal issues related to pay scales and working conditions, and it offers mentoring, coaching, and advice. The Higher Education Teachers' Association Germany is a professional organization whose membership consists exclusively of professors working at universities of applied sciences. It represents the interests of its members in areas of legislation, public administration, in courts and in public debates. The association focuses on pay, teaching load, technology transfer, expanding the subjects taught at universities of applied sciences, and supporting the introduction of master's-level study programs.

The second way for academic staff to exert influence on higher education policy making is by becoming a member of a trade union. There are two unions in Germany that are open for academic staff working in higher education institutions: the Unified Union for Services (*Ver.di*) and the Trade Union Education and Science (GEW). The former is the result of a merger in 2000 of several smaller unions with the big Trade Union for Public Services, Transport and Traffic. In 2015, this union had slightly more than two million members, of which academic staff constituted a small subgroup due to their either being civil servants or employees in the civil service. GEW had a membership of slightly less than 281,000 at the end of 2015. In this union as well, academic staff did not constitute the core group of members because the GEW is known as the (school) teachers' union. Both unions represent the interests of their members in the public and vis-à-vis their employers. Generally, unions in Germany are well organized and can exert a relatively strong influence on public policy and employers, that is, in the case of universities and universities of applied sciences, the respective state. Ever since the end of the Second World War, unionization and the inclusion of union representatives in many important policy decisions have been seen as part of the idea of a social market economy and the welfare state.

The third way to influence policy is by becoming a member of a learned society. Each discipline has its own learned society, which represents its members in matters related to teaching and research. Most learned societies have subgroups covering the various disciplinary areas or specializations. Learned societies typically organize one conference per year in order to discuss state-of-the-art developments in research and teaching, enable networking, and mentor junior academic staff. Learned societies issue public statements and try to exert influence if members feel that there are developments in the political and institutional realm that they don't agree with. For example, several learned societies in Germany have advised their members and the related institutional departments to boycott rankings. Academic staff (including professors) can become members of a union, but they are more often members of the learned society of their subject. Professors at universities of applied sciences (*Fachhochschulen*) and professors at universities have their own guildlike organizations, which are influential stakeholder and lobby organizations. However, most of the lobbying of these organizations is directed toward public policy. The decision-making power of the professoriate within universities is (although weakened to some extent) still strong enough to exert considerable internal influence independent of unionization.

Salary and Contracts

All professors (W1–W3 on the pay scale) are civil servants in Germany. Those on fixed-term contracts are usually civil servants for the duration of their contract;

however, they can opt to be employees in the civil service.[9] The differences between the three categories of professors (W1, W2, W3) are mainly related to the
salary level and the available research infrastructure. As mentioned earlier, there
are fixed salary scales for all civil servants and employees in the civil service in
Germany. These are determined by the relevant state ministries and are not unified across the country. There is very little room for salary negotiations above the
fixed scale. Only in exceptional cases are universities allowed to offer a salary outside these scales but have to seek permission from their respective state ministry
first. In the framework of recruitment for professorial positions, some negotiating
power is available on both sides, especially when a university wants to lure a highly
reputed professor away from his or her current home university. However, the
room for maneuvering is less high in terms of salary than it is in terms of infrastructure, that is, the number of research assistants, postdocs, and secretarial support directly associated to the chair (or position), teaching load, library and IT
budget, and the like. Salaries increase automatically with the number of children
in the family and with seniority as well as after annual pay rise negotiations with
trade unions.[10]

A pay scale reform introduced in 2005 shifted the traditional pay scales to a
lowered basic salary and introduced performance-related components. However,
a lawsuit by a group of professors complaining that they were being underpaid in
relation to their qualifications was decided in favor of their claim and universities
had to re-increase the basic salary to such an extent that the budget for performance-
related pay was more or less depleted.

An academic salary at the postdoctoral level is typically high enough to allow
for a middle-class lifestyle, upper middle class for professors. However, businesses
and companies pay their senior employees considerably more than universities pay
their professors and other employees. This salary disadvantage in universities is
counterbalanced by generous fringe benefits, flexible working hours, and high social
status (Herzog & Kehm, 2012).

Typically, university professors will only work at one institution at a time. If they
accrue income from elsewhere, they must seek official permission from institutional management (universities and universities of applied sciences). However, in
certain subjects or disciplines (e.g., law, architecture, psychology, medicine), university professors often have their own practice, business, or consulting agency.
This is tolerated—especially in the case of medicine—because otherwise it would
be impossible to find candidates for professorial positions. Additional income in
the form of honorariums, royalties, or likewise does not have to be approved but

has to be submitted with the individual professor's tax declaration. Because professors are civil servants, they typically have a moral obligation to be truthful in their tax declaration because if caught it might cost them their civil servant status.

The retirement age in Germany is currently 65 years of age. Recent new laws reacting to changed demographics (i.e., an aging society) have stipulated a gradual increase of the retirement age up to 67 years. This includes the population as a whole, though with some exceptions for workers who have carried out physically heavy work during their employment. However, for professors the official retirement age is not necessarily mandatory. Often professors at the threshold of retirement are asked whether they would like to continue with some teaching or supervision duties. Also, third-party funded projects often run for some time beyond the retirement age. In general, some kind of arrangement is made (sometimes paid, sometimes unpaid) between the institutional management and the professor. Civil service pensions allow for a reasonable standard of living and, as a rule, retirees do not need to find another job.

Conclusions

Professorial pathways in German higher education are a combination of the right qualifications and serendipity. Many professorial positions no longer require the candidate to have a habilitation in order to become eligible for such a position. While a junior professorship may in a small number of cases provide such an alternative route, the substitute is mostly an unspecified number of publications plus teaching experience, which are then deemed to be equivalent to a habilitation.

The Federal Ministry for Education and Research is currently very concerned about the lack of proper career progress because it is fears that the best talent does not remain in academia (Konsortium Bundesbericht Wissenschaftlicher Nachwuchs, 2017). Furthermore, it is typical that during the late phase of a doctorate or during the postdoc phase, young people start a family and have children. The need to change institutions for career progress leads to many young families having one partner commuting, often for many hours, resulting in a family life that can only take place during the weekends. Dual career options for couples are very rare in Germany. In addition, the long, drawn-out insecurity at the beginning of an academic career leads many young academics to opt for positions in the nonacademic labor market in order to have better job security.

The other side of the coin is the discussion about introducing tenure-track models. There is some reluctance to do this because it is associated with inbreeding and less competition. Currently, the federal ministry is funding a major report to be issued every two years about developments related to academic career progress in order to provide more evidence on which to base future decisions about reforms to staff structures and academic career progression. The first three reports have been published (Burkhardt, 2008; Konsortium Bundesbericht Wissenschaftlicher Nach-wuchs, 2013, 2017) but no decisions have been made yet. Furthermore, in 2012 a research-funding program was established on the same issue by the Federal Minis-try of Education and Research to come up with new evidence. It is anticipated that within the next three to five years a public policy and a model to improve career progress will be established to improve the current situation.

Still, the German nonacademic labor market has always been rather open to doctoral degree holders. This has improved even more during the last few years as the idea of living in a knowledge society and economy has taken hold. Except perhaps for some subjects in the humanities and social sciences with no clearly defined professional target area in the nonacademic labor market (for example, philosophy), most doctoral degree holders in Germany will be able to find ade-quate jobs in which they can use their acquired competences and skills.

NOTES

1. Furthermore, professors at universities of applied sciences do not have to have a *ha-bilitation* (a form of second doctorate) but are required to have worked professionally outside higher education for at least five years.

2. The Federal Statistical Office only provides figures for the public system and does not take into account any figures for private higher education institutions.

3. The higher education sector in Germany is regarded as quite separate from the vo-cational education and training sector. Student enrollment increased over time and is currently at 59 percent of the 18–24 age cohort. This is still considerably lower than the Organisation for Economic Co-operation and Development (OECD) average of 65 percent and lower than in many other OECD countries, some of which have reached a participa-tion rate in higher education of 70 percent or more (e.g., Denmark 87 percent, Switzer-land 76 percent). This is largely accounted for by the fact that the (postsecondary) voca-tional education and training sector in Germany is neither viewed nor counted as part of higher education (OECD, 2016).

4. This is why Germany has no statistics about the actual number of doctoral candi-dates. Statistics are available only for doctoral degrees awarded. The fact that Germany cannot provide statistics on the number of doctoral candidates has become a political con-cern, and universities are currently encouraged to come up with a solution, i.e., some type of registration system for all doctoral candidates.

5. A specificity of the German higher education system is the chair system. Originally, the word "chair" in this context referred to the elevated chair or pulpit from which the

teacher in the medieval university read his texts. So the most senior teachers were chair holders. In modern times the chair holder represents a particular subject area within a discipline (e.g., within physics one might find a chair for solid state physics or within German literature one might find chairs for medieval and for modern literature). A chair does not only consist of the chair holder but encompasses the whole group of junior academic staff and postdocs that are associated with the chair. In most cases, it also includes a secretary, and in the laboratory sciences technicians are part of the chair as well. In most German universities, chairs are part of a department or institute. Every chair holder in a German university is a full professor, but not every full professor is necessarily a chair holder, despite full professors being commonly referred to as chair holders. It is not possible to compare a chair holder with an endowed professorship as in a US university, as endowed professorships are very rare in Germany. In the newer Germany universities (those established after the mid-1960s), the chair holder system was basically abolished, but it is still in place in the older, more traditional universities. Chair holders simply constitute the most senior (and often most influential) professorships.

6. Due to the traditional civil servant status of professors, German universities used to have few noncitizens among their professoriate. With the growing internationalization of higher education, this has been recognized as a flaw in the system and relevant regulations have been loosened. Currently, the proportion of non-German professors at German higher education institutions is around 6 percent (Neusel et al., 2014), which is considerably lower than the proportion of foreign professors in the United States, United Kingdom, or France. It is, however, not possible for professors with a nationality other than German to become a German civil servant. At public universities and universities of applied sciences, they would be employees in the civil service.

7. While the junior professorship is only n = 800, its explicit purpose was to reduce the number of postdoctoral assistants.

8. That is part of the Humboldtian model of higher education, which is defined as education *through* research. Thus, professors as the most experienced researchers have the highest teaching load, with the exception of teaching-only staff.

9. The main differences between a civil servant and an employee in the civil service is that civil servants cannot be dismissed (unless they commit a criminal offense), and as a consequence they do not have to pay for unemployment benefits, which are normally deducted automatically from salary. In addition, the state will pay for their pensions and they do not have to pay into any pension scheme. Civil servants have private medical health insurance and can claim any health expenses that are not covered by their insurance from the state. Civil servants can unionize but do not have the right to go on strike. Employees in the civil service have the usual fringe benefits that are normal for Germany (i.e., health insurance, paid vacation time, accruing pension money, maternity leave, right to claim unemployment benefits, etc.), but contributions to their health insurance, pension claims, and unemployment benefits are automatically deducted from their salaries.

10. *Kindergeld* (money for children) is paid monthly by the state and increases per child with every child that is born. The parent with whom the children are living gets the money. As a rule, that money is paid from birth until age 18 or longer when the child is still going through education and/or training. It ends with age 24 at the latest.

REFERENCES

Burkhardt, Anke, ed. 2008. *Wagnis Wissenschaft: Akademische Karrierewege und das Fördersystem in Deutschland.* Leipzig: Akademische Verlagsanstalt.

Burkhardt, Anke, and Sigrun Nickel. 2015. *Die Juniorprofessur: Neue und alte Qualifizierungswege im Vergleich.* Baden-Baden: Nomos.

Buschle, Nicole, and Carsten Haider. 2016. "Private Hochschulen in Deutschland." *Wista* 1:75–86. Wiesbaden: Statistisches Bundesamt.

Destatis. 2014. Personal an Hochschulen. Fachserie 11, Reihe 4.4. Wiesbaden: Destatis.

Herzog, Marius, and Barbara M. Kehm. 2012. "The Income Situation in the German System of Higher Education: A Rag Rug." In *Paying the Professoriate: A Global Comparison of Compensation and Contracts,* ed. P. G. Altbach, L. Reisberg, M. Yudkevich, G. Androuchchak, and I. F. Pacheco, 145–54. New York: Routledge.

Kehm, Barbara M., and Peer Pasternack. 2009. "The German 'Excellence Initiative' and Its Role in Restructuring the National Higher Education Landscape." In *Structuring Mass Higher Education: The Role of Elite Institutions,* ed. D. Palfreyman and T. Tapper, 113–27. Abingdon: Routledge.

Konsortium Bundesbericht Wissenschaftlicher Nachwuchs. 2013. *Statistische Daten und Forschungsbefunde zu Promovierencen und Promovierten in Deutschland.* Bielefeld: W. Bertelsmann Verlag.

———. 2017. *Statistische Daten und Forschungsbefunde zu Promovierenden und Promovierten in Deutschland.* Bielefeld: W. Bertelsmann Verlag.

Musselin, Christine. 2012. *The Market for Academics.* London: Routledge.

Neusel, Aylâ, Andrä Wolter, Ole Engel, Marianne Kriszio, and Doreen Weichert. 2014. *Internationale Mobilität und Professur: Final Report to the German Ministry of Education and Research (in German).* https://www.erziehungswissenschaften.hu-berlin.de. Accessed October 10, 2016.

OECD. 2016. *Education at a Glance.* Paris: OECD

Schimank, Uwe, Jürgen Enders, and Barbara M. Kehm. 2015. "Turning Universities into Actors on Quasi-Markets: How New Public Management Reforms Affect Academic Research." In *The Changing Governance of Higher Education and Research,* ed. D. Jansen and I. Pruisken, 89–103. Dordrecht, Netherlands: Springer.

Statistisches Bundesamt. 2009. *Fachserie 11, Reihe 4.4: Personal an Hochschulen 2008.* Wiesbaden: Statistisches Bundesamt.

———. 2014a. *Fachserie 11, Reihe 4.1: Studierende an Hochschulen im Wintersemester 2013/14.* Vorbericht. Wiesbaden: Statistisches Bundesamt.

———. 2014b. *Fachserie 11, Reihe 4.4: Personal an Hochschulen 2013.* Wiesbaden: Statistisches Bundesamt.

3 | France

Marginal Formal Changes
but Noticeable Evolutions

CHRISTINE MUSSELIN

In 2009, the French minister for Higher Education, Valérie Pécresse, issued a new decree regarding faculty at universities. After six months of demonstrations and negotiations, this decree was signed in April 2009 and it somewhat modified the 1984 decree. The French academic profession, however, has rarely been at the center of the many reforms in higher education within the last decade. These recent reforms addressed the governance of French universities (the LRU Act of 2007: Loi Responsabilites et Libertés des Universités [Responsibilities and Freedom of Universities Act]) and the institutional organization of research funding and evaluation of higher education and research (the LOPRI Act of 2006: Loi d'Orientation pour la Recherche et l'Innovation [Research and Innovation Act]), which led to the creation of a national research council, the Agence Nationale pour la Recherche (ANR) and a national agency for evaluation, the Agence d'Évaluation de la Recherche et de l'Enseignement Supérieur (AERES), today called Haut Conseil pour l'Evaluation de l'Enseignement Supérieur et de la Recherche [HCERES]).

A number of the novelties present in the 2009 decree have still not been implemented, such as the four-year evaluation of all permanent faculty members in universities, which has long been opposed by the national university body, the Conseil National des Universités (CNU) (National University Council), which was supposed to implement it.[1] As a result, the adjustment of (shift in) the balance between teaching, research, and service duties that university presidents could have negotiated with each faculty member, based on the results of his or her evaluation, did not occur.[2] The main formal change that finally came into effect was the composition of hiring committees that, since the LRU Act, could now include from 8 to 16 members, half of which must be faculty members from universities different from the recruiting one (thus emphasizing the presence of external expertise).

Although not a focal point of the reforms, the French academic profession has nevertheless been affected by the transformation of the French institutional setting. The career paths stay the same and competitions remain the principal device for access to and promotion within the academic profession. However, while the number of available faculty positions decreased, a new group of permanently temporary knowledge workers emerged. In parallel, among the permanent faculty members, differentiation increased through the increase in project-based research, and the relationships between academics and their university has evolved.

The French Higher Education System and the Main Recent Reforms

The French higher education system is a public system consisting of three institutional sectors: universities, *grandes écoles*, and national research organizations. Their emergence and development are strongly linked to historical junctures.

THE ATYPICAL TRAJECTORY OF FRENCH UNIVERSITIES

The French Revolution was foundational to the development of the French higher education and research system. In 1793, the revolution closed the universities in most of the main cities, and it was only thirteen years later, in 1806, that Napoleon created the Imperial University, that is, one university for all of France. In between, a few *grandes écoles* were created with the objective of offering more operational training and better serving the economic development of France. With the new Napoleonic university, *facultés* were rebuilt, but they were first and foremost aimed at training and teaching.[3] While the individual faculties may have been located in the same city, the faculties were not integrated into a single university structure. This conception of French higher education was therefore completely different from the one imagined at about the same time by the German Wilhelm von Humbolt, and that would give rise to the research university in many countries— starting with the United States—in the twentieth century (Renaut, 1995).

This faculté and teaching-based model, despite some reforms, remained in place until the 1968 Faure Act that followed the students' movement of May 1968.

The Faure Act suppressed the former facultés, led to a complete restructuring of universities, and gave birth to the French institutions as we know them today. The act also provided the faculties with the possibility of electing their president and making decisions in bodies in which students, administrative, and academic staff (and in some cases, stakeholders) had a say.

Most of the reforms since 1968 (e.g., the Savary Act of 1984 and the LRU Act of 2007) aimed at strengthening the power of the president and increasing the institutional autonomy of the newly created universities. The emergence of French universities as stronger institutions was especially brought about by the implementation of four-year (now five-year) contracts between the ministry and each university at the beginning of the 1990s. A further important milestone was passed in 2007 with the LRU Act when universities became responsible for their payroll and therefore were able to decide on the management of human resources without obtaining an approval from the ministry for the creation or renewal of positions, as was the case before.

Because of the LRU Act, French universities can select their own staff and administer a lump-sum budget.[4] They can also decide their academic programs, although they still need them to be accredited by the ministry in order to deliver national diplomas. All universities deliver national diplomas called bachelor's, master's, and PhD and are all considered research universities. Their tuition fees are very low (less than 300 euros per year), and they are mainly funded through public resources. However, they cannot select their students or decide the level of tuition fees, and are still considered to have relatively low institutional autonomy in European comparative studies (European University Association, n.d.). They represent the larger share of the higher education system (over 1.5 million students out of 2.4 million), but they are not the most attractive or the most prestigious higher education institutions in France.

Elite Training and Research Developed outside Universities

The development of French universities did not deter the continual emergence of grandes écoles in either the nineteenth or twentieth century. The grandes écoles became, for the best of them, the main reproduction system of the French elite, although until recently (and with the exception of the *Écoles normales supérieures*), they were professionalized and not research-oriented. The grandes écoles train only a small share of students, but they select them either after the baccalaureate or after two years of intensive preparation in the *classes préparatoires* (preparatory classes). Today, there are 71 universities in France but 222 grandes écoles are registered and recognized by the French Conférence des Grandes Écoles (the grandes école equivalent of the CPU, the Conference of University Presidents). They are rather differentiated, some of them considered to be highly prestigious while others are less reputed; nevertheless, many parents prefer that their children attend them rather than go through the university system.

Grandes écoles focused on business were the first to become international and research oriented. They were more subject to international competition and adopted global standards and norms for academic programs and faculty recruitment such as the PhD credential and a publication record. As quasi-private institutions, they also sharply raised their fees.[5] Grandes écoles focused on engineering started their transformation in the 1990s, and the public ones remain almost as inexpensive as universities. They claim that they should be allowed to raise tuition fees. Despite the academic drift of grandes écoles, their links to universities remain rather weak, and the flow of students from engineering schools to the university sector remains rare, even as it is increasing at the master and PhD levels.

Another consequence of the historical trajectory of French universities is their teaching orientation. Despite the 1896 Act[6] that aimed at transforming them into research universities, research activities were still rather limited in the twentieth century, and national research institutions—starting with the CNRS (Centre National de la Recherche Scientifique [National Scientific Research Center]) in 1936, followed by many others[7]—were created to foster French research. Some of these institutions are still not very closely linked to universities, and even less to grandes écoles, but others—like CNRS or INSERM (National Institute for Medical Research)—have been providing a research label as well as human and budgetary resources to research teams located within universities since the mid-1960s. As a result, more than 90 percent of CNRS researchers currently work in university labs and research has become increasingly important for French universities.

Despite this cross-fertilization (i.e., grandes écoles becoming more academic, research institutes located within universities, and so on), the French higher education system is still often considered to be too segmented in ways that undermine system performance.[8] Some recent evolutionary reforms have aimed at changing that.

RECENT REFORMS AT THE SYSTEMS LEVEL

Two main developments have characterized the evolution of the French higher education system since 2000. The first is the increase in competition between institutions, research units, and individual academics. A large share of the budget is now allocated through selective national calls, and recurrent budgets are proportionately declining.

The second development is the creation of policies aimed at bringing universities, grandes écoles, and national research institutions together. The 2006 LOPRI Act created the possibility of establishing consortia of higher education institutions, called PRES (Poles for Higher Education and Research), in which universities, grandes écoles, and national research institutions located in the same city or region could coordinate and share some common activities or programs—for example, delivering a "joint" doctoral degree at the level of the PRES or relegating to PRES the international strategy of the different institutions.

In 2010 and 2011, these two evolutions were combined in a national program called the Grand Emprunt, or PIA (Programme d'Investissement d'Avenir, or initiative for the future). Some highly selective national calls for proposals were organized by the state to identify the best PRES and allocate a substantial amount of funding to them (16 billion euros in 2010) with the goal of fostering French research and, at minimum, maintaining France's place in the world. Only PRES (no single institutions) could apply for this funding. One of the calls for proposals—IDEX (*initiative d'excellence*)—aimed at identifying consortia of universities with high potential, labeling them as IDEX, and providing them with more resources. Eight consortia were selected; three of them were composed of already-merged or about-to-merge universities, probably because mergers was seen by the international jury in charge of the selection as a proxy for the strength of the governance of the consortium: Aix-Marseille, Strasbourg, and Bordeaux. The Fioraso Act of 2013 went a step further: it required each higher education institution to be part of or associated with a consortium of institutions, now called COMUE (Community of Universities and Institutions), also including grandes écoles and national research institutions. These huge consortia are expected to become the main institutional pillars of the French higher education system in the future.

A Co-Managed Governance of the Higher Education and Research Systems

These recent reforms, like the previous ones, are never simply brought about by administrative or governmental decisions. They always involve some members of the professoriate having access to the politico-administrative sphere. As I described elsewhere (Musselin, 2009), there is a long tradition of co-management between the ministry and part of the academic profession. Decisions at the ministry level involve academic experts solicited to review the projects submitted by universities for accreditation or funding.

Certain members of the academic profession are very active in pushing particular reforms and even implementing them when they occupy important functions at the ministry level (such as ministers themselves, members of cabinet, or directors of one of the administrative directorates of the ministry). The role of labor unions for higher education, although sometimes more visible than the discrete action of influential academics, is often not very efficient. The demonstrations of 2009, for instance, lasted more than six months but did not succeed in blocking the 2009 decree mentioned at the beginning of this chapter.

The role of professional associations (like the French Sociological Association, AFS, for instance), remains rather weak. There is no tradition of strong lobbying and they are also rather limited in scope and activities for their members.

A Pyramidal Organization of Academic Careers and of Allocation of Work

A complete description of the French academic profession would require comparing the faculty (academic staff) of the universities, grandes écoles, and national research institutions such as the CNRS or INSERM. While I will sometimes refer to the CNRS, this chapter will mainly focus on French universities because aggregated data exist for this sector but not for the other ones. I will not deal with the sector of the grandes écoles since very little data are available about the staff and the career framework of these schools.[9]

At French universities and national research institutions, the permanent faculty hold civil servant positions;[10] therefore, academic careers are organized by national rules voted upon by the parliament. The structure of the French academic profession is very different from the German system (Enders & Bornmann, 2001; Enders & Teichler, 1995), where secured positions are very rare and restricted to the highest status only—that of the professor, all other positions being temporary. Among this "temporary" workforce, only some survive the long road to professorship and securing a permanent post. France is also very different from the US system and its two tracks (Finkelstein & Schuster, 2006): the tenure track that starts with six or seven years based on the up-or-out rule and can lead to a tenured position but is restricted to fewer positions over time, and the non–tenure track, where adjuncts and post-doctoral students are employed in temporary positions until they either get a tenure-track position, decide to continue to work in contractual roles or pursue a career outside academia. Although France has evolved in

Table 3.1. Academic Positions in Higher Education in France

Status	Professors	Maîtres de Conférences	High school teachers in universities*	Doctoral fellows with teaching duties and ATER**	Associated professors***	Other
Number	20,353	36,555	13,069	13,321	2,993	5,981
%	22.1%	39.6%	14.2%	14.5%	3.2%	6.4%

Note: Shaded areas = permanent staff

*Some high school teachers are "loaned" to universities with teaching duties that are much higher than those for professors or MCF: 384 hours a year versus 128 or 192, respectively.

**ATER (*Attachés temporaires d'enseignement et de recherche*) are doctoral fellows who have just completed, or are close to completing, their doctorates, with a two-year non-renewable contract. They teach 196 hours a year.

***Associated professors are individuals working half time as professionals or in a firm and half time as professors at the university. They have three-year contracts that can be renewed twice.

the last decade, as will be explained below, the majority of the French academic profession consists of those who are civil servants.

It is possible to enter the group of permanent university staff after obtaining a PhD by applying to a first tenured position as a *maître de conférences* (called *chargé de recherche* at national research institutions).[11] Only some will become professors (or *directeurs de recherche* at national research institutions): in 2014, there were 20,353 professors and 36,555 maîtres de conférences (MCF). The French academic profession consists therefore of a pyramid structure, with a base that is much larger than the top: the way to the top is not for everyone, but those who do not reach professorship are not excluded from the system and remain maîtres de conférences until they retire. The first subsection below will describe how one can go from one level (PhD) to another (MCF) and the mechanisms that regulate this trajectory.

Finally, maîtres de conférences and professors enjoy academic freedom, which in France means that they can choose what they teach and research, and also that they can freely organize their time, except for the number of hours they have to teach each year, which is fixed by their status: professors 128 hours annually, MCFs 192 hours annually.

Before Access to a Permanent Position

In a study in which we compared cohorts of faculty members who obtained a first permanent position in 1976–77, 1986–87, 1996–97, and 2006–7, biographical interviews[12] with some members of each cohort (100 in total) showed how this first step toward an academic career has evolved over the last 40 years (Musselin, Pigeyre & Sabatier, forthcoming).

The first important transformation is that the PhD degree has become compulsory for an academic since the 1970s. Preparing for a PhD has also become more structured: the time that should be dedicated to it is not supposed to be more than three years (even if this is far from being followed in the social sciences and humanities); more doctoral fellowships were allocated in the late 1980s to permit full-time work on research (but they are still rarer in the social sciences and humanities); and doctoral schools were created in the mid-1990s and classes were formally introduced at the doctoral level with the Bologna Process. An increasing number of specific classes are offered to PhD candidates to help them find a job in academia or in firms; the idea that PhDs should not only be oriented toward academic jobs has spread in France. The doctoral period should therefore not only be dedicated to writing a thesis but also to prepare the student for a future job, and supervisors are expected to be more attentive to whether their doctoral students "check all the boxes" necessary to succeed after they finish their doctorate.

This professionalization of the training process for PhD candidates goes hand in hand with a decrease in interpersonal mechanisms and relationships. Most of the academics recruited in the 1970s and 1980s whom we interviewed explained that they entered the academic profession because one of their professors had asked them to work as a research assistant for them, and they finally decided to obtain a PhD and got a first tenured position after—or even before—they graduated. Such narratives were less common among the interviewees recruited in the mid-1990s, and never occurred among those recruited in the mid-2000s. Within universities, such interpersonal relationships were replaced by more collective decision making: committees select their PhD candidates from among the best candidates with master's degrees applying for a fellowship; the candidates are hosted in research units (even if it is still far from being the case in social sciences and humanities); and they are encouraged to exchange with faculty other than their supervisor. As for the PhD candidates themselves, we more frequently observed strategic behaviors: the rather passive enrollment of their older colleagues ceded the path to a more active choice of the place from which they wanted to graduate, the supervisor with whom they wanted to work, and the positions they would seek once they graduated.[13]

Nevertheless, and despite these evolutions, the preparation of a PhD is still considered a period of apprenticeship (Musselin, 2009). Although France signed the European charter stating that PhD candidates are young researchers, they are still "in-between": they are simultaneously potential future colleagues (integrated in the labs, sitting at meetings, producing knowledge) and students (taking classes, training in professional competences, being supervised).

Upon receiving a doctorate, they are confronted with a decrease in positions available at universities. The following figures show this phenomenon during the last decade, but this situation will worsen in the coming years as retirement rates are slowing down and the state budget cannot support the creation of many new positions.

In France, not all PhD holders are allowed to apply for academic positions. Holding a PhD is a necessary, but not a sufficient condition for entering the academic profession. Doctoral graduates have to be "qualified" by a national council of universities (CNU), which is organized around discipline-based committees. Each committee may have quite different qualification strategies: some are very selective and even model the number of candidates that they qualify on the number of positions that are opened (e.g., private and public law, information and communication technologies, and protestant theology qualify less than 35 percent of their candidates); others are less Malthusian (for example, mathematics, astronomy, and theoretical chemistry qualify more than 90 percent of the applicants).[14] Nevertheless, all committees expect the same things from the candidates: an excellent PhD dissertation, diverse experiences in teaching, and some publications, which are qualifications that must have been acquired during the PhD program.

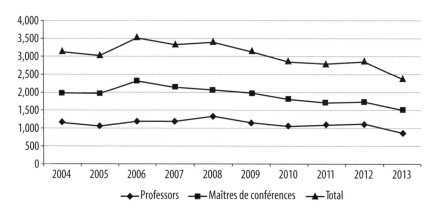

Figure 3.1. Evolution of the number of positions opened for each academic category and total since 2004. *Source:* Based on http://cache.media.enseigne mentsup-recherche.gouv.fr/file/statistiques/00/6/bilrec13_327006.pdf.

Being "qualified" by the CNU is mandatory to apply for academic positions, and the qualification is valid for four years; however, it does not guarantee a position. In 2013, 15.2 percent of those who applied for a position of maître de conferences were offered and accepted the position. However, among the 1,294 recruited in this category in 2013, almost 44 percent received their qualification the same year (this ratio was 46.52 percent in 2012 and 46.08 percent in 2011).[15] That is, selection favored the most recent doctoral graduates.

THE INTERMEDIARY AND AMBIGUOUS SITUATION OF THE MAÎTRES DE CONFÉRENCES

Those who are lucky enough to be recruited get a first permanent position as a maître de conférences. It is the largest category in terms of numbers (around two-thirds of the total number of permanent academic positions). This category is structured into two grades (maître de conférences and maîtres de conférences classe exceptionnelle). Some academics remain in this category their entire professional life. In terms of salary, civil servants are paid according to a national scale and progress according to seniority on the one hand and promotions on the other. They start at 2,070 euros per month gross.[16] If they remain in this category until the end of their career, they can leave with a monthly salary of 4,390 euros. This is not a very attractive profession and probably one of the least interesting intellectual professions, if you disregard the advantages you have as a public servant (in terms of pension or employment security). But, even with these generous benefits, after at least eight years of university training, starting with a salary that is only 1.4 times higher than the French minimum wage (1,466 euros/month) is not very attractive, especially if you consider that the mean starting salary for a student trained at the École Polytechnique (the best engineering school) is 3,750 euros per month gross and for a student trained at HEC (the best business school) is 3,340 euros/month, both having spent only five years as a student.

In the history of the French academic profession, the maîtres de conférences (called *maîtres-assistants* until 1984) were a category of academic staff working under the supervision of professors. But as the 1984 decree reads, the differences between the tasks and duties of maîtres de conférences and professors are marginal, except that the former are not allowed to supervise PhD candidates unless they defended a sort of second PhD called an *habilitation à diriger des recherches* (habilitation to supervise research). Therefore, this professional category is ambiguous: it is a step toward professorship for some, but it is also a "career" for those who will remain in this category until they retire. It is a lower position in the career trajectory: while for those starting in this category it is still considered a stage of apprenticeship during which one has still to prove one's abilities, for those who are in this category for years and will never leave it, it does not make sense to speak of an apprenticeship.

Because of this ambiguity, and because the decrees of 1984 and then 2009 are themselves not very clear in pointing out what makes a professor different from a maître de conférences, the level of autonomy and responsibility of the latter and the type of relationships they have with the professors very much vary from one department to another, and even within the same department may vary from one activity to another. As shown with V. Becquet (Musselin & Becquet, 2008), some history departments maintain a hierarchical relationship between the two categories, but these dependent relationships mostly concern teaching activities and administrative responsibilities such as department heads but not research activities. Meanwhile, in hierarchical departments of physics, maîtres de conferences will also be dependent on professors for their research. Nevertheless, in these two disciplines, we also found departments where versatility prevailed at all levels, and where maîtres de conférences and professors were engaged in the same activities.

The seniority in the position also plays a role in the content of the tasks and in the nature of the relationships: almost everywhere newly recruited maîtres de conférences are not in a situation of negotiating what they will teach and what responsibilities they will assume. Most of their colleagues—professors as well as more senior maîtres de conférences—generally consider that the newcomer should take over what the others no longer want to do.

In such matters, the place where one gets a first position plays an important role, although French universities are supposed to be equivalent. The relationships between professors and maîtres de conférences vary, the pressure for teaching (or research) varies according to the student-to-faculty ratio, and the attention paid to the career development of faculty members also varies as some departments try to encourage their young colleagues to become professors (for instance, by reducing their teaching load and leaving them time to write their habilitation), while others do not care.

The Professorship, at the Top of the Pyramid

Professors represent about one-third of the academic profession. Access to a professorship does not follow the same procedure in all disciplines. In law, economics, management, and political science, access to a professorship first of all relies on applying for and being successful at a highly selective national exam called the *agrégation du supérieur*.[17] For all other disciplines, one has to pass an ha-bilitation à diriger des recherches and then be qualified by the CNU. The rate of qualification at this level is as diverse as for maîtres de conferences: in 2013, it reached more than 90 percent in English literature, mathematics, and structure and evolution of earth, but less than 40 percent in urbanism, information and communication technologies, sport, and Catholic theology. The "qualified" can then apply for professorship positions. Again, those who are qualified the year they apply have quite a high success rate: 46.25 percent of those newly recruited as pro-fessors in 2013 were qualified in 2013 (this rate was 44.34 percent in 2012 and 45.61 percent in 2011).[18]

Within the professor category, there are three career levels—*seconde classe, pre-mière classe*, and *classe exceptionnelle*—and the progression from one to the other occurs through promotions granted either at the national level by the CNU or at the local level by universities. Each year, the ministry allocates 50 percent of the promotions to distribute to the CNU and 50 percent to the universities. In terms of salary, in 2016 the first grade started at 3,100 euros per month gross (but most are already higher as maîtres de conférences and do not start at the bottom of the scale) and could reach 6,149 euros per month gross if they rise to the highest pay grade.

In their activities, professors enjoy an even greater autonomy than maîtres de conférences and can balance their time between teaching, research, and other ac-tivities. They benefit from a long tradition of professional individual autonomy within institutions that in the past were weak. Professors are often described as being part of a *profession libérale d'etat*, meaning that they are in a way like lawyers in terms of their independence but at the same time are civil servants and enjoy state security.

This description of the French academic career framework for university fac-ulty shows it is hybrid. The university system is regulated at the national level, rules for civil servants apply to French maîtres de conférences and professors, and the state is still the employer. However, universities have become increasingly re-sponsible for recruitment of their faculty, even if they can only choose among those who were qualified by the CNU. They cannot decide the salaries (even if it now happens in disciplines such as economics), but they can decide on the posi-tions: they may transform a professor position into a maître de conferences po-sition or an administrative one, or they can outfit a computer lab if they prefer. Finally, universities are also responsible for half of the promotions (the other half still being at the national level), and they allocate funding to the departments

based on the evaluations by the AERES, which directly impacts the research capacity of the individual faculty member.

After this rather formal description of the French academic profession, I will
now turn to a more analytical point of view and explain the mechanisms underlying mobility from one professional category to another and what changes these
mechanisms have undergone in recent years.

A System of Vacancy Chains and Competitions

Along with the stability of the structure of the French academic profession, two
fundamental characteristics of the French system have not been challenged over
the last years.[19] First, the system continues to work according to a dynamics of
vacancy chains. Second, the centrality of competitions over an academic's entire
career remains high: applicants wait for a slot (for recruitment or promotion
within a category) to be opened and when a slot is opened, many candidates apply and only one is selected. The combination of these two characteristics favors
the constitution of a secondary labor market.

THE SUPREMACY OF COMPETITIONS AND THEIR RESULTS

In France, positions are opened if one becomes vacant or if a new position is
created. There must be an existing slot available for a person to move up. Transforming a position of maître de conferences into a position of professor (as an associate might become a full professor in the United States, for instance) is not
completely impossible,[20] but it is very rare because the basic principle is that in order to apply for a professor position, one post in this category must be vacant. This
in turn liberates a position of maîtres de conférences, for example, and allows those
who have no position or who want to get a position elsewhere (mobility) to apply
for it. They are all competing with one another to fill the slot.

This system of vacancy chains and competitions is the modus operandi in the
French system. It starts with the first position as maître de conférences, after one
has been successful with the qualification process. The average number of candidates applying for any one position is 38, but it varies according to the location of
the position. Large universities in big cities receive more candidates. The type of
department offering a position also plays a role: positions in a department within
an IUT (a two-year vocational college located within universities) are generally less
attractive than those in traditional departments. Paris and its suburbs are also
usually more attractive than other parts of France, and the chance for universities
to recruit through position vacancies is higher in this region than in others. In

2013, 11 universities were unsuccessful in their recruitments: 5 vacant positions received no applicants and 32 others remained vacant because all the ranked candidates opted for a position at other universities. The same competition process applies when one moves from maître de conférences to professor, even if most of the time there are fewer candidates for professor positions than for positions as maîtres de conférences. In 2013, the statistics provided by the ministry account for seven applications on average for each vacant professor position.

Despite this rather low level of competitive pressure, when we compared the four cohorts, and more precisely when we compared access to professorship of the first three cohorts after their first 10 years as maîtres de conférences, we observed that access to professorship was quicker for the 1976–77 and the 1986–87 cohorts than for the more recent cohort (1996–97)—despite the most recent cohort having published more than the earlier cohorts. One explanation for this is because in the past most candidates were applying for a professorship at the university where they were employed as maîtres de conférences and the number of slots opening was higher, thus providing more opportunities to apply and succeed. Today, there may be fewer openings; also, inbreeding (i.e., becoming a professor where you are already employed) is increasingly criticized: only those able to leave for another place may apply.

From a Transitory Labor Market to a Secondary Labor Market

This system of vacancy chains is very sensitive to changes in the number of position openings. What happens when the number of positions decreases and the supply of new doctoral graduates is stable or even increasing? One could expect that those who get an MCF position would have waited longer because recruiters would prefer candidates who have more experience and stronger dossiers and whose competence would also be easier to appreciate because of their seniority. However, this is not what we observed when we compared the profiles of those recruited in history, management, and physics in the mid-1970s, 1980s, 1990s, and 2000s. Except for the cohort of the 1980s, we observed a strong stability of the profiles of those who obtained a first MCF position.

In some aspects, evolutions can, of course, be seen. For instance, more women are hired now (and more also apply), the newly hired have a higher number of publications, and they are less often hired where they graduated (again a consequence of the critiques against inbreeding). But in many other aspects, it is striking to observe that the characteristics of those getting a first position have not changed over time, despite the changes in the process described above. First, the average age of the newly recruited is astonishingly stable, varying from 32 to 33, with an exception in the mid-eighties when the market was completely blocked (I will come back to this point). Second, these new recruits generally had a very linear trajectory, from the *lycée*, to the university, and finally obtaining a PhD. Finally, the delay between when they received their PhD and their first tenured position was, most of the time, short—often less than three years. While today so many PhD holders are struggling to obtain a position, those who succeeded in getting one generally did not wait long before they got it. According to the most recent statistics provided by the ministry, 44 percent of those who got a first position of maître de conférences in 2013 got their qualification in 2013: as most new doctorates seek (pursue) their qualification just after their PhD, it means that these individuals generally obtained their PhD in 2012. If one considers that 28.4 percent of those who got a first position of maître de conférences in 2013 got their qualification in 2012, and 14.1 percent in 2011, this means that 86.5 percent of the newly recruited in 2013 were qualified within the three years preceding their appointment, thus quite rapidly obtaining a position. This figure is decreasing but nevertheless remains rather high.

How to explain this stability of the trajectories despite the changes in the focus and character of doctoral study (advent of doctoral schools with formal programs of coursework) and the variations in the number of vacant positions? In the 1970s, the high number of positions created to meet rising enrollment numbers could explain the youth, rapidity, and precocity of the newly recruited staff. Until 1984, temporary staff could stay at the same institution until a permanent position became vacant, and in the 1970s vacancies were frequent. For those holding such temporary positions, two main possibilities existed: either they decided to step down and to go on the job market for business firms, or they waited until a slot opened at their university and they worked in temporary positions until then. So the logic was either you finally entered the academic profession by getting a permanent position, or you stepped down and entered another job market. In this system, temporary positions were a transitory period. Rather than a pure secondary labor market (Doeringer & Piore, 1971), the temporary positions held before becoming a maître de conférences were a transition toward the primary labor market (Rosenfeld, 1992; Rosenblum & Rosenblum, 1996).

A vacancy chain system only functions if a certain number of positions at the top become vacant and allow the recruitment of new applicants. In France, the system was quickly stressed in the late 1970s and the beginning of the 1980s when fewer permanent positions were available because fewer were created (due to the stabilization of student numbers) and more senior positions were occupied by young professors, which meant that retirements became rare. The vacancy chain was blocked, and temporary academics early in their career stood long at the door of the permanent academic profession. The length of the transitory period expanded. For this reason, in our study, the 1986–87 cohort is rather different from the other three: for example, the age of entry is higher and the time between the end of the PhD and the first position is longer. Temporary staff generally stayed at their university, working with their former supervisor, in a temporary position that was renewed every year. This constituted a group of "permanent temporary staff" that was expanding and which led to protests. At that time, a few years after the first election of François Mitterrand as president, the socialist government agreed to transform many of these temporary positions into permanent ones, but in order to avoid the repetition of such a situation they created new temporary positions that were either renewable only once or could not easily be renewed multiple times in the same place.

In the 1990s, even if the situation of PhD holders remained uneasy, the second massification that took place between the end of the 1980s to the mid-1990s led to the creation of new positions, and the system functioned quite well again. Unsurprisingly, the profiles of the new entrants in the 1990s are very close to those of the mid-1970s. However, in the early 2000s, when the academic labor market again faced a tense situation, surprisingly we did not observe the change in profiles that we noticed for the mid-1980s. The 2006–7 cohort is still young and received their position early and rapidly: as explained above, most of those who obtained a position got it close to the time they earned their PhD and did not wait long before being hired. But the number of positions per candidate declined and all PhD holders did not have this chance. Therefore, many newly obtained doctorates remain post-docs.[21]

In the 2000s, the number of temporary positions is increasing, favored by the development of more project-based research and the reliance on post-docs.[22] But this new population of casual workers is rather different from those at the beginning of the 1980s. While their predecessors were immobile and could wait for a position to be vacated in their department, the temporary staff of today is obliged to move from one post-doc to another, when not abroad, and no one feels responsible for their career when their mission is over. In some disciplines (e.g., life sciences or physics), undertaking one or two post-docs has even become quasi-required before getting a permanent position. But as we observed in our own study, and as confirmed by the recent ministry figures, it is not the candidates with more experience who have a better chance at getting a position: recruiters prefer young, newly minted doctoral graduates. As a result, the longer a candidate is a post-doc, the less chances he or she has to be recruited.

After the PhD, three trajectories now exist: there is always the possibility to leave for the nonacademic job market (and young PhDs are encouraged to opt for this solution); some young PhD holders still experiment with a short period of transition before they get a permanent position, but there is also an emergent secondary labor market—a group of precarious, lower paid, and less prestigious positions develop and have their own trajectory but do not lead to permanent positions. Those hired in such positions are, from this point of view, comparable with the "permanent adjuncts" of many US universities who will never get access to a tenure track. The positions these individuals hold is rarely transitory, and the longer they occupy it the less transitory it becomes. These temporary academic workers are engaged in a professional trajectory of their own, different from the career of the permanent staff, until they finally decide to leave the academic profession and find another professional path.

This is a rather silent but important transformation of the academic labor market in France (even if many times criticized and denounced by the French labor unions). Nonetheless, competitions and vacancy chains remain the central mechanisms at play.

The Haves and the Have Nots

Along with this structural transformation of the French academic profession, three other processes affected it in recent years. These are linked to some of the reforms that were introduced in the last decade. First, in 2005, the Agence Nationale de Recherche (ANR), a national research council, was created, which led to an increase in project-based research funding and a decrease in recurrent budgets (inciting academics to apply for competitive grants). The ANR was also in charge of the organization of the French Initiative of Excellence (Grand Emprunt) that aimed to very selectively allocate resources to a restricted number of projects (e.g., clusters of excellence, Idex, etc.). Second, in 2006, an agency for the evaluation of higher education and research was created to centralize all already-existing evaluation bodies into one. The main novelties introduced by this agency were to give grades (A+, A, B, or C) to labs and training programs and to make these results public on its website, thus providing funders with evaluations they could (and did) use to selectively allocate resources. Third, and as a result of the two preceding processes, performance-based funding was proportionately increased.

These changes were partly justified by the development of international rankings that occurred at the same period. The rather low results of French institutions legitimized the claims of critics who, for years, had said that the French academic system was declining. Reforms, performance, and excellence became key words in the French higher education system.[23]

Three main consequences derived from these transformations. First, the competitive pressure for publications and grants became stronger and, even if criticized, was internalized by many academics. Second, differentiation increased within the French academic profession between those who published and got grants and those who did not. Finally, the latter were more dependent than ever on their university as the relationship between academics and their university approached an employer-employee relationship.

INTERNALIZATION OF NEW NORMS

In a 2011 study of three French universities, where we interviewed administrative and academic staff involved in its governance (N=100),[24] we observed that the evaluation from the AERES, the success in obtaining project-based funding from the ANR and, more broadly, the scientific productivity of the academic staff were taken seriously, despite the many critiques about these reforms by the interviewees themselves (Musselin, 2012).

The interviewees considered the evaluations led by AERES to be of particular importance, even when they were skeptical about the methods of evaluation. They were therefore very attentive to the reports sent by their labs and training programs, and centralized them and checked them before sending them on to AERES. They even sometimes modified what the programs or labs proposed, or imposed decisions. For instance, in one of the universities, the vice president imposed English-as-a-second-language (ESL) classes in the law training programs even though the jurists were against it. Some universities also organized mock evaluations before the visit of the AERES evaluators to try to improve their results when AERES came.

The pressure for publication also increased, as only academics reaching a certain level of publications were considered by AERES to be active in research. Emphasis was also put on publications in English and in peer-reviewed journals. Some of the directors of labs in social sciences whom we interviewed complained that their colleagues were not sufficiently aware of the changing context and some even developed indicators to follow the activity of their unit.

These directors also stressed the increasing importance of grants and the new pressure, especially in disciplines where grants were less frequent, to apply for these grants and to obtain external funding. Again, even if interviewees, especially in the social sciences and humanities, criticized this trend, many of the directors of research units nevertheless tried to pressure their researchers to apply for grants.

An Increasing Differentiation

With the creation of the ANR and AERES, budget allocations and the distribution of research-based rewards have become more selective but also more visible because the evaluation results are made public and many universities, labs, or departments publicize their success to national (Grand Emprunt) or international (European Research Council) research funding agencies.

I have argued (Musselin, 2013) that the declining influence or diminution of the academic profession only affects one segment of it. The ANR and AERES, in fact, strengthened the role of peer review in decision making and in day-to-day activities. Academics solicited to assess research projects or evaluate labs and training programs produce scientific judgments but also establish the norms according to which an entity or a project will be considered excellent or not. Such norms are more transparent and explicit than before, but they are also not only "purely" academic: the impact of the project, its governance, or the accuracy of its budget are also part of the assessment. French academics, especially in the humanities and social sciences, had to learn how to fill out templates designed by the evaluation and funding agencies and, with the decrease in recurrent budgets, the ability to obtain grants became more important than ever before.

While the peers involved in the evaluation as well as the academics rewarded by the evaluation and by receiving grants benefited from the new systems (Münch, 2008; Whitley, 2009), the distance between them and those who did not receive grants increased, thus accentuating the internal differentiation within the academic profession.

This was especially visible when the calls for the initiative of excellence were launched in 2010 and concentrated a flow of supplementary resources to a certain number of projects. The map of the LABEX (LABs of EXcellence, i.e., scientific clusters) that were selected reflects a strong imbalance between Paris and the east and south of France on the one hand, and the west and north of France on the other. Although this imbalance already existed (the map is very similar to the distribution of the labs that are simultaneously affiliated to the CNRS and a university), the allocation of more resources to sites where they were already concentrated increased this imbalance. It also radically changed the content of the political narrative on higher education in France: instead of arguing that the imbalance between different territories should be addressed, higher education policies from 2005 to 2012 stressed that research performance and excellence should be the primary goals. The theoretical equivalence between each university and each professor was no longer a legitimate goal and was replaced by rewarding the best.

Who Is the Employer? The State or the University?

All of these broad-based developments have had concrete implications within universities for two reasons. First, the 2007 LRU Act made French universities responsible for their payroll: until then, academic positions were managed by the ministry. That is, when a post for professor became vacant, the university had to ask the ministry whether it could open it again. This devolution of human resource management to universities raised many budgetary problems[25] and also changed the relationship between the university and its staff.

Indeed, French academics are still civil servants, and the president of the republic still signs the recruitment papers of French professors. Their employer remains the French state, but because of the devolution of payroll to the universities, positions are no longer managed by the ministry but by universities. Even if they are not officially the employers, universities can now be more active in managing their staff. They can use the results of the AERES evaluation and/or the allocation of ANR grants as a management tool.

Those who do not succeed in getting grants or who do not receive good evaluations are under pressure by university management, which uses these results to reduce their budgets or not replace vacant positions. As stressed at the beginning of this paper, competitive academic pressures (through evaluations and grant allocations) are now aligned with—and compounded by—local university managerial pressures.

In contrast, those who get excellent evaluations and are successful in obtaining grants are in a much better situation and are less dependent on university management: they can negotiate with administrators and resist managerial pressure. Nevertheless, there has been a transformation from their previous individual autonomy to a more "performance-based autonomy"; that is, their autonomy depends on their capacity to be productive.

Conclusions

The overall architecture of the system has not changed, but the new focus on selective excellence and its associated modus operandi have been introduced and are at work. Although they are often actively criticized by collectives like Sauvons la Recherche (Save Research) or Sauvons l'Université (Save the University), they are accepted and appropriated by part of the academic profession, especially when they benefit from them. Therefore, they provoke controversies and divergent views among French academics.

The divide is not only ideological; the focus also increases the level of differentiation among French academics. Although far from being systematic and shared, new practices are also emerging in the grandes écoles—even public ones. Forms of tenure tracks are introduced, some universities are starting to offer start-up research funds to some of the newly recruited staff, and salary negotiation have been introduced in some places for some disciplines (especially economics).

The basis on which the development of academic careers relied is also changing. While the secondary labor market still plays the role of a "holding pattern" or transition from temporary to permanent positions for the few that are hired a few months after the end of their PhD, most of the time it becomes a "trapped" situation. Academic job seekers are going from one post-doc to another and the more post-docs they accumulate, the less their chance of securing a permanent position. Paid less, unsecured, they also often do not have autonomy to work on their own projects but instead work on the research programs of those employing them. This process grows as the number of opened positions declines. As a result, the egalitarian principals of the French higher education system are slowly being encroached upon. Differentiation gains ground for access to, as well as progression in, the academic career.

NOTES

1. This is a national body organized in discipline-based sections with faculty members, two-thirds of which are elected by their peers and another third appointed by the ministry. Their main task is to examine the dossiers of those who would like to apply for a first position and to decide whether they are "qualified" to do so or not.

2. One of the points of discord in the 2009 movement against the decree was that it suggested that the president could decide and impose what the balance between teaching and research would be for each academic, according to evaluation results. Until now this balance was the same for all: 50 percent for teaching and 50 percent for research. According

to the most recent version of the decree, this can be proposed but cannot go against the will of the faculty member in question.

3. In France, universities are composed of *facultés* (a potential translation could be "schools"). At that time, they were discipline-based (faculté of humanities, of sciences, of medicine, of law, and of theology until the end of the nineteenth century. These facultés were re-created in 1806 but not integrated into comprehensive individual institutions (university) in the city in which they were located. The facultés communicated directly with the national government.

4. A lump-sum budget permits reallocation across budget categories at the local level.

5. The grandes écoles rely on revenues generated by tuition fees and supplemented by revenues from the chamber of commerce as well as industry, which are quasi-public institutions.

6. By the end of the nineteenth century, French higher education experienced a series of reforms inspired by the Humboldtian German system. These reforms led to the 1896 Act and the re-creation of universities, regrouping the facultés located in the same city, but the facultés remained the main organizational pillars and universities were a purely administrative entity.

7. For example, INSERM for the life sciences in 1964, INRA for the agricultural sciences in 1946, CEA for nuclear research in 1945.

8. Journalists, politicians, and even scientists speak of the decline of the French system, of the problems of French universities, and believe universities should do better.

9. Faculty members at the grande écoles often work on private contracts with tenure-track systems similar to those in the United States.

10. In contrast to all other civil servant positions in France, these are open to foreigners.

11. Recruitment at the CNRS is very different from that at universities: discipline-based national committees make the decisions; universities and research units have very little to say. When recruited, *chargés de recherche*—with the agreement of the recruitment committee's CNRS institute—will choose the research units they will join among the two or three they contacted before the recruitment and which declared they would be ready to welcome this candidate.

12. In a "biographical" interview you ask people to describe their trajectory, how they became a faculty staff member and developed a career as an academic. It is different from interviews in which you ask people to describe their current activity, how they work with their colleagues, etc.

13. Traditionally, doctoral students in the humanities and social sciences work at home because they are not hosted by their labs.

14. Figures for 2013 are based on DRGH (2014), http://cache.media.enseignements up-recherche.gouv.fr/file/statistiques/00/6/bilrec13_327006.pdf.

15. Figures for 2013 are based on DRGH (2014), http://cache.media.enseignementsup -recherche.gouv.fr/file/statistiques/00/6/bilrec13_327006.pdf.

16. That is, before social security tax and before income tax.

17. For those who do not succeed or do not apply for the aggregation, it is possible to apply to specific professor positions opened by the ministry, if one has a seniority of at least

ten years as a maître de conférences. Nevertheless, very few of these positions open each year, and those who get them are always regarded as "second-class professors." The current ministry is trying to reform this by decreasing the weight of the aggregation and increasing the number of positions opened without passing the aggregation.

18. Based on DRGH (2014), http://cache.media.enseignementsup-recherche.gouv.fr/file /statistiques/00/6/bilrec13_327006.pdf.

19. Unless other sources are cited, the figures in this section are based on the statistics of the ministry, DRGH (2014), http://cache.media.enseignementsup-recherche.gouv .fr/file/statistiques/00/6/bilrec13_327006.pdf.

20. This is called a position transformation, but it rarely happens.

21. Hiring committees still prefer "recent" candidates hired just after earning their PhD. But only a fraction of those who recently obtained their PhD have this opportunity.

22. With the development of project-based research, permanent staff can rarely conduct all the research work themselves and post-docs are recruited by project managers using grant money. There is also the development of post-doc positions such as the EU Marie Curie programs, or regions or municipalities fund positions on a selective basis. Post-docs are recruited on time-limited contracts.

23. With the election of François Hollande in 2012, the emphasis on excellence and performance decreased, but the belief that the institutional restructuring of the French system was crucial to being competitive became even stronger, and the 2013 Fioraso Act promoted the creation of regional consortia of higher education institutions called COMUE.

24. University presidents and vice presidents, deans, members of deliberative bodies, senior administrators, and directors of labs and departments.

25. Budgetary problems arose because the calculation of the budgets needed for the positions run by the university was not well led (for instance, the increases in budgetary requirements linked to promotion, seniority, or merit were underestimated); the administrative staff of universities was not sufficiently trained to face this new responsibility; or some university presidents made inconsequential decisions.

REFERENCES

DGRH (Direction Générale des Ressources Humaines). 2014. *Campagne de recrutement et d'affectation des maîtres de conférences et des professeurs des universités Session 2013*. Paris: MENESR.

Doeringer, P., and M. J. Piore. 1971. *Internal Labor Markets and Manpower Analysis*. Lexington, MA: Heath.

Enders, Jürgen, and Lutz Bornmann. 2001. *Karriere mit Doktortitel? Ausbildung, Berufsverlauf und Berufserfolg von Promovierten*. Frankfurt: Campus Verlag.

Enders, Jürgen, and Ulrich Teichler. 1995. *Der Hochschullehrerberuf im internationalen Vergleich. Ergebnisse einer Befragung über die wissenschaftliche Profession*. Bonn: Bundesministerium für Bildung, Wissenschaft, Forschung und Technologie.

European University Association. N.d. *France*. http://www.university-autonomy.eu/ countries/france.

Finkelstein, Martin, and Jack H. Schuster. 2006. *The American Faculty: The Restructuring of Academic Work and Careers.* Baltimore: Johns Hopkins University Press.

Münch, Richard. 2008. "Stratifikation durch Evaluation: Mechanisms der Konstruktion von Statushierarchien in der Forschung. " *Zeitschrift für Soziologie* 31, no. 1:60–80.

Musselin, Christine. 2009. *The Markets for Academics.* New York: Routledge. Originally published in French as *Le marché des universitaires: France, Allemagne, Etats-Unis.* Paris: Presses de Sciences Po, 2005.

——. 2012. *Libertés, responsabilités et . . . centralization des universities, monography.* Paris: CSO, Sciences Po and CNRS. http://cso.edu/upload/dossiers/Rapport_LiberteR esponsabiliteCentralisationUniversites_2012.pdf

——. 2013. "How Peer Review Empowers the Academic Profession and University Managers: Changes in Relationships between the State, Universities and the Professoriate." *Research Policy* 42, no. 5:1165–73.

Musselin, Christine, Frédérique Pigeyre, and Mareva Sabatier. Forthcoming. *Devenir universitaire en France, hier et aujourd'hui.*

Musselin, Christine, and Valérie Becquet. 2008. "Academic Work and Academic Identities: A Comparison between Four Disciplines." In *Cultural Perspectives on Higher Education,* ed. J. Välimaa and O.-H.Ylijoki, 91–108. Dordrecht, Netherlands: Springer.

Renaut, Alain. 1995. *Les révolutions de l'Université. Essai sur la modernisation de la culture.* Paris: Calmann-Lévy.

Rosenblum, Gerald, and Barbara R. Rosenblum. 1996. "The Flow of Instructors through the Segmented Labor Markets of Academe." *Higher Education* 31, no. 4:429–45.

Rosenfeld, Rachel A. 1992. "Job Mobility and Career Processes." *Annual Review of Sociology* 18, no. 1:39–61.

Whitley, Richard. 2009. "The Impact of Changes in the Governance of Public Science Systems on Intellectual Authority and Innovation." In *Exploring the Worlds of Mercury and Minerva,* ed. L. Wedlin, K. Sahlin, and M. Grafstrom, 291–316. Uppsala: Uppsala University.

4 | United Kingdom

Institutional Autonomy and National Regulation, Academic Freedom and Managerial Authority

PETER SCOTT

The academic profession in the United Kingdom has been shaped by the general forces that have influenced the evolution of all professions and has been reshaped by socioeconomic, political, and technological change. But it has also been shaped by characteristics particular to higher education in the UK. These include both "traditional" characteristics, such as a high degree of institutional autonomy and a shared memory of and affection for collegiality, but also "modern" characteristics, such as the rapid advance of a more explicitly managerial organizational culture in universities and the widespread adoption of entrepreneurial, and market, practices.

National Context

Although the UK was a unitary state until the 1990s, the reestablishment of a separate Scottish parliament and government and the establishment of the National Assembly and government in Wales have moved it closer to becoming a federal state (although, confusingly, the UK parliament and government continue to act as the parliament and government of England, the largest component of the UK). This process of "devolution" has had particularly pronounced effects in higher education where substantial policy convergence has taken place—most controversially with regard to tuition fees (none in Scotland and £9,000 and rising in England). More broadly, Scottish higher education remains an overwhelmingly public and managed system, while in England there has been a shift toward a market-oriented system (albeit subject to more intrusive state regulation). However, so far this policy divergence has had limited effects on the conditions of academic employment, partly because most research funding has remained a UK-wide or unitary state responsibility and partly because these conditions are determined by institutions not by governments.

The degree of functional differentiation in UK higher education is also difficult to characterize. In a formal sense, it has been reduced. In 1992, the distinction between (traditional) universities and most other higher education institutions (notably the former polytechnics) was abandoned. However, the formal unity of the system is compromised in a number of ways. First, there is a clear reputational hierarchy among institutions (as there always had been even among traditional universities, now often labeled "pre-1992" universities). Second, "league tables" of universities, constructed by newspapers and other media organizations, have assumed a new importance within a more competitive and consumerist culture, a worldwide phenomenon. Third, UK universities have grouped themselves into informal clubs, now called "mission groups." The most prominent of these is the Russell Group, composed by the 25 leading research-intensive universities led by Oxford and Cambridge. However, in terms of academic employment, the abolition of the so-called binary system in 1992 led to an increasing convergence of employment structures and conditions.

These new, informal modes of differentiation have not produced a full reversal of that trend. Of much greater significance has been the increasing differentiation of academic roles within institutions—between research-oriented and teaching-oriented academic staff, between traditional academic and new para-academic roles, and between managers and staff, both academic and professional. A new element, however—the impact of which is difficult to assess—is the growth of private for-profit institutions that do not employ their academic staff on conventional and quasi–public sector contracts. So far, despite active encouragement by the government in England, they have played a peripheral role in the higher education system.

The degree to which institutions enjoy autonomy is also unclear. In historical terms universities were, and in formal terms still are, exceptionally autonomous. According to a recent European University Association scorecard, they are among the most, if not the most, autonomous in Europe (EUA, 2016). They own their buildings and other assets and appoint and employ their own staff (up to, and including, full professors). No members of their governing boards or councils are appointed by the government; instead, their membership is wholly within the discretion of the university itself. However, this autonomy has been constrained in a number of ways. First, they are required to meet certain conditions before they become eligible for government funding (and these conditions have tended become more detailed and intrusive). Although direct government funding has been reduced and replaced by tuition fees paid by students (in England), similar conditions must be met if their students are to be eligible to receive state loans to pay these fees. Second, the government has taken more direct power over higher education. The new Higher Education and Research Act (UK Parliament, 2017) gives the secretary of state the authority to strip even traditional universities of their power to award degrees granted under royal charters, as part of a package of new powers to regulate higher education in England (primarily directed at private, for-profit institutions). Finally, universities' freedom is constrained by a proliferation of codes and guides on governance, management, and a range of other issues, none of which is legally mandatory but in practice cannot be ignored.

Consequently, the most accurate characterization of academic employment would be to describe it as a hybrid system. In a formal sense, decisions reside with the institutions, but in practice these are heavily influenced at intermediate and national levels by funders' requirements (research councils and funding bodies), by collective habits (on the part of universities acting as an employers' group and of academic and other trade unions), and by a growing burden of regulation and legislation (which may not be principally focused on either higher education or employment matters, for example, freedom of information or health and safety).

UK universities and other institutions of higher education currently enroll 2.5 million students, and they make up one of four European systems with more than 2 million students (the others are France, Germany, and Poland). It remains an overwhelmingly public system in its fundamental values and majority funding. But it has never been a state system. During the past three decades, the UK system has undergone radical change in both quantitative and qualitative terms.

The Changing Face of UK Higher Education

There have been four major changes in UK higher education: growth and expansion; differentiation replaces segmentation; audit, accountability, and regulation; and fees and funding.

GROWTH AND EXPANSION

As has already been indicated, the UK did not acquire a truly mass system of higher education until the 1990s, later than most other western European countries and much later than the United States. Previous bursts of expansion had taken place in the 1960s when the new campus universities such as Sussex and Warwick were established and the former colleges of advanced technology became (technological) universities. Expansion also occurred around the time of the Robbins report (which offered authoritative support for expansion at a time when many argued that "more means worse"). Student growth slowed in the mid- and later 1970s with the end of the postwar boom. In the 1980s, traditional universities' budgets were sharply reduced by the new Thatcher government. In response, the universities reduced the number of students admitted, and the consequent unmet demand was met instead by the polytechnics that had been established in the previous decade (Scott, 1989, 1994). But it was only with reforms in secondary school examinations, which produced many more qualified applicants in the late 1980s, and the abandonment of the binary distinction between universities and polytechnics in 1992 that growth really took off (Shattock, 2013).

Expansion was further fueled by increased funding following the election in 1997 of a new Labour government, which was more actively committed to "widening participation" among less privileged social groups (HESA, 1999, 2009). Initially the bulk of the additional funding was in the form of increasing public expenditure (which remained at high levels throughout the 2000s). But starting in 2001 students were also expected to pay tuition fees of one thousand pounds (fees had effectively been abolished in 1962), which were increased to three thousand pounds in 2005 and then to a maximum of nine thousand pounds by the new Conservative-led coalition government elected in 2010. That cap is now due to be raised, provided institutions score well in the new state-sponsored Teaching Excellence Framework (TEF), which measures student satisfaction, entry grades, and employment outcomes. The result was that burgeoning demand for higher education did not end in a reduction of average unit costs.

However, it is possible that the very ease with which the UK has been able to accommodate large-scale expansion without serious funding pressures has meant that the transition from elite—or, at any rate, restricted—forms of higher education to more open and mass forms took place without the necessary reflection on, or adjustment to, its multiple consequences in terms of student motivation and success, graduate employability and rates of return, the pattern of courses, curriculum, and delivery methods; and the need for greater heterogeneity of institutional missions (and types). For example, completion rates have remained high and wastage rates low, and commitments to a degree of intimacy in relations between students and their teachers—perhaps more appropriate in an elite system and the close embrace of teaching and research—have remained strong. For these reasons, it has been said that the UK has acquired a mass system in "a fit of absentmindedness."

DIFFERENTIATION REPLACES SEGMENTATION

The second major change has been the development of new forms of differentiation. The formal segmentation of UK higher education into universities and polytechnics (central institutions in Scotland) was abandoned in 1991–92. The result was to create a formally unified and allegedly more homogeneous system. The polytechnics became universities. All, bar one, entered the subsequent Research Assessment Exercise. However, this change was perhaps less dramatic than it appears. The original motive for establishing the binary system in the 1960s had been the government's reluctance to agree to the open-ended expansion of the university sector, revealingly labeled the "autonomous sector," and its desire to build up a "public sector" (the polytechnics) instead. In other words, it was about political control, or accountability, more than about differentiation of educational missions. By the later 1980s the universities were subject de facto to much greater control, and were as "public" as the polytechnics, so this overriding rationale of the binary policy ceased to apply (Scott, 2014).

Indeed, the abandonment of the binary system on balance may actually have encouraged greater differentiation. Much has been made of the phenomenon of so-called academic drift—the desire of less prestigious institutions to achieve greater academic respectability by adopting more traditional forms and practices. Although this has certainly happened in the UK, for example, in terms of the intensification of a more pronounced research culture across the whole system, other factors apart from academic drift were also significant—not least the growth of a more competitive quasi-market system, which may have stimulated conformity more than it rewarded differentiation. It is also important to recognize a reverse phenomenon—the broadening of the university tradition as a result of the incorporation of the former polytechnics into the university system. Practices and behaviors that had once played almost no part in that tradition became accepted, even mainstream—for example, more flexible patterns of study (including part-time courses) and more applied forms of research. As a result, the UK higher education system has become more of a "broad church" than it was two decades ago.

More recently, some overt forms of differentiation have emerged, notably since the election of the Conservative-led coalition government in 2010 (BIS, 2011; Callender & Scott, 2013). This trend has accelerated further with the election in 2015 of a purely Conservative government. The threshold for achieving full university

status, in terms of minimum student numbers and subject range, has been lowered. As a result, a number of smaller specialist institutions, previously focused on
teacher training or art colleges, have become universities. A still small number of
private providers, including two for-profit institutions, have become universities.
But that number is expected to increase sharply as a result of the 2016 white
paper and subsequent Higher Education and Research Act of 2017 (BIS, 2016).
Consequently, the traditional conception of the "university" has been diluted
still further. Another significant shift has been the development of so-called
'mission groups within the UK higher education system. These first emerged in the
1990s as informal interest groups formed by vice-chancellors of similar types
of universities without any formal mandate. But they have now become perhaps
the most important element in a powerful new taxonomy of institutions. The
most prominent is the Russell Group of 24 research-intensive universities, now often glossed as the UK's "top universities."

The interpretation of this drift toward greater differentiation in the UK system,
therefore, is far from straightforward. According to one account, the drift toward
greater homogeneity represented by the abandonment of the binary system has
been thrown into reverse as institutions have had to accommodate to the realities
of an increasingly heterogeneous mass system (intensified perhaps by the development of quasi-market policies and practices). But, according to an alternative
account, the abandonment of this top-down segmentation of the higher education
system with different "classes" of institutions was a prerequisite for the emergence
of a more flexible and responsive system.

Audit, Accountability, and Regulation

The third big change has been the increasing burden of audit, accountability,
and regulation, which in turn has obliged universities to become more "managed"
institutions. This has taken many forms. The most prominent has been research
assessment, successive Research Assessment Exercises (RAEs) and now the Research Excellence Framework (REF). Research in UK higher education is now
subject to more scrutiny and review than in any other comparable higher education system. It is difficult to underestimate the impact on the habits, mentalities,
and practices of universities—and of the academic profession. But some of its practical effects have been contradictory. For example, the results of successive RAEs
have demonstrated that excellent research is widely distributed across the system,
with three-quarters of institutions having at least one unit (department) with the
highest possible grade. As a result, a high-performance research culture has been

generalized. But RAE results have been used to concentrate research funding, thus creating (for the first time in the UK, at any rate explicitly) an elite of research-intensive universities. As a result, the links between research and teaching, once regarded as axiomatic, have tended to be eroded.

Parallel attempts to assess the quality of teaching have been less decisive. Initially the Quality Assurance Agency (QAA) carried out detailed subject-by-subject reviews (Teaching Quality Assessments). But these have now been replaced by whole-institution audits that concentrate instead on the systems institutions use to assure (and enhance) quality. The possibility of moving to an even lighter-touch system based on perceived risk is now being considered, which would mean teaching quality in most institutions would only be reviewed rarely (if at all). Now greater reliance is placed instead on the National Student Survey, a mandatory survey of satisfaction among final-year undergraduates. This represents a key shift from peer-review-based quality assurance to customer satisfaction surveys, and is consistent with the increasing emphasis on market mechanisms as a guarantee to standards. Attempts have also been made to introduce funding rewards for excellent teaching, to balance the very substantial funding rewards attached to excellence in research, initially when a limited number of well-funded Centres of Excellence in Teaching and Learning (CETLs) were introduced in 2003. But this experiment was abandoned. A more interventionist instrument has now been introduced in the shape of the Teaching Excellence Framework (TEF) based on entry standards, satisfaction rates, and employment outcomes.

In addition, there is a raft of other forms of regulation to which UK institutions are subject. Many of these are related to the conditions attached to the receipt of public funding. For example, universities are required to demonstrate their financial health; if institutions are unable to demonstrate this they are subject to more detailed scrutiny (and, in extreme cases, external intervention—despite their formal legal independence). There are also extensive requirements in terms of reporting the number of students who are enrolled and complete their courses, to ensure that funding allocations are accurate. However, as institutions receive more of their income from tuition fees and less from direct State grants and as more private (often for-profit) providers enter the higher education marketplace, the balance of regulation will need to shift away from conditions attached to the receipt of these grants (although regulations determining the eligibility of students for state loans to pay tuition fees will still need to be policed) and toward more general regulatory regimes such as exist in the banking and energy sectors. However, the future shape of regulation in UK higher education remains in a state of flux as governments veer between greater intervention and control on the one hand and on the other a laissez faire market approach.

A major impact of this rising tide of audit, assessment, and regulation has been to require universities to develop stronger governance and management structures. Lay-dominated university councils (and governing bodies) have been encouraged to take on more active (and interventionist?) roles instead of acting in a more passive manner as trustees of charities. Senior management teams have expanded, with vice-chancellors now firmly regarded as chief executives (and rewarded as such) supported by a growing number of full-time executive academic and professional managers. The traditional practice of part-time rotating pro-vice-chancellors and deans is in a sharp decline in all but a handful of UK universities (Smith & Adams, 2007; Kennie & Woodfield, 2008). More generally, a pronounced managerial culture has permeated the system partly in response to the growing scale of institutions and complexity of their missions in a mass system, but substantially in response to the rising tide of regulation.

Fees and Funding

The fourth major change has been the introduction of tuition fees as a major source of income, and also the wider development of entrepreneurial practices in areas such as internationalization (where fees paid by non-EU students provide a key income stream), and applied research and knowledge exchange. Students now pay fees of up to a maximum of nine thousand pounds a year (a flat rate for all disciplines regardless of the actual cost of the provision). But they are entitled, without any means test, to receive state-provided loans from the Student Loans Company. Because payback only starts when students graduate and their earnings exceed a minimum level, the fees market is not at all price sensitive. In fact, current calculations suggest that more than 40 percent of loans will never be repaid in full, with the result that the new fees structure costs as much in public expenditure as the former grants system. Nearly all institutions charge at, or close to, the maximum allowed, although when the new funding regime was introduced the government had hoped fees would be variable. The government's latest proposals will allow further, although modest and inflation-rated, increases in fees.

Nevertheless, headline fees are higher in UK higher education than in any other European higher education, and also higher than in nearly every state system in the United States. The introduction of fees, or cost-sharing between students/graduates and taxpayers, has been a gradual process. At the beginning of the 1990s, students did not pay fees, and they also received grants for their living expenses. Higher education in the UK was free, at the point of use, and all funding was provided through general taxation. In the early 1990s, grants were replaced by repayable loans. In 1998, following the Dearing report, tuition fees were introduced—initially at the low level of a thousand pounds. In 2005–6 they were increased to three thousand pounds, although in a further tightening of the regulatory system an Office for Fair Access (OFFA) was established to ensure that institutions made adequate provision for scholarships and bursaries for poorer students. The current nine thousand pound maximum was introduced in 2011 following the election of the new coalition government. Although sharply contested by students and others, these fees in effect are the culmination of a long process that witnessed the inexorable erosion of the commitment to funding higher education out of general taxation. Both major political parties, Labour and Conservative, have accepted the inevitability of fees.

However, a number of consequences has flowed from this acceptance. First, overall limits on the number of students have been lifted; institutions will now be free to recruit as many students as they are able. This is likely to lead to significant turbulence as some struggle to fill their places, in contrast with the managed system of student numbers that has prevailed until now and was designed to reduce turbulence. Second, active measures will need to be taken to help a genuine market develop in terms of fee levels by finding ways to increase price sensitivity. One route is likely to be the development of lower-cost forms of higher education, offered perhaps by new private providers. Links between teaching and research are liable to erode as a result. Third, institutions will be forced to compete more aggressively by developing stronger "brands" and investing more heavily in marketing (at the expenses of core academic functions?). This trend is already being vigorously stimulated by the growth of "league tables" (Marope, Wells & Hazelkorn, 2013; Marginson, 2014). The overall effect could be that English higher education (higher education has remained "free" in Scotland) will become a less "public" system, not so much in terms of its funding—which will still be drawn predominantly (although indirectly) from public sources—as in its practices, values, and ethos. But whether this can accurately be labeled "privatization" is less easy to determine at this stage.

Evolution of the Academic Profession in the United Kingdom
Distinctive—and Exceptional?—Characteristics

Academic employment in the United Kingdom has two important features that distinguish it from such employment in many other countries, particularly in the rest of Europe, many parts of Asia, and Latin America.

- First, academic staff possess very few rights (or responsibilities) in addition to those possessed by other employees. In no sense do they constitute a separate caste with protected status. An important reason for this is the paucity of specific legislation on issues such as the protection of academic freedom—or, indeed, on higher education generally. Only in recent years have any statutory safeguards of academic freedom been developed, and mainly as grudging exceptions within legislation designed to prevent "radicalization" and "extremism." Matters that would be regulated by law in many other countries are instead guided by convention (or determined by archaic documents such as university charters). The last distinctive feature of academic employment (at any rate for staff on permanent contracts in traditional universities), tenure, was abolished in 1987. Significantly the abolition of tenure has made little practical difference to security in academic employment (for the categories of staff who previously enjoyed its protection).

- Second, academic staff in the UK have never enjoyed the status of being public officials or civil servants. Instead, they are directly employed by their institutions, which are all independent legal corporations (although the legal details and constitutional arrangements vary). As a result, UK professors may have never enjoyed the social prestige once enjoyed, by repute, by professors in Germany because their salaries and conditions of employment are not the same as those of senior civil servants. The distinction between full professors and other academic staff is less marked than in many other systems. Professors are not grand figures with exceptional status and authority. But another consequence is that the conditions of academic employment in the UK have been more flexible than in many other countries. Universities are free to establish their own promotion criteria. There are no state-imposed conditions that must be met before promotions can take place; nor are there any state examinations or tests to be passed to determine eligibility. Institutions are also free to establish new chairs without seeking the permission of any state or intermediary body. Also, possession of a PhD is an almost universal prerequisite for appointment to a permanent academic post, but it is not mandatory. Institutional employment policies are not constrained by state regulations. These two effects-the more limited social prestige enjoyed by academic staff and the much higher degree of institutional discretion over conditions of employment—have perhaps helped the UK respond more quickly to the evolution of new and flexible forms of academic employment.

In the past, however, limited use was made of this discretion. It was held in check by a number of inhibiting factors, which in practice made it more difficult to vary significantly the conditions of academic employment in the UK. These included: (1) de facto national collective bargaining on salaries and conditions, even though the outcomes of such negotiations were in theory not binding on individual institutions; (2) quasi-civil-service salary grades and common conditions of service, with a broadly consistent nomenclature of academic ranks; (3) a strong academic stake in institutional governance, at any rate in the more traditional universities (a stake that was—and largely still is—near-absolute in Oxford and Cambridge); (4) weak demarcation between (senior) academic staff on the one hand and on the other institutional leaders and other senior managers (many of whom were senior academics on temporary and rotating appointments); and (5) strongly shared professional norms that, while accepting the legitimacy of rivalry for academic esteem, were reluctant to endorse differential reward systems in different institutions. As a result, conditions of academic employment within the UK system were close to those that might prevail within nationally regulated systems, even though in formal and legal terms it was not such a system.

Although these inhibiting factors on the conditions of academic employment remain strong, their cumulative effect has been reduced over the past two decades by a number of new factors.

- First, professional solidarities have tended to be eroded by the growing heterogeneity with UK higher education. Even the abandonment of the binary system in 1992 and the incorporation of the former polytechnics within the university system, although formally a move toward a uniform system, created greater diversity of values and practices within the enlarged university system (and specifically introduced new employment regimes). The increasing differentiation between research careers and general academic careers, in most if not all universities, has compounded this diversity.
- Second, this differentiation has taken the form not only of growing demarcations between senior and junior, permanent and temporary, research-focused and teaching-focused roles but also the emergence of

paraprofessions in universities; the development of hybrid (or blended) roles; the increasing importance of other established professions within increasingly large and complex institutions (for example, accountants and human resources managers); and, perhaps most significantly, the growth of a full-time executive management class that, although still drawn overwhelmingly from the ranks of the academic profession, has increasingly adopted corporate norms (Deem, Hilyard & Reed, 2007).

- Third, higher education has imported more corporate employment practices from the private sector (as UK local government and health services have as well). For example, professors are now likely to be paid market rates, derived from analogous roles in the private sector or reflecting their importance in securing high research "scores" in the REF, while the salaries of vice-chancellors and other senior managers have also been substantially increased. More general efforts to introduce performance-related pay to the majority of academic staff have—so far—been less successful. But their effect has been to promote a new and harsher employment culture expressed in terms of organizational development, process review (or reengineering or transformational change). These changes have been accompanied by a general decline in the power and influence of trade unions.

However, this drift from patterns of academic employment that, although flexible in theory, were in practice constrained by powerful conventions of mutuality to new patterns that make fuller use of this flexibility needs to be qualified in two respects. First, there have been convergent as well as divergent pressures. The powerful unifying effect of the RAE/REF has already been mentioned. Moves to professionalize university teaching through induction and training courses (now typically accredited by a national body, the Higher Education Academy) have produced a similar, although less powerful, effect. The development of employment law has also led to greater uniformity of practice in areas such as gender discrimination, unfair dismissal, bullying and harassment, and (most recently) retirement ages. Second, this shift toward flexible conditions of academic employment has taken place without significant changes in formal structures and regulations. Legislation has played only a limited part. Instead, two different types of driver have been important. The first is the rise of regulation (and, more generally, the growth of what has been called an "audit society"), which has already been discussed. The second is changes in organizational cultures and professional behaviors that in turn have been stimulated by larger transformations such as the massification and (still far from complete) marketization of UK higher education. In a very real sense, nothing has changed, but many things have changed.

General Characteristics

The UK academic profession has traditionally been characterized by high degrees of collegiality, although the extent to which has been a comfortable myth and to which it has been a reality is a matter of controversy. However, myth or reality, it has shaped habits and behaviors within the profession, contributing to significant levels of professional solidarity. In most traditional universities nominal job title distinctions have been retained; entry-level academics who have teaching and research responsibilities are typically appointed as lecturers and then progress to become senior lecturers and finally, if they are fortunate, are promoted to be readers or professors. The proportion of professors has increased as new types of chairs have been created—personal and developmental chairs in addition to existing established chairs. In the so-called post-1992 universities, the former polytechnics, a slightly different nomenclature prevails because, in practice, the entry-level grade is senior lecturer and promotion is to principal lecturer. In a growing number of UK universities, the US grades of assistant, associate, and full professors have been adopted.

As a result, the hierarchy of the profession may be less categorical and rigid than in some other systems. A strong, and strengthening, research culture that tends to emphasize disciplinary and professional loyalties (in the form of "invisible colleges"). The levels of unionization, which are still comparatively high even among senior professors, have led the majority of UK academics to define themselves as "employees." And, since the abolition of tenure, there has not been a clear-cut distinction between tenured (or tenure-track) academics and other instructors. However, this comparative absence of hierarchy, and consequently higher levels of collegiality and solidarity, should not be exaggerated. It does not mean that the majority of academics can expect to be promoted to chairs. Despite the increase in the number of chairs, competition for promoted posts has increased. Indeed, institutions have tended to tighten promotion criteria, particularly with regard to past and future research performance. Yet there remains an expectation of reasonable progression among staff on permanent contracts. However, this does not apply to many research staff who are appointed on fixed-term contracts linked to specific research programs (that are often externally funded), nor to the increasing number of (often part-time and fractional) academics appointed on teaching-only contracts. But, once again, there are dangers in emphasizing this distinction as a new, and decisive, fault-line in the UK academic profession. Although there is a widespread assumption that the number of research and teaching-only staff has increased sharply, this assumption is not—categorically—supported by the available data.

SIZE AND SHAPE

UK higher education institutions currently employ 404,000 staff, of whom 198,000 (49 percent) are academics and 206,000 (51 percent) are managers, administrators, and clerical and manual staff. The number of academic staff increased by more than 33,000 between 2005–6 and 2014–15, broadly keeping pace with the growth in student numbers. Two points are worth emphasizing. First, the growth in the number of academic staff was especially rapid between 2005 and 2010. Then growth slowed significantly when higher student fees were introduced, only to pick up again. Second, the growth in the number of nonacademic staff was slower and actually declined after 2010, only recovering its 2009 total in 2015. The details are given in table 4.1) (HESA, 2016)

Just under half of academic staff have contracts requiring them both to teach and research, traditionally regarded as the "standard" contract, while 31 percent have teaching-only contracts (75 percent of whom are employed part-time) and 23 percent have research-only contracts (table 4.2). Half of academic staff also work part-time, and a third are employed on fixed-term rather than permanent contracts (table 4.3). Overall, there is a reasonable gender balance among aca-

Table 4.1. Staff in UK Higher Education Institutions, 2004–5 to 2014–15

Year	Academic staff	Nonacademic staff	Total
2015–16	201,380	208,750	410,130
2014–5	198,335	205,550	403,835
2013–14	194,245	201,535	395,780
2012–13	185,585	196,935	382,515
2011–12	181,385	196,860	378,250
2010–11	181,185	200,605	381,790
2009–10	181,595	205,835	387,430
2008–9	179,040	203,720	382,760
2007–8	174,945	197,510	372,455
2006–7	169,995	194,165	364,160
2005–6	164,875	190,535	355,415
2004–5	160,655	185,650	346,305

Table 4.2. Academic Staff by Academic Employment Function, 2015–16

Function	Full-time	Part-time	Total
Teaching only	13,405	39,185	52,590
Teaching and research	80,305	18,315	98,620
Research only	40,290	8,360	48,645
Neither teaching nor research	1,015	505	1,525

Table 4.3. All Staff by Function and Mode of Employment, 2014–15

Activity	Full-time	Part-time	Total
Academic staff	132,865	65,470	198,335
Managerial, professional, and technical staff	75,195	20,680	95,870
Clerical staff	43,745	23,855	67,595
Manual staff	20,445	21,585	42,030
Total	272,250	131,585	403,835

Table 4.4. Academic Staff by Contract Level and Sex, 2015–16

Contract level	Female	Male	Total
Senior academic	2,155 (35%)	4,065	6,160
Professor	4,775 (24%)	15,195	19,975
Other contract levels	84,215 (48%)	91,030	175,245
Total	89,225 (48%)	109,110	198,335

demic staff with 55 percent male and 45 percent female (table 4.4). But two qualifications are needed. First, women make up a significant majority of the total student population. Secondly, less than a quarter of (full) professors are women. The proportion of black and minority ethnic staff remains very low, especially (as with women) in the senior ranks of the profession and the most prestigious universities.

SPECIALIZATION OF ROLES

The notable trend is toward an increasing specialization of roles. The proportion of academic staff with generic teaching-and-research responsibilities has declined, and almost half now have either research or teaching-only contracts. However, this not a straightforward phenomenon. Although the number of research-only staff has grown substantially as the focus on research performance has become more intense and pressures to increase external research funding have become greater, the major change may have been that the balance of responsibilities of general academic staff, especially perhaps the most senior and those in the more research-intensive universities, has shifted toward research. Most UK institutions now have elaborate workload models for all academic staff; one effect has been to encourage the most productive researchers to concentrate more on their research. It is revealing that many professors are now casually labeled "research professors." Their traditional roles as senior scholars and scientists who "profess" their discipline as teachers and public intellectuals as well as researchers now receive less emphasis. A similar focus on teaching-only roles has been slower to develop, despite the emphasis on student satisfaction. Although there has been much talk of increasing the number of academic staff on teaching-only contracts, they still fall into three main categories—first, part-time teachers who are also often practitioners in professional disciplines (for example, clinicians or architects); second, academic staff whose research performance has been judged not to be adequate by the higher standards of the RAE/REF; and third, teachers in what are still peripheral institutions—in new private (especially for-profit) providers and teachers of higher education courses in local colleges.

The Rise of Management

The second trend is the rise of a management class in UK higher education. Again, this is not a straightforward phenomenon that can be tracked through the data. It has not taken the form of an increasing proportion of managerial and administrative staff at the expense of academic positions; in fact, the proportion of nonacademic staff has declined slightly (although some of this is explained by a smaller number of clerical and manual labor staff in UK institutions—partly the result of "outsourcing" routine services to external contractors). Instead, three things appear to be happening. First, a cadre of executive senior managers has solidified and expanded. Although most are academics, their commitment to teaching and research has been sharply reduced (and their organic links with their—former—academic colleagues have tended to atrophy). Second, all academic staff have taken on an increasingly administrative burden, either directly in terms of their involvement in course and portfolio reviews, academic audit, and quality assurance or indirectly because of their involvement in the greatly expanded apparatus of peer review that is now needed to service the growing needs for assessment and accountability. Third, new hybrid roles have developed that are part academic and part administrative in areas such as information and student services (which have been labeled "blended professionals") (Whitchurch, 2013). The impact of higher consumerlike expectations among students has perhaps been reflected more in the elaboration and professionalization of such services than in the transformation of teaching itself.

INTERNATIONALIZATION

Other trends are also important. One is that the academic profession in the UK is becoming more international. In the mid-1990s, 8 percent of academics were from outside the UK; by the mid-2000s this had increased to 13 percent, and currently it is 16 percent (Sastry, 2005). This internationalization of the UK academic workforce is most pronounced among (full) professors, which is a common feature of higher education systems in other countries where access to senior academic positions is not restricted by civil service regulations, but also among early-career researchers, which reflects the large number of international students recruited by UK institutions. This raises an important question about the sustainability of the current academic workforce in the UK. There is little doubt that more lucrative (and apparently more exciting) career opportunities are available to many UK graduates, especially in banking and financial services. The PhD has become a career path no longer for the best and brightest but for second-tier achievers in some key fields. It is unclear whether the internationalization of the academic workforce in the UK should be seen predominantly in positive terms, as evidence of the wider internationalization of the system, or in negative terms, as evidence of a deficit in demand from within the UK for academic positions.

DISCIPLINARY AND INSTITUTIONAL LOYALTIES

Another significant trend is the tension between the ambitions of individual academics and institutional imperatives. According to an international research project on the Changing Academic Profession (CAP) undertaken in the mid-2000s, the primary allegiance of UK academic staff was to their discipline, followed by their department, and lastly their institution (Locke & Bennion, 2010). Their major concerns were "cumbersome administration," "top-down management" and an exaggerated "performance orientation," all hallmarks of a tighter institutional focus. Whether this tension between individual aspirations and institutional imperatives is evidence of the pains of transition to new models of higher education—and, therefore, a temporary phenomenon—or evidence of an enduring structural contradiction characteristic of all modern higher education systems remains unclear. This can only be answered by considering, first, the special conditions that apply in the UK (where the academic profession, despite its formal autonomy, has become more—or perhaps too—heavily "policed," even if much of this takes the form of "self-policing"); and then, wider considerations regarding the changing nature of academic work in mass higher education systems in knowledge-intensive societies.

SALARIES

The average salary of a full-time academic staff member in the UK in 2012 was £47,609, and of full professors £76,214. In most institutions, academic salaries up to the grade of full professor are determined by a process of collective bargaining conducted between the University and College Union (UCU) and the University and College Employers Association (UCEA). The government is not involved. Institutions have made limited efforts to introduce performance related pay for nonprofessorial staff, many of whom are also entitled to annual increments on agreed salary scales within their grade (lecturer, senior/principal lecturer, reader). However, promotion to a higher grade is tightly policed and often the proportion of promoted posts in effect is rationed, even when they are not "new" positions. Institutions are free to determine the salaries of full professors above a minimum level, according to their individual performance or market conditions. In the past five years, nationally negotiated increases in academic salaries have been low, typically 1 or 2 percent.

Two areas of debate have emerged with regard to academic salaries in the UK.

1. The first is the extent to which academic salaries have kept pace with salaries in similar occupations and professions. Here the evidence is ambiguous. While academic salaries certainly fall behind in the boom years leading up to the 2008 banking crisis, more recently increases in salaries in comparable occupations (particularly in the traditional professions and in the public sector) have been as sharply curbed. However, the Changing Academic Profession project found that levels of job satisfaction were comparatively low in the UK. Part of the explanation may have been a perception that salaries are too low, although a larger part of the explanation was likely to have been the impact on the status and autonomy of academics of market-oriented reforms (and other forms of "modernization") that have been discussed in the preceding section of this paper. Particularly notable has been the widespread adoption of

transparent "workload models," designed to allocate workloads more equitably but also used as a tool of management control.

2. The second is the increasing inequality of rewards and promotion prospects within the profession. The most troubling is the emergence of a sharp divide between a privileged professoriate, especially in certain disciplines and within the most highly regarded universities) and a so-called "precariat" composed of teachers with part-time and/or temporary contracts. There are also troubling variations between the salaries of men and women; in the case of full professors, women were paid on average £4,817 less than their male colleagues. But these variations have been attributed to differences between salaries across academic disciplines, which are substantial. The average salary of a professor in the London Business School was £215,709 while in the nearby University of the Arts London, an institution focused on art and design, it was only £65,423. Also, an issue of growing controversy is the rapid increase in the salaries of vice-chancellors and other senior management, in contrast to the pay restrictions imposed on the majority of higher education staff. This trend is an inevitable outcome of the rise of a more sharply demarcated management class, which has also already been discussed.

An academic profession appears to be emerging that is more sharply divided between highly paid executives and research "stars" on the one hand and a growing number of teachers and researchers who are paid less, often on temporary, fixed-term, and insecure contracts, on the other. As a result, the traditional solidarity of the academic profession in the UK, whether myth or reality, may now be being undermined. However, it is important not to overstate these changes. The divisions within the academic profession in the UK are not strongly structured in terms of research-intensive universities and more teaching-oriented institutions. As I have already argued, the impact of an increasing emphasis on research performance has tended to sharpen the self-identification of UK academics as researchers (some argue at the expense of their role as teachers); this impact has been general rather than confined to academics in more research-intensive universities. Nor has the substantial increase in the number of academic staff, accelerated of course by the designation of the former polytechnics as universities in 1991–92, led—yet—to far-reaching modifications in the structure of the profession. The overall impression remains of an academic profession still strongly committed to traditional norms and behaviors, and still structured in comparatively conventional forms—although, perhaps, a profession on the brink of profound change.

Drivers of Change

The changing nature of academic work, and evolving characteristics of the academic profession, in the United Kingdom during the last 30 years have been shaped by a large number of influences, some of which have been specific to the UK and some more generic trends affecting all higher education systems (although the intensity of their influence has in turn been shaped by national contexts). In conceptual and practical terms, it is often difficult to distinguish between national and generic influences. The three national influences identified here in the context of the UK clearly have also been influential in other national systems.

In the UK, three national influences have been particularly prominent since 1990.

- The growth of more overt competition: A system that had always consisted of highly autonomous institutions but typically operated on the basis of collaborative (and collegial) coexistence has moved some way toward becoming a "market" driven by more competitive behavior. As a result, a system that was seen as convergent, because disciplinary affiliations and professional values were regarded as more important than institutional loyalties and locations, has tended to become divergent under these new market pressures. The implications for the academic profession have been profound—including the rise of a managerial class in universities and the specialization of academic roles (and consequent erosion of professional solidarities). In addition, new ancillary professions have emerged that restrict the competence of mainstream teachers and researchers and compete with them for resources, for example, in marketing or "business analysis."
- An increasing emphasis on students as "customers": Growing competition between institutions to recruit students, higher tuition fees, and the proliferation of instruments designed to measure—comparative— performance (whether formal instruments such as the National Student Survey, or informal instruments such as "league tables") have focused attention of student/customer satisfaction—in contrast to earlier conceptions of academic quality as measured by various forms of peer review. As a result, mutuality has tended to be crowded out by markets.

Again, the implications for the academic profession have been far-reaching. They include a shift toward the corporate management of teaching (or, at any rate, its outcomes), pressures on teachers to please their students, and a rapid increase in new professional roles designed to enhance the "student experience."

- An intensification of research culture: Although now a mass system, the UK system has also become more focused on research performance. While this is true of many other higher education systems because of the increasing emphasis on securing competitive advantage within a global "knowledge" economy, specific UK factors have accelerated this shift. Successive Research Assessment Exercises (RAEs), now superseded by the Research Excellence Framework (REF), have had multiple impacts, including the growth of corporate management of research performance (and growth of research strategies), the segmentation of the academic profession into the "research active" and "research inactive" (which has had the paradoxical effect of lodging research esteem even more strongly at the core of professional identities), and the intensification of competition between universities (because RAE-REF scores are a key input into league tables). Once again, it has spawned subprofessions such as research managers and bid writers. This intensification of the research culture has also provoked a reaction. Successive UK governments, Labour and Conservative, since 2000 have developed a range of measures to measure, and reward, teaching—for example, nationally funded Centres of Excellence in Teaching and Learning and, most recently, the Teaching Excellence Framework, which has already been discussed.

There is also a number of "generic" trends that have also decisively influenced the development of the academic profession in the UK. Five deserve special emphasis.

- The first is the expansion of higher education, in terms both of the number of students enrolled and the number (and type) of institution embraced within mass systems. The size of the academic profession has increased, approximately on the same scale. At the same time, it has become more heterogeneous. So there have been both quantitative impacts—for example, on the nature of teacher-student relations—and qualitative impacts, such as the incorporation of more vocationally oriented institutions with less stake in critical academic enquiry (and scholarship and research). In the UK, the impact of mass expansion may have been particularly marked for two reasons. The first is that expansion has been a more recent phenomenon than in many other peer countries; the most rapid growth was experienced between 1990 and 2006. The second is that teaching, at any rate in more traditional UK universities, has depended on a certain "intimacy" between students and their teachers less marked in other systems.

- The second is the combined effect of new learning technologies and student cultures, which together have revolutionized the classroom. The impact of high-profile initiatives, such as the development of e-learning platforms and now massive open online courses (MOOCs), has probably been less than the accretion of more mundane tools, whether the sophisticated presentation techniques students now expect or the email forums, social networking, and novel forms of communication that have radically changed study habits (Gaebel, 2014). However, student behavior and expectations have also changed, partly as a result of their eager adoption of these new communicative lifestyles and partly because of changing articulations between higher experience, graduate skills, and the labor market that may no longer be fully consistent with older ideas of professional or expert society. The effects on the academic profession have been multiple, including new patterns of student learning (to which teachers must adapt) and (again) the emergence of new professional roles (mainly associated with the application of new learning technologies).

- The third is more familiar—the effects of scientific dynamism on disciplinary taxonomies, and so on professional roles and identities. As a result, disciplines have splintered and also been reconstituted, even more rapidly (and randomly?) than in the past. The impact has been particularly dramatic and direct in the context of research. But the content of teaching programs has also been fundamentally influenced. Similar effects have also been stimulated by broader intellectual developments—for example, the influence of neoliberal ideas in economics or business and management. As a result, the nature of academic work and the shape of the academic profession have been in constant flux. The "acceleration" of science has transformed what had previously been (comparatively) stable and evolutionary intellectual— and professional—structures into more fluid and volatile environments.

- The fourth generic trend has been toward greater emphasis on the applications and impact of research and also on wider engagement between higher education and society (and the economy). To some extent, this is an endogenous phenomenon, reflecting the greater weight now placed on interdisciplinary and transdisciplinary fields of inquiry as a result of scientific dynamism (and have been theorized under a variety of labels such as "Mode 2" or the "triple helix") and also the multiple societal engagements inherent in mass higher education systems (Gibbons et al., 1994; Nowotny, Scott & Gibbons, 2001, 2003; Etzkotwitz, 2008). But it is also imposed from outside. For example, in the current UK REF research, rankings will be determined by assessments of the "impact" of chosen outputs as well as their scientific "quality" (Bekhradnia, 2007; Martin, 2011). The implications for the academic profession of this fourth shift are considerable. Once again, new subprofessions have emerged, notably roles that might be termed as "knowledge brokers." Researchers themselves have been transformed into "knowledge entrepreneurs." And priorities in, and also modes of, research and teaching have inevitably changed.

- The fifth and final generic trend is the impact of globalization. This has been felt in a number of ways. The advance of free-market economic globalization has tended to depress state budgets, leading to pressure on institutions to search for alternative funding streams. It has also emphasized the role of universities and research in the generation of wealth in an increasingly knowledge-intensive global economy. The academic profession itself has become more international where national restrictions on access to the profession have not been relaxed. Many PhD programs depend for their viability on the flow of international students. Universities in many countries are now staffed by those born elsewhere, from early-career researchers to professors. Global league tables of universities, despite challenges to their methodology, have become increasingly influential in measuring performance.

The distinction between "national" and "generic" influences shaping the future of academic work and the development of the academic profession is to some degree arbitrary. The three "national" influences that have been defined as specific to the UK have also shaped policy and practice in other higher education and research systems—although less intensely perhaps. The drift toward increasing competition, if not to higher student fees, the tendency to define students as "customers" and the intensification of research cultures are really worldwide phenomena—all of which can be traced back to neoliberal accounts of how global markets operate (Slaughter & Rhoades, 2004). Similarly, the four "generic" influences have had different impacts in different national environments.

The key to understanding how academic work and the academic profession is being reshaped is perhaps to be found both in the interplay, and differential balance, between national and generic influences and their combined effects. The UK may represent an interesting case study in this respect, because of the speed and scale of the transformation that is under way.

- Until recently, despite spurious claims of insular exceptionalism, UK higher education was in most respects a standard European "public" system of higher education. Its historical origins were similar to those of France or Germany, with the state (both national and local) playing an increasingly significant role in endorsing, regulating, and funding provision. Although universities enjoyed greater formal and legal autonomy, and their association with state bureaucracies was looser than was usual in the rest of Europe, this was more than compensated for by robust traditions of strong academic (self) government, which expressed in other ways a profoundly "public" ethos to the UK system.

- Today, UK (or, more accurately, the English) higher education offers the most advanced European example of the shift from an essentially public to a market (or marketlike) system. English students are charged the highest fees in Europe (and, as has been pointed out, higher fees than in most US state systems). English universities are among the most regulated in Europe (and perhaps the world) with elaborate systems of quality assurance and research assessment that are more developed, and more intrusive, than is common elsewhere. It even appears that they are sometimes regarded essentially as "delivery organizations," mandated to satisfy externally imposed objectives (whether determined through political or market mechanisms), and the autonomy is now justified in terms of operational effectiveness rather than in the context of their fundamental critical responsibilities in an open society. Increasingly they seem to be conceived of as knowledge organizations (even businesses) rather than as educational institutions. The tradition of academic self-government has been eroded by the advance of so-called managerialism, with important—and largely negative—consequences for the standing of the academic profession.

The scale of this transformation has dismayed many critics. The question that arises is whether UK higher education is a trailblazer or whether its current trajectory is exceptional, an aberration. The answer is probably to be discovered as much on deeper structural shifts as in political change. It probably remains true— even in the UK/England—that the academic profession is shaped at least as much by the changing nature of academic work, which in turn reflects more profound scientific, cultural, and social change, as by the surface turbulence of political and market discourses (Scott, 2006). Of course, these more profound changes are played out with different degrees of intensity in different national contexts. But, even in these nationally modified forms, they represent the most powerful drivers of transformation.

REFERENCES

Bekhradnia, Bahram. 2007. *Evaluating and Funding Research through the Proposed "Research Excellence Framework."* Oxford: Higher Education Policy Institute.
BIS (Department of Business, Innovation and Skills). 2011. *Higher Education: Students at the Heart of the System.* London: BIS.
———. 2016. *Higher Education: Success as a Knowledge Economy.* London: BIS.
Callender, Claire, and Peter Scott, eds. 2013. *Browne and Beyond: Modernizing English Higher Education.* London: Institute of Education Press Bedford Way Papers.
Deem, Rosemary, Sam Hilyard, and Mike Reed. 2007. *Knowledge, Higher Education and the New Managerialism: The Changing Management of UK Universities.* Oxford: Oxford University Press.
Etzkowitz, Henry. 2008. *The Triple Helix: University-Industry-Government Innovation in Action.* London: Routledge.
EUA (European University Association). 2016. *University Autonomy in Europe.* https://www.university-autonomy.eu.
Gaebel, Michael. 2014. *MOOCs: Massive Open Online Courses.* Brussels: European University Association.
Gibbons, Michael, Camille Limoges, Helga Nowotny, Simon Schwartzman, Peter Scott, and Martin Trow. 1994. *The New Production of Knowledge; The Dynamics of Science and Research in Contemporary Societies.* London: Sage.
HESA (Higher Education Statistics Agency). 1999. *Students in Higher Education Institutions, 1996–97.* Cheltenham: HESA.
———. 2009. *Students in Higher Education Institutions 2007–08.* Cheltenham: HESA.
———. 2016. *Staff in Higher Education: 2014–15.* Cheltenham: HESA.

Higher Education Better Regulation Group. 2011. *Annual Report 2011*. https://www.univer
sitiesuk.ac.uk/policy-and-analysis/reports/Documents/2012/hebrg-annual-report
-2011.pdf.

Kennie, Tom, and Steve Woodfield. 2008. *The Composition, Challenges and Changes in the
Top Team Structures of UK Higher Education Institutions*. London: Leadership Foundation for Higher Education.

Locke, William, and Alice Bennion. 2010. *The Changing Academic Profession in the UK and
Beyond*. London: Universities UK.

Marginson, Simon. 2014. "Social Science and University Rankings." *European Journal of
Education* 49, no. 1.

Marope, Mmantsetsa, Peter Wells, and Ellen Halzelkorn, eds. 2013. *Ranking and Accountability in Higher Education: Uses and Misuses*. Paris: UNESCO Publishing.

Martin, Ben. 2011. "The Research Excellence Framework and the 'Impact Agenda': Are We
Creating a Frankenstein Monster?" *Research Evaluation* 20, no. 3:247–54.

Nowotny, Helga, Peter Scott, and Michael Gibbons. 2001. *Re-Thinking Science: Knowledge
and the Public in an Age of Uncertainty*. Cambridge: Polity Press.

———. 2003. "'Mode 2' Revisited: The New Production of Knowledge." *Minerva* 41:179–94.

Sastry, Tom. 2005. *Migration of Academic Staff to and from the UK: An Analysis of the HESA
Data*. Oxford: Higher Education Policy Institute.

Scott, Peter. 1989. "Higher Education." In *The Thatcher Effect*, ed. Dennis Kavanagh and
Anthony Seldon. Oxford: Oxford University Press.

———. 1994. "Education Policy." In *The Major Years*, ed. Dennis Kavanagh and Anthony
Seldon. London: Macmillan.

———. 2006. "The Academic Profession in the Knowledge Society." In *The Formative
Years of Scholars*, ed. Ulrich Teichler. London: Portland Press.

———. 2014. "Robbins, the Binary Policy and Mass Higher Education." *Higher Education
Quarterly* 68, no. 2:147–63.

Shattock, Michael. 2013. *Making Policy in British Higher Education, 1945–2011*. Maidenhead:
McGraw Hill—Open University Press.

Slaughter, Sheila, and Gary Rhoades. 2004. *Academic Capitalism and the New Economy:
Markets, State and Higher Education*. Baltimore: Johns Hopkins University Press.

Smith, David, and Jonathan Adams. 2007. *UK Universities and Executive Officers: The
Changing Role of Pro-Vice-Chancellors*. London: Leadership Foundation for Higher
Education.

UK Parliament. 2017. *Higher Education and Research Act*. http://services.parliament.uk/bills
/2016-17/highereducationandresearch.html.

Whitchurch, Celia. 2013. *Reconstructing Identities in Higher Education: The Rise of "Third
Space" Professionals*. London: Routledge / Society for Research into Higher Education.

5 | Russia

Higher Education, between Survival and Innovation

MARIA YUDKEVICH

One cannot overestimate the importance of the national context of a higher education system nor its institutional features for higher education research and policy. Indeed, national context helps us to understand individual and organizational incentives (for faculty, administration, and students or academic structures such as chairs, departments, etc.) as well as individual and organizational behavior in the higher education market. Understanding and taking into account institutional features also help to estimate outcomes of potential policy changes and plan any interventions in such a way that make them more realistic and efficient.

What are those characteristics in the Russian university system? While there are quite a number of them, the following could be the most important:

- High level of institutional diversity among universities in terms of size, quality, mission, legal status (public and private), etc.
- Separation of the university sector from the academies (thus, to a large extent, institutional separation of teaching and research)
- Centralized higher education system (with a dominant role of state control over finance, employment, curriculum as well as accreditation, licensing, etc.)
- Internal academic labor market (dominance of internal labor markets for academics over external ones and corresponding insularity of the

universities as organizations, associated with a specific system of reproduction of academics based on inbreeding and single-university careers)

It is quite complicated to get nuanced and reliable data—both statistical and survey data—on the Russian higher education system. In this chapter, I use three sources of data: (1) the Russian Statistical Agency (Rosstat), (2) the Monitoring of Educational Markets and Organization Project (MEMO),[1] and (3) the national survey of university faculty conducted as part of the "Changing Academic Profession Study" (2012).

Diversity

The Russian system of higher education is characterized by a substantial degree of diversity. This includes institutional diversity, but it also includes diversity in terms of the faculty they employ and the students they enroll.

HIGHER EDUCATION INSTITUTIONS

Today, the Russian system of higher education includes 548 public and 402 private institutions and slightly more than 1,300 related regional branches, approximately two-thirds of which are linked to public and one-third to private institutions. Currently, the total number of faculty at public institutions of higher education is estimated to be around 300,000.

According to the typology fixed in the Russian Law on Higher Education in 1996, there are three types of higher education institutions (HEIs): universities, academies, and institutes. Universities offer educational programs in a wide range of areas, offer postgraduate programs (PhD level), do research, and coordinate research activities in their key areas of expertise. Academies[2] differ from universities by offering educational programs in a narrower range of disciplines as well as undertaking narrower areas of research. Institutes are different from universities and academies in that they offer an even narrower range of ongoing educational programs and research activities. In the first years following the introduction of the law, many institutes converted to universities, seeking a more prestigious status and the extra benefits related to it (such as greater government subsidies or better marketing opportunities). As a result, at the moment, there is no clear substantial delineation between higher education institutions of different types based on this typology, and quite often this distinction is rather formal and does not reflect any quality or governance differences.

The largest number of institutions—just over half of all public HEIs—are affili-ated with the Ministry of Education and Science. There are 22 other ministries and agencies that have HEIs under their jurisdictions. Among the largest HEI opera-tors are the Ministry of Agriculture, the Ministry of Health and Social Develop-ment, the Ministry of Culture, the Ministry of Transport, and the Ministry of Sport and Tourism.

The private sector of the higher education system is generally associated with education of low quality, which is reflected in at least three aspects. First, its student quality is low (Unified State Examination[3] scores for students admitted to private HEIs are significantly lower than for those admitted to public HEIs). Second, its infrastructure and material support are quite poor, and expenditures per student are lower than in the public sector. Finally, the faculty core at these institutions is rather small—most teachers work part-time or are on hourly based contracts while working full-time at public higher education institutions with little time left for research.

At the same time, the public university sector is not homogeneous. During the early 2000s, the Russian government implemented initiatives designed to create stronger, research-focused institutions by designating selected universities with a special mission and mandate.

Thus, two new types of public institutions of higher education were introduced: federal universities and national research universities. Federal universities are the main universities in a federal district. Their mandate includes providing the dis-trict with a highly competitive professional staff who meet the requirements of the business and public sectors in the respective region. Having a federal university status provides the institution with opportunities for research (both fundamen-tal and applied) in priority scientific fields, and for receiving relevant financing. Today in Russia, there are 10 federal universities, organized mainly through the mergers of several smaller universities in respective regions. National research universities received their status in 2008–9 on a competitive basis, based on their programs for institutional development. As of today, this status has been awarded to 29 institutions, each for a 10-year period.

The largest share of higher education institutions (especially high-quality re-search universities) is concentrated in Moscow and Saint Petersburg. In addition, there are regions where the government has made major investments in higher education infrastructure in different parts of Russia (the most famous and impor-tant ones being in Siberia, Krasnoyarsk, and Novosibirsk, founded in the 1950s and 1960s) and where there are quite a few high-quality educational institutions.

As employers, HEIs situated in these peripheral regions are also significantly less attractive than those in Moscow and Saint Petersburg in terms of quality of academic conditions, salaries, access to information, cultural diversity, and career opportunities for young faculty.

FACULTY

Today, there are about 300,000 faculty in Russia's public universities—50,000 less than in 2005 when the number of Russian faculty reached its maximum. Such a negative trend is related both to the decrease (due to demographic decline) in the number of young people who can seek higher education and to the decrease in the number of higher education institutions, which is the result of the government policy seeking to close and restructure inefficient institutions.

A substantial percentage of the faculty has doctoral degrees. The Russian degree system, like the German, has two levels of doctoral degrees—the Candidate of Sciences, which is often considered to be equivalent to the Western PhD, and the Doctor of Sciences, which is analogous to the *habilitation* in the German system. Today, the share of faculty with the Candidates of Sciences is about 55 percent, which is the result of a positive trend that started in the earlier 1980s. An even more positive trend can be seen in the percentage of faculty who are Doctor of Sciences degree holders. In the earlier 1980s, the share of Doctors of Sciences was around 5 percent; now it is about 15 percent. In the context of the shrinking number of faculty, this means that faculty who do not hold a doctoral degree are the first to leave. The share of faculty with doctoral degrees is substantially higher in public universities than in private ones.

Other important recent changes include the age structure and gender balance of faculty. There has been a significant decrease in the share of young faculty and a relative growth of senior-age faculty (i.e., the share of faculty over 65 was 11.7 percent and 17.5 percent in years 2005 and 2015, respectively, while the share of faculty under 30 was 16.1 percent and 8.6 percent in those same years). As for the gender balance, recent decades constitute a period of feminization of the academic profession in Russia: while in 1995, the share of men was 60 percent, around 2000 it reached about 50 percent, and in 2010 reached a stable level of 44 percent.

STUDENTS

There are 5.2 million students in the Russian higher education system, of which 85 percent are enrolled in public universities. Until quite recently, 65 percent of secondary school graduates enrolled in HEIs. Participation rates have continued to increase, and in 2009 the share of all 17-year-olds who became first-year university students was 89 percent. Given the high participation rates and low level of selectivity, there are concerns from those within the higher education system that the average level of academic preparation of incoming students is lower than it should be.

While 45 percent of students in Russian HEIs are enrolled in full-time study, 4 percent are enrolled in part-time study, and the rest (over 45 percent) are enrolled in distance learning programs. The quality of part-time and distance learning programs differs strikingly from full-time programs, and, in most cases, part-time and distance programs have very low academic standards but provide a formal education credential.

There is a dual-track tuition system: some students pay tuition fees while others are accepted into tuition-free, state-subsidized spaces (latter available only in public institutions). Distribution of tuition-free openings is merit-based, not income-based.

Admission to state-funded places is based solely on the results of the Unified State Exam (USE). Students pass the USE in the final year of high school; USE results are comparable across schools and among students. Students can apply to up to five different universities by sending in application forms with USE results to the universities of their choice. Universities collect students' applications and rank applicants on the basis of the total score of the required subjects. So students with the highest cumulative USE scores get accepted. There is always competition for state-funded slots, while there often is no competition at all for self-funded openings (especially at institutions that are perceived to be of medium or low quality). As a result, the academic level of the student body within an HEI may differ substantially between state-funded and self-funded students. This has an obvious impact on the quality of work for faculty: in some HEIs, faculty have to teach rather weak students with low motivation while at other HEIs, which are highly selective, the student body is rather strong. There is currently a perception that faculty in low-quality institutions often have to compromise on quality and not expel students with inadequate performance in order to keep collecting tuition fees.

This system means that HEIs have no control over the composition of the student body (i.e., letters of motivation, extracurricular activities, or high school grades are not taken into account).[4] Such rules were introduced in 2009 as a mechanism to diminish the scope of admission decisions made under HEI discretion and thus to prevent entry-level corruption, which has been widespread in the post-Soviet period and was supported by a system of university-run examinations. Indeed, the current system was introduced to deal not only with corruption but also to improve equality in terms of access to high-quality education, and it certainly had such an impact.

As can be seen from the foregoing, the system of higher education in Russia is characterized by diversity in terms of types of HEIs, their status, their faculty body, and student motivation and quality. This variety should definitely be taken into account in any discussion on specific features of the Russian system of higher education.

Separation of the University Sector from the Academies

There is a long-standing separation between the university sector and the academy (nonteaching, pure research) sector. Fundamental research is nearly always carried out in the Academies (a similar separation exists, for example, in the French and Indian systems). Currently, there are six different Academies, the largest of which is the Russian Academy of Sciences.[5] The scientific institutions of the Academies of Sciences can provide doctoral and postdoctoral professional education, but as a rule they do not have undergraduate or master's programs. Fundamental research funding most often goes to the scientific institutions of the Academy of Sciences. Only a few universities in Russia receive state funding for fundamental research on an annual basis.

As a consequence, there is a clear dominance of the teaching mission within most HEIs. According to data from the Changing Academic Professions project, a large share of faculty at Russian HEIs are primarily interested in teaching. They were asked, "Regarding your own preferences, do your interests lie primarily in teaching or in research?" (see table 5.1 for results).

Table 5.1.   Professional Orientation toward
Research or Teaching (valid percent)

Preferences	%
Primarily in teaching	18
In both, but leaning toward teaching	43
In both, but leaning toward research	33
Primarily in research	6
Total	1,566

Source: Sivak and Yukdevich (2017).

Moreover, among the 20 countries that took part in the CAP study, Russia has the lowest percentage of faculty who are primarily interested in research. HEIs hire faculty predominantly as teachers (the Russian word for faculty—*prepodavatel*—means "teacher"). In most cases, hiring decisions are based on teaching needs and the ability of the prospective candidate to teach certain courses. Faculty positions carry quite heavy teaching loads, and heavy teaching loads are the main reason for rather low research involvement and performance by faculty. Indeed, according to CAP data, 65 percent of surveyed faculty either agree or strongly agree with the statement "teaching and research are hardly compatible with each other."

Higher education institutions are mainly aimed at professional education; they receive funding according to the state plan on professional education of specialists (based on the number of admitted students). The total numbers in this plan are determined by the Ministry of Education, while the ministry also decide how these planned numbers will be divided among higher education institutions. This creates strong incentives to increase enrollments. HEIs are mostly evaluated by how they fulfill their teaching obligations. They also report to the ministry about "faculty quality," which is measured in terms of share of faculty with doctoral degrees and in terms of nominal faculty productivity. While in recent years the research performance of universities has become an increasingly important component in asserting university efficiency by the public authorities, the role and place of research in the "average" public university is still under question. This new policy trend, however, already affects both university recruitment policy as well as faculty perceptions and expectations.

Rudiments of a Centralized Higher Education System

In general, there is a paternalistic type of relationship between HEIs and the state. Public institutions are fully dependent on the state in almost all important matters and, in turn, the state institutionally shapes and controls all important aspects of HEI functioning. This "principal-agent" type of relationship suffers from all kinds of problems that arise due to asymmetry of information. Below we consider the following aspects of this relationship in detail: planning for state-funded places, financial planning, curriculum design and assessment, and PhD programs.

Planning for State-Funded Places

First, since most of the funding that HEIs receive is aimed at the teaching function, it is profitable for them to increase enrollment (all other factors remaining the same). This, of course, supports the trends toward increasing participation in higher education, but raises questions about the quality of education, as we will see below.

The Russian higher education system revolves around so-called admission quotas. As mentioned above, each institution has a certain number of students it can admit to state-funded places in each program. Institutions apply for the quotas well in advance of the enrollment period; relevant ministries review the applications and determine allocations. Decisions are usually based on the previous period (in other words, planning is based on prior enrolment numbers). If a certain program has low state-funded enrollment numbers in one year, the institution risks having lower admission quotas for the next year (which, of course, also means lower state funding). It is, therefore, beneficial for HEIs to admit as many students as possible to occupy all state-funded places, including students who performed poorly in the Unified State Exam. This may result in implications about quality, as such a system creates incentives for an HEI to sacrifice quality for money, and only rather strong universities care about reputation enough to prevent enrollment of insufficiently strong students. Government, in turn, uses quotas to regulate the number of specialists to be trained in particular disciplines (taking into account state priorities and labor market demands). It therefore also indirectly affects the composition of the faculty body as the reduction or increase in admission quotas in some disciplines may force an institution to seek a corresponding reduction or increase in the number of faculty members.

Educational programs continue to be characterized by high levels of specialization, even in the first year, a phenomenon that could be interpreted as being a legacy of the Soviet planning system. Indeed, under the former planning system, the state decided the number of specialists required in different disciplines. Students were admitted to specialized programs to be trained for specific types of job and then centrally assigned to those jobs. Today, such a system of obligatory distribution does not exist, but early specialization still persists. So, 17-year-olds have to decide which field they are interested in and to make a choice of educational program according to that decision. Normally, for the first two to three years they will be taught a predetermined sequence of courses with little (if any) room for individual student choice. At the same time, many graduates do not work in the field in which they were trained and early specialization might be one reason for that.

Financial Planning

An important feature of financial planning for the HEIs is its short-term nature. Budgets are assigned for one year only (including those allocated for some government projects such as university excellence initiatives run by the Ministry of Education and Science). There is no long-term financial commitment from the state, even in the case of some long-term government initiatives. For universities, then, it is hard—or even impossible—to support long-term, large-scale projects and to make long-term commitments. For example (keeping legal constraints aside), it is impossible for the university to offer tenure-track and tenure contracts if it is not certain about future funding and cannot secure funds for this purpose, and therefore many faculty members are given contracts rather than permanent positions.

Curriculum Design and Assessment

Since the Soviet period, it is the responsibility of the state to maintain standards of professional education. This means that the set of core courses to be taught in each specialization is the same for all HEIs who train students in a given field and this set is approved by the Ministry of Education and Science. Institutions have to adhere to these standards and only some selected (i.e., top-quality) universities are given the authority to set their own standards. However, so far these universities have not devoted much attention to exercising this freedom to develop their own curriculum.

While curricular standards are the same across the system, the real quality of courses can be quite different due to variations in the quality of faculty and of students (to which universities have to adjust). Inbreeding and insularity of the system also add substantially to this difference: many courses are taught with basic textbooks written by the course lecturer and published in university publishing houses.

PhD Programs

Graduate education and the degree system in Russia have several specific features. PhD degrees are issued by the Ministry of Education and Science, not by the institutions themselves, although HEIs conduct the thesis defense. One implication of this feature is an adverse selection problem, with many weak institutions "selling PhD diplomas," which then leads to the problem of validity of academic degrees and the quality of the degree system. The PhD degree has become a positioning good and an important signal of status rather than a signal of academic quality. Indeed, the number of PhD degrees awarded has been growing rapidly over the past few years, especially in certain areas of the social sciences and humanities, mainly due to the lowering of academic standards to meet the rising demand for the degree from people in the nonacademic sector. This has resulted in a continuous depreciation of the system of doctoral degrees in Russia.

In general, doctoral education is no longer competitive in a number of fields. Moreover, most postgraduate students have no intention of working in academia. The majority of them, even those enrolled in full-time programs, also work full-time in the business sector. As postgraduate scholarships are low in value, young graduates cannot afford to not earn a salary through regular work. That being said, full-time postgraduate programs do not really involve rigorous study, which is particularly attractive for male students, as being full-time students means they can avoid being drafted into the army.

The problems of postgraduate education are even deeper due to the absence of any real national academic market and a lack of academic job prospects outside one's own institution. This means that HEIs have no stimuli to train high-quality students whose competences will not be appreciated in the market anyway. Together with inbreeding, this contributes to a situation where students do not compete for the best positions and have no incentive to develop their academic skills so as to pursue an academic career.

At the same time, the Ministry of Education and Science still considers the number of PhD defenses and the "efficiency" of graduate programs at the HEI (measured by the share of enrolled students that completed a degree within four years after the start of the program) as an important indicator of university efficiency. This creates even stronger incentives for HEIs to compromise on quality.

In general, the system of reproduction of academics to a large extent determines the prevalence of inbreeding and many other characteristics of an academic university system in Russia. State control of important aspects of university life is rather strong. Such a paternalistic approach makes universities weaker in those activities that are usually considered an essential part of the academic governance system (see Rosovsky, 2013).

Internal Academic Labor Market

In order to understand academic careers within the Russian higher education system, it is important to understand academic career pathways, the chair system and academic contracts, the salary structure, inbreeding, and academic governance arrangements.

ACADEMIC CAREER PATHWAYS

The standard way to start an academic career in Russia is to enter a graduate program—usually at the same institution where the bachelor's and master's degrees were obtained—and start working as a teaching assistant at the same time as well. It is also common to start teaching tutorials and classes for courses that your thesis adviser is teaching. Such a system is both the source and the consequence of inbreeding in the Russian university system: by the time the PhD is obtained, the young fellow is already deeply integrated into faculty life, has his or her own social connections (often facilitated by the PhD adviser) and teaching loads, and does not find it necessary to move to another place.

There are many academic ranks in a standard career ladder: teaching assistant, lecturer, senior lecturer, associate professor, professor. When moving up from teaching assistant (this position is often held by PhD candidates who teach in their departments), people experience an increase in academic status, a nominal (not really substantial in many cases) increase in salary, and may have less heavy teaching loads. An upgrade in rank depends on the number of years of teaching (in a particular institution), the degree level (Candidate of Science or Doctor of Science), and is subject to availability of vacancies at the department or chair level. The distribution of ranks is presented in figure 5.1, where one can easily see that for many faculty, the level of associate professor (docent) is the highest rank they can reach during their career.

CHAIR SYSTEM AND ACADEMIC CONTRACTS

HEI teachers are not civil servants and there is no lifetime employment. Contracts are temporary and are supposed to be renewed on a competitive basis. Until recently, the level of competition was quite low and one could say that the external market for academic labor did not work since it was dominated by an internal labor market. However, recent policy initiatives as well as social changes have affected this balance substantially.

The smallest organizational unit and, at the same time, the center of decision making in everything related to the educational process (including faculty recruitment) is a chair. Formally, a chair is defined by a narrow research area. It is a highly hierarchical structure ruled by the head of the chair who, in practical terms, makes all the important decisions. Therefore, when new faculty members

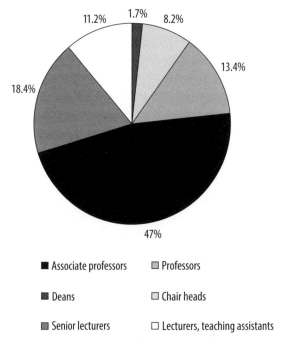

11.2%   1.7%   8.2%

13.4%

18.4%

47%

■ Associate professors   ▨ Professors

■ Deans   ▢ Chair heads

▨ Senior lecturers   ▢ Lecturers, teaching assistants

Figure 5.1. Distribution of ranks in public and
private higher education institutions in 2014.
Source: Indicators of Education, 2016, 230.

are hired, they are employed by a specific chair rather than a department. Another
hierarchical level in Russian universities is departments (which may be called institutes in some HEIs, usually engineering ones). The departments essentially unite
chairs that provide courses within one educational program. Unlike departments
in US universities, chairs in Russia are considered to be teaching units characterized by a concentration of power and strong hierarchical patterns.

To coordinate, plan, and control the educational process, chairs use individual
teaching loads, which indicate the amount of instructional work a teacher needs to
provide during an academic year. The annual load is calculated in hours: a teaching assistant's workload is around 750–900 hours per year; that of a professor,
600–700 hours. Such a workload means that a teacher has at least three full days
of teaching a week, sometimes even four, which leaves considerably less time for
research.

The number of faculty positions assigned to each chair is defined by aggregate
teaching loads that a chair is responsible for in the university curriculum. Each

chair is therefore interested in maximizing the number of courses it teaches within the educational programs at a university so as to get more faculty positions. These incentives are clearly counterproductive. Once given the privilege and duty to deliver lectures (normally a PhD is required for this), people teach the same courses for many years and become highly specialized. Since it is hard for them to switch over to other areas and deliver new courses, the curriculum becomes rigid and is prone to stagnation. To delete a course from a program would often mean leaving someone without their long-standing job, and chair heads know this all too well. They are, therefore, interested in keeping the status quo, which ensures that all chair teachers keep their jobs.

The recruitment system is organized as follows. In order to hire a new faculty member, a chair has to have an open, relevant position available with a guaranteed teaching load. Formally, it is a competition-based recruitment. If a university has a vacant position or if faculty term contracts are about to expire, the university advertises the vacancies. Such advertisements are published on the university's website, in mass media, or through employment services, including private ones. Finding new faculty on the "open market" usually takes place when a university is opening new educational programs. In all other cases, in practice, there is no open competition (or any competition at all). Despite information about new positions being advertised, no one regards it as a real opportunity for anyone outside the university. In fact, the head of the chair and his or her connections (including informal ones) determine the extension of existing contracts and make decisions about new hires. Teaching assistants and teacher positions are usually filled by young graduates or postgraduate students of the same chair (for reasons mentioned above).

Only in exceptional circumstances would an existing contract not be extended. Yet, meeting formal requirements (such as published research and methodology papers or positive feedback from students) is important too because these are some of the parameters used when assessing the chair's (the academic unit's) performance as a whole, which the chair is responsible for. At the same time, the chair's publications—both research and didactic ones—are important at the university level, too.

Full-time faculty sign a standard employment contract for one, three, or five years. The first contract is usually signed for one year, the next one for three years, and then it is extended once every five years, if there are no complications or complaints on either side. Until recently, the extension of a contract did not cause any substantial change (regarding workload, wages, etc.). Tenure did not exist, but, in reality, due to the lack of any real competition for teaching positions and the fact that contracts were extended nearly automatically, faculty considered their contracts to be permanent. While there is an official retirement age, many people continue working even after reaching it (there is a rather small pension provided by the state).

The faculty's main function is teaching, which is heavily regulated by the teaching-load calculation. Yet lecturers are supposed to do research, too, so they work under the looming imperative that "one has to do research in order to be a good teacher." However, the labor contract defines neither the volume of research to be done nor the results expected. Any attempt to formalize the time split between teaching and research, or even research results, is unlikely to succeed in a situation where most faculty members do not even have their own work offices and usually only come to the academic unit in between classes. Within such a system, quite often people teach the same courses for many years, as mentioned above, and get attached to them.

Research performance, in many cases, does not serve as a significant factor when it comes to extending academic contracts. University chairs and departments are, however, interested in impressive research results of their faculty, which are needed for external reports, so they create opportunities for the improvement of such criteria by publishing internal paper digests, internal conference proceedings, and so on.

The contract system, which was originally designed to maintain stability since contracts were almost automatically renewed, is now experiencing tensions in the face of the new realities of competition for students, for academic vacancies, and for resources, as well as growing demands for increasing efficiency. While there was no tenure system de jure, a tenure system existed de facto. Peoples' expectations, and hence strategies, were formed under an assumption that their job positions (not job conditions or remuneration) were secure. Now, the situation is changing: the competition for places is increasing and the university administration, facing uncertainty and increasing performance requirements from the ministry, tend to offer one-year contracts to the majority of faculty. This creates substantial tension within the academic profession.

Since the research performance of universities is becoming more and more important as a general imperative imposed by the ministry, at the micro level, individual research performance becomes an important criterion for recruitment and promotion. In determining salaries and the real total income of faculty, research performance starts to play an important role as well.

Salaries

During the 1990s and the beginning of the 2000s, earnings in the university sector were dramatically low (see Androushchak & Yudkevich, 2013)—25 to 50 percent lower than average earnings in the economy. However, during the last decade, the gap has been decreasing and now the average faculty salary level is an important indicator that is used by the Ministry of Education and Science to monitor the efficiency of top management in universities. Over the last five years, real incomes of faculty at Russian HEIs have been rather stable (see figure 5.2).

There are considerable variations in wages among academic fields, which reflect the market demands for different degree programs and different opportunities for faculty to obtain outside income. The highest wages are in economics and the social sciences, which are in the highest demand both within and outside the university sector, while academic staff in the arts and natural sciences experience less demand and receive lower wages.

The main determinants of teacher salaries in the university are teaching load, rank (which determines a budget category in the wage scale), academic degree, and administrative services. These factors, on average, add up to 70 percent of academic salaries and are referred to as the basic component of the salary. The rest of the salary is referred to as the stimulating component and constitutes about 30 percent of the total salary.

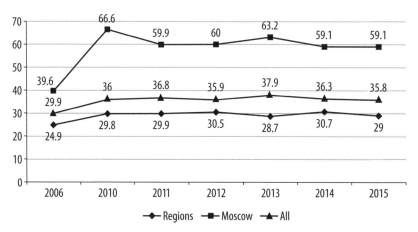

Figure 5.2. Income of faculty at Russian higher education institutions (in real terms, thousand rubles, in 2015 prices). *Source:* Faculty surveys, 2006–15, Monitoring of Educational Organizations and Markets.

In principle, universities have both the legal and financial autonomy required for the individualization of teachers' salaries and are able to compete for the best through a system of higher salaries, additional bonuses, and other items. Despite the potential to compete for academic staff, however, institutions are still rather reluctant to do so. Reasons include limited financial capacity, no market for academic research (which would provide faculty and universities direct returns for their research reputation), and the high risk of social tensions within the university's academic community. At the same time, the new trend in the university system, which puts more emphasis on the importance of research, is universities introducing bonuses for research performance. Many universities are now initiating a new faculty remuneration system that implies that a part of the faculty salary is determined according to different criteria and measurable achievements, such as research performance, external grants, etc.

Recent demographic trends (i.e., the decline in the age cohort that resulted in a sharp decrease in the number of prospective students) as well as current reforms in the higher education system have had an important impact on the system. First, fewer faculty are needed to teach students and vacancies are becoming more competitive. In addition, senior management is interested in cutting down faculty size in order to pay higher salaries to the rest—under the new rules, university rectors are monitored and judged on their ability to keep average faculty salary at a level that is double the average salary in the region). As a result, faculty feel considerably less secure, sense more competition, etc.

Inbreeding

As mentioned earlier, one of the key features of the university system in Russia is widespread inbreeding, with doctoral students moving into positions at their degree-granting university. This is supported by various cultural, infrastructural, and academic factors (see Sivak & Yudkevich, 2015 for a more detailed analysis).

There are several reasons for this widespread inbreeding, one being the financial factor. Relatively low starting salaries in many fields make full-time university employment unattractive for young people who have already entered the labor market and enjoy better salaries, and who will not (for a rather long time) get comparable money at a university. It, therefore, becomes important for universities to hold on to the students and postgraduates who are inclined to do teaching and research work.

Inbreeding tends to produce another negative result: the graduates who stay at their home universities may not be the best, as they have very little external work experience, are not part of wider academic networks, and have few academic connections outside their own institution or even department. It turns out that their ability is, more or less, to pass their own knowledge, received at the same university, to the next generation of students. In most cases, their academic supervisors and heads of chairs remain indisputable academic authorities for them.

There are also implications for academic recruitment. Insiders—that is, faculty members who themselves graduated from the institutions where they teach or have not worked at other institutions (at least until recently)—show stronger inbreeding-oriented recruitment strategies, whereas those faculty who graduated from other universities are more likely to support externally oriented recruitment policies and welcome "new blood," but they are usually very few, so they have little opportunity to influence the policy (see Sivak & Yudkevich, 2015 for a detailed analysis and discussion).

Inbreeding also affects many aspects of research production, since teachers without any outside experience rarely have publications in external journals (since they mostly focus on departmental or university-published editions) and rarely participate in external conferences. They are part of narrower academic networks (again, usually limited to their own colleagues within their chair or their department) and are chained to their academic supervisor or head of chair. Finally, they are much more inclined to teach rather than to do research, which seems logical because teaching includes certain "university-related investments" into work at this particular university while research (measured in publications) does not. This is consistent with Gouldner (1957, 1958) and Tuma and Grimes (1981).

As a result, insularity affects the norms that regulate research in at least three ways. First, certain local rules and standards regarding research and publications emerge and the alienation from the external peer environment may have a negative impact on research quality. Second, some "local disciplines and fields," traditionally developed within only one university, appear. Finally, developing or supporting this or that research field is defined not by external factors (such as marketability) but rather by the private interests of individuals.

To a large extent, inbreeding enables a system of informal contracts (the system of mutual responsibilities and expectations) between older and younger, senior and junior members of faculty. Inbreeding, therefore, encourages paternalism (guarding and promoting one's disciples) and a kind of clan system, as well as the formation and maintenance of tight, informal connections.

The high level of specific investments and high average time recorded at one institution lead to faculty being oriented toward internal networks. In contrast, people aspiring to a mobile career want to remain competitive in the market; therefore, they make fewer investments in teaching and administrative work and put more effort into research in order to achieve results that are visible and valued in the external academic market. It is more important for them to be involved in interuniversity networks. Thus, the latter share rather cosmopolitan values, the former prefer local values and show fidelity to their own university.

In the system based on internal labor market and reproduction from within, internal organizational rules dominate over external professional influences. In particular, external expertise is eclipsed by the internal expertise, which is not immune to the informal influence of internal networks. As a result, there are situations when promotion is based not on transparent academic achievements but on internal status and prestige. Moreover, inbreeding-oriented traditions make research performance less important than affiliations with a certain institution or school, or political groups. All of this affects research performance and its competitive potential in the global academic market.

Finally, inbreeding is associated with low mobility between institutions and the dominance of a single university career pattern of academic pathways. While HEIs formally are obliged to have their job postings open for people from outside, it is commonly believed that outsiders are strongly discriminated against when employment decisions are made.

GOVERNANCE AND DECISION MAKING

The Russian system of university governance is rather vertical (this phenomenon is closely related to inbreeding, which positively rewards seniority and tenure at one institution). There is quite low faculty participation in decision making on important university matters, and academics do not think they can really influence university policy at any level (department or university in general).

Faculty passivity is also related to the specific investment faculty members make in the current university as an employer (again, due at least partially to inbreeding) and weak links with the academic community outside the university. One could say that among the two systems of control within the university (following Gouldner, 1957), academic control is rather weak and organizational dominates.

HEI teaching staff in Russia also acknowledge the growing control functions executed by departmental and university administration (see Altbach, 1996; Sivak & Yudkevich, 2017). At the same time, they do not feel like being involved in decision making regarding important matters. It is true that university governance structures in Russia responsible for academic decision making are mostly concentrated within administrative structures. The level of academic self-governance and teachers' engagement is very low. As a result, most of the control mechanisms are vertical. Such vertically organized evaluation mechanisms have also become substitutes for peer evaluation, which would normally be a natural by-product of university staff's main activities. Faculty perceive such external (top-down) evaluations—as opposed to internal peer evaluations—as "pressure" and a sign of "bureaucratization." At the same time, scholars have generally argued that shared governance is crucial for developing a world-class university (Rozovsky, 2014).

INTERNATIONAL RECRUITMENT

On the whole, one can say that the level of internationalization in the Russian university sector is quite low. Few people have research or teaching experience abroad. According to CAP data, only 3 percent of surveyed faculty taught abroad in 2011–12, 17 percent had collaborations with foreign colleagues, 8 percent had publications (in the previous three years) with colleagues from other countries, and only 8 percent agreed that their primary research is "international in scope and orientation." Incoming mobility is also quite low: there are few foreign teachers and researchers working in Russia, and very few universities try international academic recruiting.

Russian universities, with few exceptions, do not have any specific international recruitment policy, and there are several reasons for that. First of all, universities are limited in the wages they can offer, compared to the salaries in US and European universities. Then, even if universities find sufficient funds, they face the problem of long-term guarantees and assurances of their obligations. Moreover, international recruitment risks creating social tension among the faculty, which is bound to happen when there are differences between relatively low-paid long-employed professors and attractive contracts for younger recent graduates. Finally, one can foresee a conflict between local and foreign academic norms. The latter are more transparent in terms of recruitment and promotion, and are based on individual research achievements, while the former are more "communal," more informal, and reward age, experience, and time within the university.

The state is making certain attempts to create conditions that would encourage international cooperation aimed at forming prominent university research centers and labs for potential "breakthrough" research. In 2009, the state launched its first competition aimed at attracting leading international scholars to Russian universities. From 2010 to 2013, as a result of this competition, a number of laboratories were created at Russian universities under the supervision of leading academics from abroad who received substantial remuneration in exchange for agreeing to spend at least several months a year in Russia. However, this program meant high transaction costs for both parties, particularly due to the academic and bureaucratic differences between Russia and other countries. Complex formal reporting requirements, restrictions on spending state money on equipment, databases, empirical studies, and so on, also had a negative impact on the efficiency of these research groups. At the same time, even though it is too soon to judge the program's impact, its substantial positive effect (included, among other things, the substantial growth of high-quality research output) is already evident.

Besides the financial issues, certain legal issues regarding academic employment of foreign nationals are still unresolved. Currently, this type of contract requires that HEIs apply for quotas and work permits for foreigners, and then renew the contracts periodically. In such a situation, it is quite problematic to create a tenure and tenure-track system that would be supported not only by the university's informal structure but also by legal institutions.

The new university excellence initiative (5-100 Program), which we discuss in more detail below, also puts an emphasis on internationalization. The goal of this program is to increase the competitiveness of the Russian higher education system by supporting several leading universities in their efforts to become world class. Fifteen universities were initially selected for governmental financial support (with six more added in the second round) in exchange for their commitment to substantially improve their positions in global university rankings. Key indicators of success for a university within this program include, among others, the share of international students and international faculty at the university. Universities therefore make efforts to bring international scholars into their institutions. However, to make these efforts fruitful and systemic, a number of problems have to be resolved at the national level, such as immigration issues (work permits, visa process complications, etc.), insurance and pension questions, provision of security and accommodation in places where most of the communication is in Russian, and so on. At the university level, there are problems to be addressed as well: the lack of tenure contracts, non-transparent taxing (from the foreigners' point of view), nontransparent structure of salary calculation, and the like.

Recent Transformations in the Research Support System

As mentioned in previous sections, in most cases there is no direct state financial support for university research. While several exceptions exist (among them,

Moscow State University, Saint Petersburg State University, National Research University Higher School of Economics), for large top-quality institutions there is no general rule. Meanwhile, the Academy of Sciences gets direct budgetary assignations from the state and then distributes them among the institutions of the Academy. However, in the years 2010–14, new, important trends in the organization of research in the Russian university system emerged.

MEGA-LABORATORIES

In late 2009, the Ministry for Education and Science initiated a competition for "mega-laboratories." These research labs were supposed to be headed by top-quality international scholars. This was the first large-scale targeted research support program for universities. In the period of 2010–16, there were five rounds of competition. Each lab typically received around three million US dollars for three years. It was assumed that, after this period, these labs would be able to attract external funding (or would be supported by the university itself) and would not have further financial support from the state.

The program had mixed results. On the one hand, it was quite positive as the program brought many reputable international scholars into the system and attracted bright young researchers and PhD candidates to continue academic careers. On the other hand, it proved to be unsustainable in some cases since opportunities for external funding (at least in some disciplines) are rather limited. So, without continued funding from the state, some labs are about to wind down.

UNIVERSITY EXCELLENCE INITIATIVE: 5–100 PROGRAM

At the end of 2012, Russian President Vladimir Putin signed a decree with a target that at least five Russian universities in the year 2020 should be in the top 100 positions in world university rankings. While such a target seems probably too ambitious, it clearly indicates the priorities articulated by the state. The value of strengthening the research function is also clear (at least to some extent) to the professoriate. According to the recent survey of the academic profession, in Russia almost 90 percent of Russian faculty in public universities believe that strengthening the nation's capacity to compete internationally should be among the top priorities for higher education in the country.

The total financial support for 21 selected universities is determined annually and this money is distributed unequally—according to the quality of applications and commitments that universities are ready to undertake in the first year and the annual results in consequent years. Rectors of universities that are selected for support within this program are personally responsible for the program's implementation and results. In some ways, the authority of these rectors is reduced since, in each university, an external board oversees the rector on the most important decisions. This board also includes international experts to introduce international experience and vision into the system.

The main indicators that are the basis for initial support are position (accurate up to 50 positions) in leading global universities' rankings (for universities and educational programs) that a university is targeting to achieve; number of articles in Web of Science and Scopus per faculty member; average citation index per faculty member, calculated from the total number of articles in journals indexed in Web of Science and Scopus; share of international faculty; share of international students studying in the university's main educational programs; share of revenues from nonbudgetary sources in the makeup of university revenues; and average USE scores of students admitted to the university for full-time bachelor's and specialist studies, financed by the federal government.

Some experts believe that the design of the indicators creates incentives for quick results—that is, publishing in low-tier journals to achieve quantitative targets and bringing in weak international "academic tourists." It also discriminates against humanities where journals are not the main places to publish scholarly work. There is therefore some conflict between the targeted goals of this program and the national priorities in the creation of competitive universities, not only in a limited numbers of disciplines (such as technical sciences) but in the whole range of disciplines.

The existence of such a program contributes to institutional diversity and to the differentiation of conditions for faculty in universities of different ranks. Indeed, in top research universities (especially those included in the 5-100 Program), requirements are much more demanding: faculty are expected to publish more, but at the same time financial and infrastructural conditions are better and faculty get more support for their research.

One may say that internationalization and research support are now the main milestones that had been largely ignored under previous initiatives. Whether HEIs, with almost no degree of internationalization and historically rooted separation from basic research, will be able to succeed is a moot point. While it is too early to discuss the long-term outcomes of this program, the first evidence suggests that there is a clear, positive trend in publication performance, with the number of publications in high-quality journals and peer-reviewed international journals in general growing substantially since 2012 (see figs. 5.3 and 5.4, and Matveeva, Poldin, Sterligov & Yudkevich, 2017 for detailed analysis of the program impact).

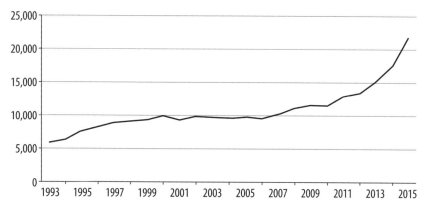

Figure 5.3. Dynamics of publications of Russian universities, research papers and reviews (SCI-E, SSCI). *Source:* Web of Science database.

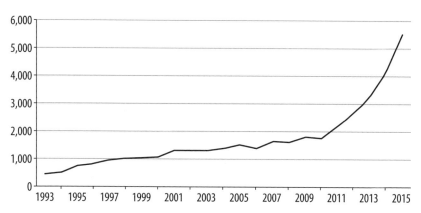

Figure 5.4. Dynamics of publications of Russian Universities in Q1 journals, research papers and reviews (SCI-E, SSCI). *Source:* Sivak & Yudkevich, 2013.

GRANT SUPPORT OF UNIVERSITY RESEARCH:
TOWARD A NEW SYSTEM

One more important recent change concerns the creation in early 2014 of the Russian Research Foundation. The current thinking is that most of the research support to the HEIs (and later to the institutions under the Academies of Sciences) will be given on a competitive basis through this foundation. The foundation has already launched several waves of grants on different scales—from grants for small teams and larger groups to grant support for university-level projects. The efficiency of this initiative will critically depend on the ability both of the ministry and the academic society to address a number of structural problems. One of the important ones is the low quality of expertise. While expertise is a key ingredient of any grant system, in the Russian case it is far from good. Namely, it suffers from a lack of transparency and has to rely mostly on domestic experts since the procedure for bringing international experts into the system (due to numerous bureaucratic constraints and restrictions) is extremely complicated both for the foundation and for the experts themselves. As a result, such a system can hardly be considered effective for research support allocation, and people complain about the unpredictability of competition results. Academic discipline organizations often consider these grant competitions as lotteries and do not trust the results, often accusing the foundation of corruption and making decisions without appropriate expertise.

Conclusion

The last two decades have been a time of constant reforms and changes in the higher education sector in Russia. While the system in general adjusts toward market conditions, it still bears some rudiments of the post-Soviet planning system, both in terms of the organization of the system in general and also in relation to academic career pathways. Distinctly "national" practices are quite rigid. The practices are changing in leading universities, but still this change does not affect the system as a whole.

Strong state control and the entire logic of state participation in the HEI sector in Russia contribute to weakening the academic community's participation in HEI governance and give little incentive for change from within. At the same time, current reforms create huge tensions for the faculty who face changing (and more demanding) expectations in terms of increased research performance and attracting external funding from grants and industry research. They also face increased uncertainty, more competition, and feel less secure.

Differentiation of higher education institutions evidently affects the working conditions as well as the academic career pathways in institutions of different quality and status.

The state certainly has an ambition to build world-class universities in Russia, to make them visible at the global academic market, and to restore the former potency and glory of the university sector in Russia. Even the recent excellence initiative by the Russian government is formulated in a global-rankings perspective (by 2020, at least five Russian universities should be in the top 100 of major global rankings). At the same time, the state wants to improve the efficiency of the system in general; this means addressing the bottom tier of the system, represented by weak institutions.

Bringing research into the HEI system is an important step in realizing these ambitious plans. To create world-class research universities it is important to improve competitive mechanisms of research support and bring HEIs and institutions of the Academy of Sciences closer together (to use the research synergy of both sectors). At the same time, it is also important to overcome the remaining rudiments of the planning system that still work in contemporary institutions.

NOTES

This chapter was prepared within the framework of the Basic Research Program at the National Research University Higher School of Economics (HSE) and supported within the framework of a subsidy granted to the HSE by the Government of the Russian Federation for the implementation of the Global Competitiveness Program.

1. The MEMO project consists of annual representative surveys of students and their families, schoolteachers, and faculty at colleges and higher education institutions, heads of colleges and HEIs, and employers. It is designed and administered by the Higher School of Economics, with financial support from the Ministry of Education and Science of the Russian Federation.

2. One should distinguish between academies as a form of higher education institution and Academies of Sciences, which represent the research (nonteaching) sector of the academic system and will be discussed later in the chapter. To avoid confusion, I will use capital letters when referring to the latter.

3. The Unified State Examination (USE) was introduced in Russia in 2009 as a set of obligatory exams for all high school graduates. The USE serves both as a final exam in high school and as a basis for admission decisions by HEIs. For example, where places are allocated to applicants with the highest cumulative scores, admissions are based on USE scores.

4. There is a recent policy trend to give some decision-making power to the HEIs, to take into account some extracurricular activities, but the emphasis is rather minor.

5. Others are Academies of Medical Sciences, Education, Agricultural Sciences, Architecture and Construction Sciences, and Arts.

REFERENCES

Altbach, Philip G. 1996. *The international academic profession.* Princeton, NJ: Carnegie Foundation for the Advancement of Teaching.
Androushchak, Gregory, and Maria Yudkevich. 2012. "Russian Higher Education: Salaries and Contracts." In *Paying the Professoriate: A Global Comparison of Compensation and Contracts,* ed. P. G. Altbach, L. Reisberg, M. M. Yudkevich, G. V. Androuschak, and I. Pacheco, 265–78. London: Routledge.

———. 2013. "Changing Realities: Russian Higher Education and the Academic Profession." In *The Global Future of Higher Education and the Academic Profession: The BRICs and the United States,* ed. P. G. Altbach, L. Reisberg, M. M. Yudkevich, G. V. Androuschak, and Y. I. Kuzminov, 56–92. London: Palgrave Macmillan.

Froumin, Isak, Yaroslav Kouzminov, and Dmitry Semyonov. 2014. "Institutional Diversity in Russian Higher Education: Revolutions and Evolution." *European Journal of Higher Education* 4, no. 3:209–34.

Gouldner, Alvin W. 1957. "Cosmopolitans and Locals: Toward an Analysis of Latent Social Roles. I." *Administrative Science Quarterly* 2:281–306.

———. 1958. "Cosmopolitans and Locals: Toward an Analysis of Latent Social Roles. II." *Administrative Science Quarterly* 2:444–80.

Higher Education in Russia and Beyond (newsletter). 2014. Issue 1: Russian Master Plan (Spring).

Indicators of Education. 2016. Informational Bulletin, HSE Publishing House, p. 230. https://www.hse.ru/en/primarydata/io2016. Accessed September 6, 2018.

Matveeva, Natalia, Oleg Poldin, Ivan Sterligov, and Maria Yudkevich. Forthcoming. "Research Performance of Russian Universities: Effect of Global Excellence Initiative." *Educational Studies Moscow,* forthcoming.

Monitoring of Educational Organizations and Markets (MEMO). "About the Project." National Research Higher School of Economics. https://memo.hse.ru/en/about. Accessed September 7, 2018.

Rosovsky, Henry. 2014. "Research Universities: American Exceptionalism?" *International Higher Education* 76:4–6.

Sivak, Elizaveta, and Maria Yudkevich. 2013. "Academic Profession in a Comparative Perspective: 1992–2012." *Foresight and STI Governance (Foresight-Russia until No. 3/2015)* 7, no. 3 (2013): 38–47.

———. 2015. "Academic Immobility and Inbreeding in Russian Universities, in: Academic Inbreeding and Mobility in Higher Education." In *Global Perspectives,* ed. Maria Yudkevich, Philip Altbach, and Laura Rumbley, 130–55. London: Palgrave Macmillan.

———. 2017. "The Academic Profession in Russia's Two Capitals: The Impact of 20 years of Transition." *European Educational Research Journal* 16, no. 5 (2017): 626–44.

———. Tuma, Nancy Brandon, and Andrew J. Grimes. 1981. "A Comparison of Models of Role Orientations of Professionals in a Research-Oriented University." *Administrative Science Quarterly* 26:187–206.

Yudkevich, Maria. 2014a. "Russian University: recovery or rehabilitation." *Studies in Higher Education* 39, no. 8:1463–75.

———. 2014b. "Leading Universities in Russia: From Teaching to Research Excellence." *Journal of International Higher Education* 6, no. 3:113–16.

6 | Brazil

An Emerging Academic Market in Transition

ELIZABETH BALBACHEVSKY

The Brazilian experience is exemplary for understanding the tensions and contradictions produced inside an emerging academic system as it faces, simultaneously, the challenges of expanding access and strengthening its academic performance. First, there are the challenges of building up a modern academic system in a situation of chronic shortage of qualified candidates to fill all academic positions. This chapter analyzes how this situation impacts the shape of the academic market and career, and also reviews the tensions created by the transition from the scenario where there is an undersupply of qualified professors to another where academic credentials become more widespread and lose their central discriminant role. As argued in this chapter, the only way to defuse the tensions generated by this changing scenario is to lessen the relevance and prerogatives attached to different positions on the academic ladder. In these circumstances, external institutions and programs are responsible for producing the signals of academic prestige. Sometimes these signals even cut across the institution's internal academic ladder.

While facing cross-pressures for expanding access and improving academic performance, an emerging academic system will commonly experience some degree of institutional stratification or diversification. In the case of Brazil, the picture that emerges is one of strong institutional segmentation, where the barriers to career mobility increase as the scholar becomes older and more experienced.

The Higher Education System in Brazil

Brazil is a federal republic, which means that the policies shaping higher education come from different and more or less autonomous levels of authority. In addition to the federal government, Brazil's 26 states, the Federal District (surrounding Brasilia, the capital), and the country's 5,570 municipalities are all officially entitled to organize their own higher education systems. Thus, in 2015, the federal system included 107 institutions, of which 63 held the status of comprehensive universities and another 40 were Federal Centers for Technological Education (vocational training centers). States owned 118 higher education institutions, of which 38 were universities; and a number of municipalities, in different states, owned 73 institutions, of which 10 also held the status of universities. The private sector was composed of 2,070 institutions scattered throughout the country, including 84 universities. Nonuniversity institutions may assume different shapes and names. They are usually smaller, but this is not always the rule. Nonetheless, being a nonuniversity institution in Brazil does not mean that it is a vocational institution. On the contrary, all institutions—universities or not—are entitled to grant the same kind of undergraduate degree: the bachelor's degree, which is also a professional certification.

The main difference between university and nonuniversity institutions is that the former are supposed to have some research activity. Thus, the agencies in charge of evaluating higher education demand indicators of research outputs. By Brazilian law, a university is also supposed to support at least three different master's programs and one doctoral program. These programs should be evaluated and approved by the Ministry of Education's agency in charge of graduate education, Fundação Coordenação de Aperfeicoamento de Pessoal de Nivel Superior or Foundation Coordination for the Improvement of Higher Education Personnel (CAPES). Once accredited as a university, the institution enjoys autonomy to establish new programs at the undergraduate level.

While the federal government is in charge of regulating and supervising the federal and private institutions throughout the country, states are in charge of regulating and supervising the state- and municipality-owned institutions inside their territories. It is usual to find three or more institutions located in the same neighborhood but subject to different rules, diverse evaluation systems, and different sources of support.

Graduate Education and System Expansion

The Brazilian experience is an interesting case for exploring how the shortage of qualified candidates for academic positions affects the institutionalization of university life. In the 1950s and 1960s, the challenge of staffing higher education institutions with competent professionals was first met by sending a significant number of academics abroad to have access to PhD training. By the late 1960s, the number of graduate personnel was enough to support the development of a domestic graduate system. Graduate education in Brazil was, since the beginning, organized in formal programs, which included completing coursework, writing a research paper, and publicly defending the thesis or dissertation.

Since 1976, a formal, nationwide evaluation based on peer review defines the level of public support each graduate program is entitled to receive. This evaluation imposes a threshold of minimum quality for graduate education, which, in turn, defines which programs are qualified to grant master and doctoral degrees. It also limits the dispersion of graduate programs across all universities. Even in the present day, despite its rapid expansion, graduate education—in particular doctoral programs—tends to be concentrated in a small number of more academically qualified institutions (Balbachevsky & Schwartzman, 2010; CGEE, 2011).

In the Brazilian experience, the success of building up a dynamic system of graduate education produced an informal stratification among public universities, which cut across the legal classification that separates federal-owned universities from state-owned ones. In the late 1960s, when graduate education was first recognized and received support from the federal government, only a few public institutions (both federal- and state-owned), and some Catholic universities, were well positioned to take advantage of the new incentives. At that time, these universities attracted a number of PhD holders from abroad, and because of that, they were able to create the first graduate programs. Since graduate programs also offered the best conditions for supporting research, these universities attracted more academics with doctorates who then educated the next generation of their academic personnel. The operation of this virtuous circle is one of the most important factors explaining the growth of a small number of "real" research universities in Brazil (Balbachevsky, 2013). As early as the end of the 1980s, these universities already had most of their academics qualified as doctors, and, what is more important, many of them started to impose informal norms demanding a PhD degree as the minimal condition for access to an academic appointment.[1]

Beginning in 1992, the Brazilian higher education landscape experienced major changes in graduate education, which have had important implications for the academic labor market. First, graduate training opportunities expanded. In 1996, all Brazilian universities together granted only 2,900 doctorates. In 2007, this number was 9,900, an increase of 350 percent in nine years. The regulatory framework also changed. A new education law, enacted at the end of 1996, reinforced the relevance of academic degrees in the public universities' academic ladder. Most importantly, from 1996 until 2003 access to the public sector was almost completely closed. During this period, the Brazilian government imposed restrictions on new contracts in all public sectors as part of its policy to control the expansion of the public budget and to fight the high inflation rates that plagued the Brazilian economy. By 2004, when the public sector started to hire again, there were a large number of young scholars holding doctoral degrees and waiting for positions within the public sector. As discussed later in this chapter, the new influx of qualified academics seeking positions in the public sector affected in various ways the shape of the academic career, and produced new dynamics in the academic market in general.

ACADEMIC LABOR MARKET ADJUSTMENTS AND MASSIFICATION

Full-time contracts were introduced in the public sector in 1968, with the first major reform of the Brazilian higher education system.[2] The introduction of this kind of contract in the public university occurred at the same time as major policy initiatives that organized, for the first time, a large-scale public funding for research and graduate education in Brazil (S. Schwartzman, 2010). In the 1970s, the public sector almost universalized full-time contracts. The combination of these initiatives created an unparalleled window of opportunity for both the consolidation of the scientific community and an increasing complexity of the institutional design of public universities. Estimates made by several specialists point out that from 1970 to 1980, the total budget allocated to the federal universities in Brazil more than quintupled, and that most of these increases were directed to support the expansion of full-time academic contracts (Velloso, 1987; Mattos, 1990; J. Schwartzman, 1993).

However, what was not foreseen by the 1968 reform was the increasing pressure for access to higher education experienced by Brazilian society at the time. From the mid-1960s to 1970, the number of enrollments at the undergraduate level grew from a little over 93,000 to more than 425,000. In 1980, the number of students enrolled in bachelor-level programs in Brazil was more than 1.2 million

(S. Schwartzman, 1992). In the Brazilian experience, it was the private sector that faced the pressures posed by this rash growth in access to higher education. The growth of the private sector happened with the expansion of many independent *faculdades*—small, family-owned, nonuniversity institutions entitled to grant bachelor degrees.

The growth of this new demand-driven private sector,[3] coupled with the expansion of full-time contracts in the public sector, created two segregated markets: from the 1970s to the early 1990s, the private and the public sectors' markets grew with almost no point of contact. Operating under different rules and with diverse goals, one sector almost ignored the other. Public institutions turned to their alumni when recruiting new academics and had the public graduate system to meet their demands for faculty qualification. Private, demand-driven institutions also recruited their academics from among their own alumni. Academic credentials were not important here. Instructors working in the private sector were poorly qualified and ignorant of the rules of academic life.

This picture started to change in the mid-1990s when a new education act, the Lei de Diretrizes e Bases da Educação (LDB—Law of the Directives and Basis of Education), was enacted. The public debate that preceded the major change in the regulatory framework of Brazilian higher education created a social awareness of the importance of academic credentials for the quality of higher education. When enacted, the new LDB imposed several changes in the private market. First, it imposed on private institutions a minimal threshold of one-third of "qualified" faculty, meaning holding at least a master's degree. Second, in order to be accredited as a university, private institutions had to have a minimal proportion of doctorate holders among their faculty and sustain some activity at the graduate level. Finally, the new law also imposed a pattern of academic careers in private universities that acknowledged and rewarded academic degrees. Together, these changes opened a new market for young scholars graduating from the ever-expanding graduate system. As mentioned, these changes happened at a time when the public sector was closed.[4] With the lack of new positions in public universities, the alternative of being employed in the private higher-education sector seemed attractive enough for the new generation.

The ways different institutions responded to the new regulatory framework created a novel differentiation within the private sector. The majority of private organizations stayed confined to a kind of "commodity-like" market of mass undergraduate education, where they compete for students by offering the least expensive education possible. For these institutions, hiring qualified academics was something they were hardly able to afford (much less interested in). In the new regulatory environment, they avoided the pressure to upgrade the profile of their academics through an intense circulation of employees. These institutions hired better-qualified academics when they sensed stronger regulatory pressure, only to dismiss them later.

The larger for-profit private universities benefited from the change in the regulatory environment through the scale of their operations. They enroll hundreds of thousands of students. Even charging low tuitions fees, they are able to amass enough resources to absorb the costs created by the government's regulatory pressure. For them, it was easier to isolate the demands for an enriched academic life posed by the better-qualified academics into small "isles of academic life," linked to a few graduate programs, while preserving the traditional per-hour paid contract in most of their undergraduate operations. By supporting these small-scale research environments, the larger for-profit private organizations also respond to the regulatory requirements. They were able to provide the figures the government demanded in order to be accredited as universities. With the status of universities, they then benefited from the autonomy granted by the new LDB.

Finally, at the top of this new hierarchy in the private higher-education sector there were a small number of highly entrepreneurial institutions catering to students from wealthier families. In addition to undergraduate programs, these institutions also offered well-regarded professional training programs, professional graduate education, consultancy, and even doctoral programs. Some are new, nonuniversity institutions; some are old, traditional Catholic and other denominational universities. For all these institutions, the academic credentials of the academic staff are a source of prestige. These institutions are what I call private elite institutions.

Growth of Institutional Diversity and Autonomy

Due to the preceding reforms, Brazil has become a well-known case of extreme institutional diversity: in the public sector, the dominant institutional profile is still the traditional comprehensive university. The federal and all state systems favor the more prestigious format of universities, each of them usually holding multiple campuses scattered to different cities. Only among municipality-owned institutions is the isolated professional school the dominant format. The huge private sector, which accounts for almost 75 percent of all undergraduate enrollments in the country, presents a myriad of different institutional arrangements and patterns of ownership. In the private sector, one can find several kinds of institutions, varying from small, isolated, family-owned professional schools, of-fering less than a dozen bachelor programs and counting less than a hundred students, up to huge for-profit universities, some of them with shares in the stock market, enrolling several hundred thousands of students.

In the last 20 years, diversity was reinforced and expanded by new initiatives and policies implemented by both the federal government and the state governments. First, there was the 1987 decision by the government of the state of São Paulo, the country's richest state, to provide complete financial and academic autonomy to its three universities.[5] Since then, the three universities owned by the state of São Paulo are supported by a fixed percentage of the largest tax collected by the state, a tax imposed over all commerce of goods and services inside the state. The strong autonomy granted to these universities created a unique opportunity for institutional development and academic development.

In 1997, the federal government also allowed the private sector to differentiate by adopting either a philanthropic or a for-profit profile. The former, usually Catholic or other denominational universities and community-owned institutions, are subject to stronger regulatory controls, especially regarding their philanthropic roles, but receive some tax exemptions. Being philanthropic (i.e., not-for-profit) also facilitates access to some programs and support from the federal government. In contrast, the for-profit sector is subjected to less regulation but does not receive tax exemptions. This change in the regulatory framework opened a window of opportunity for the private sector to expand and diversify, as described above.

In the early 2000s, the for-profit subsector experienced an intense process of consolidation, with the merging of some major organizations. These dynamics started as a response to new stringent rules and evaluation processes imposed by the federal government, which created important new costs for the private sector. These costs were easily faced with the scale created by merging small and large organizations. These organizations also profited from the government's decision to use the private sector as a safety valve to ease the increasing pressure for access to higher education (Sampaio, 2014).[6] These new mega-organizations become very large teaching-oriented, for-profit universities. Some of them are even listed on the stock market and receive investments from large international groups such as the Laureate and Kroton groups.

Finally, between 2007 and 2012, the federal government adopted an ambitious plan of expansion and modernization for the federal universities (the elite research sector universities regulated by the federal government), nicknamed REUNI. In this program, the government tried to incite the federal universities to take a more responsive role regarding the demands for access. The program provided resources for expansion and as well as the modernization of the universities. Among other objectives, the universities were asked to increase the number of first-year students enrolled each year, to provide evening courses targeting nontraditional students, and to reserve places for minorities and children from poor families. Sustained by the program, the federal university sector experienced a quick expansion, with the creation of new universities and the building of new campuses for old universities.

Academic Careers in the Public Sector

BARRIERS TO ACADEMIC MOBILITY

From the perspective of the academic career, Brazil's diverse and overlapping higher education sectors reinforce barriers to interinstitutional mobility. All academics from the public sector hold the status of civil servants. However, they serve different levels of government and are subject to different rules. Even inside the same sector, after some years, moving from one institution to another is a highly unusual event because the academic can incur some salary loss due to the lack of seniority of the contract. If the change involves crossing the boundary between two sectors (for example, from a state university to a federal university or vice-versa), the odds are definitely against such a move since the academic may lose income related to the career rank and seniority. In this context, the public higher education sector in Brazil is marked by the prominence of internal markets. Once nominated as part of the academic staff of a public university, the scholar has access to a de facto lifelong career where progression is controlled by both general rules and local uses that could raise or lower the minimum performance level demanded for promotion.

At the state level, state-owned institutions have autonomy to organize their career paths in different manners, but, in general, they tend to follow the pattern established by the federal system. The only major deviations are the three universities belonging to the richest state in the federation, the state of São Paulo.[7] These universities also impose a postdoctoral degree, the *livre-docência*—an adaptation of the old German *Privatdozent*[8]—as a mandatory requirement for an academic to be promoted to associate professor and also to apply to full professorship.

FORMAL RULES, LOCAL NORMS, AND ACADEMIC DEGREES

There are important differences between formal rules and local uses within the Brazilian system. Even though rules are general and accessible to anyone, the real operation within each university depends on a number of unwritten arrangements known by all stakeholders but seldom spelled out. The differences between general rules and local uses vary from one institution to another. Among other things, they are a result of the distance between *the real conditions* of academic life within different universities and the *formal assumptions* that organize the academic career in the public sector.

In mature higher education systems, the academic career ladder is, in several ways, beyond the control of any particular organization. In these systems, the academic's reputation, built within the national and international community of peers, plays a decisive role in defining who will fill an institutional position or have access to a promotion. In this sense, disciplines "cut across enterprise" (Clark, 1983, 29). The academic's reputation in a disciplinary community—and nowadays in the growing number of cross-disciplinary communities—is the most relevant reference when it comes to assessing the odds to win when competing for a new position. These "invisible colleges" (Crane, 1972) are organized mostly through signals in the form of publications and other outputs. In this sense, publications operate as interconnecting points of coordination linking otherwise isolated academics (Polanyi, 1968; Braun, 2003). It is this complex interplay between the rules produced inside particular organizations and the norms that organize this web of interconnected professionals nationwide (or even globally) that makes the academic career so elusive in the eyes of most organizational theories.

Thus, in these systems, it is expected that the academic's position on the organizational ladder will roughly align with his or her reputation, acquired in this global web of peers. This alignment reflects the meritocratic nature of the academic life and makes the university the best institutional environment for the growth of a flourishing research community. However, this congruence cannot be taken for granted in emerging systems (such as Brazil's). The shortage of human resources with advanced education is, in general, a well-known trait of developing societies. It is, therefore, no surprise that universities also face the same problem when it comes to finding qualified candidates for academic positions. What is seldom acknowledged in the literature, however, is the impact that such a situation has on how the academic ladder is organized within each institution and what are the conditions of access to an academic position.

First, the shortage of qualified candidates forces universities to lower the requirements for recruiting for junior academic positions. In developing countries, not only the availability of qualified personnel but also the opportunities for training are scarce. This reality means that while some young academics will have access to graduate education once employed, others will stay their entire professional life without sound academic qualifications. In this scenario, usually, the academic degree (and not performance) is the first and most relevant credential for ascending the academic ladder. However, the opposite movement is also present. Since many academics will spend their entire professional life without experiencing any regular academic training, there is a pressure to mitigate the exigency of a graduate degree for promotion. Usually, the answer to these opposing pressures is to recognize the academic degree as a sufficient condition for promotion while, at the same time, acknowledging local organizational pathways that allow academics to circumvent the legal requirement of a degree for promotion. In some countries, this situation may even create pressures to lower the knowledge and performance contents of graduate education, which ends up creating a system of hollow academic credentials.

As the academic career inside an institution becomes disconnected from the hierarchies of intellectual prestige outside, it also loses its capacity to signal academic quality or distinction, which is meant to "accrue to an individual or to a group of academics for meritorious or exemplary performance" (Moore, 1992). In many emerging systems, the role of recognizing exemplary performance is mostly performed by external entities and institutions, such as special scholarships controlled by science foundations and the prestige derived from the academic's personal ties to a prestigious research group, laboratory or research center, and the like.

In the case of Brazil, it is possible to evaluate how the relationship between career and academic degree has evolved over the last 30 years. In 1992 and 2007, the Research Center for Public Policy Studies, from the University of São Paulo (NUPPs), carried out national surveys with representative samples from the Brazilian academic profession. The first survey received support from the Carnegie Foundation and was part of its research project "The International Academic Profession." The second survey was part of the international research network, the Changing Academic Profession (CAP), and was supported by the State of São Paulo Science Foundation (FAPESP).[9] Table 6.1 presents the data from both research-oriented and regional public universities in Brazil, collected in 1992 and 2007.

The data presented in table 6.1 exemplify some of the dynamics discussed above. It is possible to assess how the relationship between career and academic degree has changed in Brazil over the last 20 years by analyzing the findings of a highly relevant statistical procedure: the proportional reduction in error (PRE),

Table 6.1.   Distribution of highest degree by academic rank in Brazilian
public universities, 1992 and 2007 (by percent)

1992	Master's Degree and Lower	Doctorate	Total
	Research Universities		
Entry-level positions	90.7%	52.7%	66.7%
Mid-career positions	6.7%	35.7%	25.0%
Full professor	2.7%	11.6%	8.3%
Total (100%)	(75)	(129)	(204)
	Regional Universities		
Entry-level positions	53.9%	6.0%	41.9%
Mid-career positions	41.6%	77.5%	50.6%
Full professor	4.5%	16.5%	7.5%
Total (100%)	(401)	(133)	(534)
2007			
	Research Universities		
Entry-level positions	93.3%	21.0%	26.5%
Mid-career positions	6.7%	66.3%	61.7%
Full professor	0	12.7%	11.7%
Total (100%)	(15)	(181)	(196)
	Regional Universities		
Entry-level positions	65.7%	11.6%	31.5%
Mid-career positions	7.4%	78.1%	52.2%
Full professor	26.9%	10.2%	16.3%
Total (100%)	(91)	(181)	(272)

Source: Brazil sample, the Carnegie Foundation, 1992; Brazil sample, CAP, 2007.

which compares the estimate of the probability of error under two rules (Silva, 1990). Thus, if $P(1)$ is the probability of error associated with the first rule, and $P(2)$ is the probability of error with the second rule, the PRE is estimated by the general formula $PRE = P(1) - P(2)/P(1)$.

Using this very simple statistic, it is possible to estimate the proportional reduction in error for predicting that an academic is placed in a given position from knowledge about his or her highest degree. By comparing the probability of error for predicting a position for an academic in the entire sample and the probability of error for predicting a position among the subset of academics with the relevant degree, it is possible to calculate the PRE for predicting the individual position in the academic ladder given the candidate's academic degree.

Consider first the PRE in estimating an entry-level position, given that the academic holds a master's degree or lower. In 1992, this reduction was 0.72 in research universities, and only 0.21 in regional universities. These data show that already at the beginning of the 1990s, research universities in Brazil were successful in confining lower-qualified academics to lower ranks. Meanwhile, in regional universities, a large number of academics were able to reach high positions without holding a doctorate.

Consider now the PRE in estimating a middle-upper rank, given that the academic has a doctorate. In 1992, it was 0.29 in research universities, and 0.81 in regional universities. Thus, already at that time, holding a doctorate was not enough to assure a promotion within a research university, while in a regional university this was sufficient.

Among research universities, the new reality created by the changes in the regulatory level described above almost erased the presence of poorly qualified academics. At the end of the 2000s, almost all academics employed at research universities had a doctoral degree; only 7 percent reported not holding one. Within regional universities, the picture is still more complicated: not only were there a large number of academics without full qualifications (33.5 percent) but also the odds of less-qualified academics reaching a top position in the institutional ladder were still high. The PRE for estimating a middle-upper position in a regional university, *given a low academic qualification*, was 0.52. This means that in these universities, tensions have been building as a new generation of young, better-qualified academics has entered institutions where the upper positions in the institutional ladder are filled by older, less-qualified academics.

Educational Qualifications, Research Involvement, and Career Mobility

One way to assess the tensions created by this new reality within regional universities is to compare the degree of commitment to research among academics in different ranks. As it is well acknowledged by the literature, in order to be a full-fledged researcher—in addition to conducting research with some regularity—an academic should be able to bring the research findings to the attention of a wider audience, meaning they should publish these findings. In the Brazilian context, researchers should also have the skills to compete for external funding since it is not usual for universities, even public ones, to set aside their own resources to support research. In the 2007 survey, a number of questions covered these dimensions of academic life. When combined, they produce a scale measuring the level of an academic's commitment to research. The scale ranks the research engagement of Brazilian academics from a nonactive role to a fully professionalized researcher with active international connections. In the middle, the scale distinguishes between those who publish but do not have access to external funds for research (classified as a partially professionalized researcher) and those who publish and have access to external funds but do not hold active international connections (classified as a full-fledged researcher with only domestic connections).[10] Table 6.2 below shows the relationship between commitment to research and academic rank in public universities, considering the more research-oriented ones and those more oriented to undergraduate education, where graduate programs, especially at the doctoral level, are few. The former I have designated *public research universities*, while the latter I have designated *public regional universities*, regardless of whether they belong to the federal government or to state governments.

Table 6.2.   Patterns of Commitment to Research, Academic Rank, and Institutional Environment in the Public Sector, in 2007

| Type of Institution | Commitment to Research | Academic rank | | | |
		Full Professor	Associate Professor & Midcareer Positions	Assistant & Other Entry-Level Positions	Total
Public research universities	Full-fledged researcher with international connections	56.5%	28.9%	19.2%	29.6%
	Full-fledged researcher with only domestic connections	26.1%	25.6%	21.2%	24.5%
	Partially professionalized researcher	8.7%	40.5%	51.9%	39.8%
	Not active	8.7%	5.0%	7.7%	6.1%
	Total (100%)	(23)	(121)	(52)	(196)
Public regional universities	Full-fledged researcher with international connections	6.3%	18.2%	4.3%	11.9%
	Full-fledged researcher with only domestic connections	6.3%	22.1%	9.7%	15.6%
	Partially professionalized researcher	45.8%	55.2%	61.3%	55.6%
	Not active	41.7%	4.5%	24.7%	16.9%
	Total (100%)	(48)	(154)	(93)	(295)

Source: CAP survey, 2007, Brazil.

As one would expect, the proportion of academics with a high research profile is much higher in research universities than in regional universities. Research universities also count with academic personnel who are more internationalized and better positioned to compete for research funds. However, what is most impressive is the way these profiles relate to the academic career within each institutional environment. In research universities, the relationship between commitment to research and rank tends to follow a linear pattern, where academics in higher ranks are also research leaders with an active and international research profile. Within regional universities, the pattern runs contrary to the expected association: there are more academics fully committed to the research role in midcareer positions than in either entry-level positions or at the end of the career ladder. The lack of commitment to research among the older, lesser qualified academics that now occupy the higher positions in these universities is something to expect. However, the presence of a new generation of academics with low commitment to research may signal a problematic situation that could reproduce the old conditions preventing the academic development of these universities.

The data presented in both tables above illuminate a system in transition. Until the beginning of the 1990s, the job vacancies in regional universities attracted mostly local candidates with little, if any, academic training. Once employed, the demands for academic qualifications could easily be by-passed using special provisions present in almost all university regulations, such as the recognition of "equivalent performance" by internal committees. For those with a more entrepreneurial profile, the usual routine was to comply with the teaching demands of the institution for a while and then ask for a leave of absence after a few years to search for academic qualifications in doctoral programs in more research-oriented universities.

After 2003, when the public sector experienced a new cycle of expansion, the new positions opening in all public universities attracted a large number of candidates, most of whom held a doctoral degree. Even if the initial salaries were not high, employment in the public sector was (and still is) highly attractive: once accepted, academics have immediate access to full-time, stable contracts and the teaching load, compared with the private sector, is very low. What is more important, as a graduated academic in the public sector, a scholar qualifies to apply for the numerous programs launched by the Ministry of Science, Technology and Innovation and State Level Foundations for support of research.

However, the internal environment these young scholars found within public regional universities was not the paradise they had envisaged. The doctoral degree had assured them access to mid-level positions in the career ladder, but access to higher positions was blocked by academics from an older generation who were less qualified and less productive but still in control of the institution's internal politics. In addition, the new academic positions created by the federal government imposed larger teaching loads since they were created under a policy framework aiming to support a quick expansion of access to the public sector.

Even when these young scholars are motivated to do research, they face harsh competition accessing funds to support research projects. Since the end of the 1990s, the Brazilian Council for Research (CNPq) had changed the way research funds were distributed. Instead of considering individual projects as they were presented to the council, it started launching bids, greatly increasing the competition for funds. For younger academics in regional universities—who could not count on the collaboration of older, more experienced colleagues—accessing these funds is a serious challenge. Since Brazilian universities have no special provisions for supporting an academic's research activities, developing an active research profile is quite difficult, in particular for academics placed far from the more dynamic academic centers and working in environments where there is a low commitment to research and graduate education.

At the end of the 2000s, this situation gave rise to an intense mobility among young scholars from the less research-intensive public institutions toward the more research-intensive ones. It was quite common for a young scholar to start his or her career employed in a more remote university and move from there to a more research-oriented department in another university. After improving a publishing portfolio, the academic would be in a position to apply to another opening, and so on, until, with luck, he or she could reach a highly competitive position within a research university.

The new scenario created by the enlarged number of qualified young academics was positive for more research-intensive universities since the more competitive environment created opportunities for selecting the best candidates. For regional universities, however, academic mobility was perceived as a sort of brain drain. The situation was particularly adverse for them because they did not have autonomy to fight for the talents they were losing. Given the uniform law regulating the career ladder in all federal universities and the strong constraints on their financial autonomy, it was not possible for them to offer fringe benefits that would tip the scale in their favor. Therefore, it comes as no surprise that, by the end of 2012, the federal government reformed the law organizing the career ladder within the federal system and strengthening the barriers against this type of mobility.[11] The new regulations succeeded in restricting mobility because by moving from one institution to another the academic runs the risk of losing the rank and seniority acquired within the career ladder in his or her former university.

ACADEMIC RANKS AND SIGNALS OF ACADEMIC PRESTIGE

The more usual alternative to defuse the internal tensions that come with the disconnection between institutional rank and academic prestige is to hollow out the meaning of hierarchies in the academic career. In most Brazilian public institutions, different positions in the academic rank alone add few prerogatives outside of the increase in salary: all academics have similar teaching loads and are subject to the same staple contract, which establishes the duties and privileges associated with an academic position in general terms. At the same time, academic credentials mean a lot: only academics holding a doctorate are entitled to give classes and advise in graduate programs; a doctorate is a requisite for an academic to be appointed as rector, dean, and in some cases, head of department. For an academic, being attached to a well-evaluated doctoral program is considered a relevant signal of prestige and is much more important for appraising the academic role within the university than the position he or she holds in the institution's academic rank.[12]

Since 1976, all graduate programs in Brazil are subject to a stringent system of evaluation strongly based on peer review and coordinated by the Ministry of Education's Agency in charge of Graduate Education—CAPES. The process of evaluation is long, mobilizing hundreds of academics in all fields and considering different aspects of each program, from the quality of the students' products and their commitment to academic activities to the academics' research profile and the quality of their publications. The main evaluation is carried out every four years, but exchange between CAPES and the programs is intense all the time. One by-product of this evaluation is an unequivocal sign of prestige attached to all academics linked to the programs that score high on the seven-point scale of this evaluation. Being an advisor in one of these programs counts for the researcher's success when applying for external support. Most importantly, such programs represent a good platform for organizing networks that help create competitive proposals for sizable research funds. On the other hand, success in applying to these programs and the level of support and resources for research that comes with them increases the potential for developing high-impact research, which is a relevant indicator that will improve (or confirm) the evaluation of a graduate program in the next round of evaluation.

Another signal of prestige highly prized by academics with an active research profile is the system of scholarships known as "scientific productivity scholarships." These scholarships are awarded by the Federal Council for Research (CNPq) and are ranked from level 2 up to level 1A, passing through 1B, 1C, and 1D. Access to these scholarships is organized through calls issued by the CNPq every year. Committees of specialists in each area select applicants to whom the scholarship will be granted. Once awarded, the researcher must submit a report of her academic production every four years. This report serves as the basis for the assessment that will decide if the scholarship will be renewed or denied and, if it is open, the academic's promotion through the scholarship's ranks. This scholarship does not add a large amount of money to the academic's income. However, it is highly regarded because of its recognition role. Because of that, there is no limit to the number of times the same researcher's award can be renewed.

The dynamics coming from the agencies in charge of graduate education and research funding add up to the formal and informal rules inside the universities and supported the development of a strong, self-refereed scientific community in Brazil (S. Schwartzman, 2010). Members of the scientific community tend to be concentrated in research-oriented universities where graduate education is a major endeavour. However, academics with this profile are found in all public universities, and, what is most relevant for our discussion, in most less research-oriented universities they are ranked in different positions on the institutional ladder. Some are full professor, but many younger academics highly committed to research occupy lower ranks, even as teacher assistants, and have colleagues in higher ranks with lower commitment to research. This situation explains why it is crucial to a member of the scientific community to be assured that different positions in the academic ranks do not imply restrictions to the academic's roles inside the university. It is also important to sustain the academic's autonomy regarding her research agenda, and it is imperative to limit the reach of the university's administrative hierarchy so that it does not have a say regarding the way the researcher will expend the hard-earned money that will support the academic's research activity and graduate programs. In the same way, it is also essential to assure that differences in rank are not translated into differences in academic responsibilities, like teaching lead and research autonomy. That is why, inside the Brazilian universities, advising master's and doctoral degree candidates is a prerogative of academics holding a doctorate, whatever their institutional rank, but it is not a right attached to the full professorship position. It is perfectly possible, for example, for a teacher assistant with a PhD to become a full member of a doctoral program, while an older, less research-oriented colleague, even with a full professor position, is blocked and has no role in the same graduate program.

This describes the situation for active members of the Brazilian research community. However, most of the academics in public universities occupy a more peripheral position regarding the web of researchers that organizes the core of Brazilian science. They hold stable, full-time contracts but do not meet the standards of professional achievements usually expected from a member of the scientific community. Some do not hold a doctoral degree; others have a low publishing profile and thus are not accepted as a full member of a graduate program because of the exigencies posed by CAPES.[13] Others even are employed in departments with few qualified academics and thus do not reach the minimum threshold that would enable organization of a graduate program. In these circumstances, regardless of their position in the academic rank, researchers' academic responsibilities tend to be circumscribed to teaching at the undergraduate level. Because of the lack of academic credentials and/or limited performance as researchers, they are almost entirely disconnected from their national and international community of peers. For these academics, the only acceptable grounds for differentiation are those produced by externalities that are in principle accessible to everyone, such as seniority. Thus, for different motives, they also contribute to making the academic ranks less relevant for identifying leadership and as a tool for the institution to recognize and reward academic performance.

Therefore, within most of the public sector, the formal ranks that organize the academic career have little relevance. They do not differentiate roles and responsibilities. The prestige and hierarchical positioning of an individual academic are a function of decisions that take place outside the university and are by-products of the operation of the complex machinery that supports research and graduate education in Brazil. The informal hierarchies created by these mechanisms are more fluid and less conspicuous than the ranks recognized by the university, but they are much more effective. They regulate the level of support the academic is able to mobilize from external sources. On the other hand, being capable of mobilizing significant resources for research is a major factor contributing to the scope of the academic's research network, which in turn has consequences for the frequency of citations to their work.

Career and Market Dynamics in the Private Sector

Diversity is a pervasive trait of the institutional environment in the private sector. While a mix of collegiality and democratic modes of governance mark the public sector, the private sector is much more hierarchical (Balbachevsky & Schwartzman, 2011). The department is usually the academic's home base, as the smallest academic and administrative unit in the public sector. In the private sector, academics tend to identify themselves as being attached to an undergraduate program or teaching discipline. In both cases, the relevant authority who organizes the academic's daily life in the private sector is the coordinator of the program or discipline. The coordinator is, usually, a position filled by direct appointment by the organization's senior administration and is in charge of organizing the schedule of courses and distributing the teaching responsibilities among the academics. This decision is central. The most common contract in the private sector is a per-hour paid salary. Nevertheless, besides the time spent in class, the actual paid hours may also encompass other activities such as coordination of programs, advising students, or even doing some research. The coordinator also acts as a buffer between students and academics, and between the academics and the organization's senior administration and vice-versa. It is also the coordinator's responsibility to enforce the central administration's decisions and to enforce the decisions and demands coming from the senior administration. Finally, a coordinator fulfills a central role ensuring that the program as a whole meets the targets posed by the public agencies in charge of overseeing and evaluating the undergraduate program.

Access to an academic contract in the private sector is mostly done through informal means. Selecting the new academic is the direct responsibility of the coordinator, after consultation with senior administration. The private sector does not offer tenure-track contracts, but each institution offers full-time contracts to a restricted number of academics, usually the ones with major responsibilities within the institution. Promotion is usually through the external market: it is by moving from one institution to another that an academic improves his or her employment and contract conditions.

Even the elite-oriented institutions cannot afford to extend the generous terms of contracts found in the public sector to all academics. Yet, in order to increase their attractiveness in the eyes of families from the upper-middle class, they have to sustain a rich and dynamic academic environment. To accommodate these diverging drives, these institutions usually opt to diversify roles and contracts among their academic staff. They usually have an academic core, composed of well-regarded teachers, distinguished scholars, and acclaimed professionals, who work side by side with a larger number of peripheral staff, composed of academics hired to give a fixed number of classes. A small number of these institutions formally differentiate the academic career into three different profiles. Some academics are hired in the role of scholars and researchers, with their teaching load concentrated in graduate education and their performance measured by the number and quality of articles published. Others are hired as teachers, with their performance measured by their popularity among students. Finally, some academics are hired as consultants, with their performance measured by the number of projects contracted in the external market (Balbachevsky & Botelho, 2015).

Academics hired by nonuniversity demand-driven institutions face the worst contract and work conditions. These institutions offer the same contractual terms to almost all academics and do not differentiate ranks or support mechanisms for promotion other than to the position of coordinator. Salaries are low, and there is no support for other academic activities beside class hours. In contrast, the 1996 Education Law demands that private, for-profit universities organize an institutional career track that includes ranks based on academic credentials and a percentage of academic positions in nontenured full-time contracts. However, only a few academics in each university have access to these positions. The decision about who will fill these positions is the responsibility of the university's senior administration. Usually this decision balances the academic's profile, his or her engagement with tasks outside the classroom, and the degree of trust the senior administration has regarding the academic's commitment to the institution.

Some academics employed by mass-oriented private organizations view their employment as a transitional placement while waiting for an opening in the public sector or an opportunity to move to an elite, private institution. In the large metropolitan areas, it is more or less usual for doctoral candidates or fresh doctorate holders to combine evening lectures in mass-oriented private organizations with a fixed-term, part-time, informal arrangement as an assistant researcher in a research team directed by a senior academic in a public university. While this is regarded as an acceptable alternative for a young, ambitious academic, this choice may create a dead end for the young scholar. The large teaching load that comes with contracts in mass-oriented private organizations sometimes prevents young academics from amassing enough research experience and outputs to build a competitive profile necessary for succeeding in the competition for access to the more dynamic academic environment.

Private, elite institutions have different strategies for selecting new academics. Some are selected inside the institution's alumni networks. In this case, the academic is a former student, known by the coordinator, and called to be in charge of a number of classes, usually as a substitute for a colleague on leave. From this provisional beginning, the new academic can prove his or her worth and, as time goes by, have access to a more stable contract with the institution. In other instances, especially when the selection aims to fill a permanent position or attract a more mature scholar, the institution publicizes a new opening and organizes a hiring committee that will be in charge of selecting the new faculty member. In this case, the selection is conducted through an open competition where candidates are asked to present an open lecture, pass through an open inquiry on their curriculum vitae, and even, in some cases, perform a written examination.

In all circumstances, private, elite institutions offer a more dynamic and diverse academic environment. However, the contractual conditions may vary greatly from one person to another. Usually, an entry-level position is a per-hour paid teaching position, not essentially different from those offered by mass-oriented private organizations. Access to the institution's career ladder is negotiated on a case-by-case basis with the academic, coordinator, and senior administration. The promotion decision depends on an assessment of the candidate's performance as a teacher, researcher, and/or consultant. Again, if the new academic accepts a large teaching load at the beginning of his or her contract, this decision may compromise the ability to improve performance in other areas deemed necessary for access to the academic career path.

Conclusions

This paper reviews the dynamics that have shaped and changed the academic market in Brazil. As argued above, the Brazilian experience could be seen as an example of the tensions and contradictions produced in an emerging academic system that simultaneously faces the challenges of expanding access and strengthening its academic performance.

Building up a modern academic system is a challenge when there is a chronic shortage of qualified candidates to fill academic positions. In this context, as argued, not only is the availability of qualified personnel small, but the opportunities for training are also scarce. This reality means that while some young academics will have the opportunity to continue their academic studies once employed, others will spend their entire professional life without sound academic qualifications. In these circumstances, it is the academic degree (and not performance) that is the first and most relevant criteria for advancing in the academic ranks. However, the opposite movement also is present. Since many academics will spend their entire professional career without experiencing regular academic training, there is pressure to mitigate the absence of a graduate degree for promotion.

In mature systems, the expected situation is a relative congruence between the academic's institutional ranks and scholarly reputation, acquired among peers in the wide scientific community. This congruence cannot be taken for granted in emerging systems where it is more or less usual for the academic's position in the institution's career ladder to not correspond to his or her prestige among peers. Thus, the role of recognizing exemplary performance (Moore, 1992) tends to be performed by external institutions and bodies. In the case of Brazil, the recognition given by special kinds of scholarships and being accepted as advisor in well-evaluated graduate programs are deemed more central to establishing an academic's worth than the position he or she occupies in the institutional rank.

As academic credentials become more widespread among the country's new generation, tensions arise. As described above, in the last two decades, the number of new academic positions opened in the Brazilian higher education grew quickly, in both the public and private sectors. Nevertheless, as graduate education has spread and the number of qualified candidates has expanded, the requirements for filling these positions have also increased dramatically. While in the past graduate education was, typically, an experience that came after employment, the would-be academic nowadays must finish graduate studies before applying for an academic job, especially if his or her focus is on the more reputed positions in the public sector (Schwartzman & Balbachevsky, 2013). However, once accepted to an academic position, many scholars discover that even if the doctoral degree is enough to ensure monetary gains, the upward movement in the career ladder is blocked by an older, less qualified, and less productive generation still in control of the institution's internal politics. As argued above, the only way to defuse the tensions generated by this situation is to disconnect prerogatives from the institution's rank. However, this disconnection also means that institutions lose a central tool for stirring the academics toward their goals.

Emerging systems face cross-pressures for expanding access and improving academic performance and will always experience diversification. In the case of Brazil, the picture that emerges is not only diversification but also strong segmentation, where the barriers to mobility become stronger as the academic becomes older and more experienced. Different sectors in the Brazilian academic market support diverse professional portfolios. What is valued in one segment is not even relevant in another and, with time, the professional profile produced by working in one segment closes the opportunity for success in another. Thus, while mobility in the Brazilian academic market has increased in the last decade, and there are signals that the academic market in the private and public sectors is more connected today than in the past, mobility is still an experience confined to the first years of academic life. In such a segmented market, many young, well-qualified academics, formed by the expensive public system of graduate education, will fail to secure a place in a nurturing academic environment that could support their further development.

NOTES

1. In 1988, the University of São Paulo (USP) was the first Brazilian university to officially require the doctorate as a minimum requirement for access to faculty ranks across the entire university. That year, USP reformed its academic career path and eliminated all academic positions that did not require a doctorate. In 1989, that decision was also adopted by the State University of Campinas (UNICAMP) and, a few months later, by the State University Júlio de Mesquita (UNESP). Until 2014, federal universities did not officially require doctorates for those entering their academic ranks. Nevertheless, this requirement had become the norm in some research-oriented federal universities since the end of the 1990s. In 2014, the Ministry of Education enacted a decree imposing a doctorate as the minimal requirement for a candidate being accepted as an academic in federal universities. However, a provision was made for accepting lower degrees in "exceptional cases." This provision is frequently used by regional universities because of the lack of qualified candidates, also because local candidates, even if holding lower qualifications, are preferred since they have more incentives for not moving away after a few years.

2. The 1968 reform also replaced the old chair system with a new departmental organization. It also opened alternatives for internal diversification by allowing the old faculties of science, humanities, and philosophy to split into different specialized institutes. For an overview of the 1968 reform, see Klein, 1992.

3. Private higher education has a long history in Brazil (See Sampaio, 2000). Since the beginning of the twentieth century, denominational learning centers were organized in the country by the Catholic Church and other religions. The first Catholic university was founded in Rio de Janeiro in 1940. Besides these elite institutions, another traditional form of private higher education in Brazil was the trade school, a kind of tertiary-level vocational school catering to children from the lower middle class interested in training for the clerk positions created by the ever-expanding tertiary sector in the Brazilian economy. Up to the 1960s, it was common for an academic, especially at the beginning of his or her career, to hold two or more part-time appointments, both in public and private institutions.

4. In the middle of the 1990s, the federal government imposed a hiring freeze on new civil servants in order to gain control over public spending, regarded as a major source of inflationary pressure that plagued the Brazilian economy at the time.

5. The autonomy granted to the São Paulo state universities resulted from a long and aggressive strike that united the academic staff, students, and employees' unions from the three universities. From the unions' and university authorities' point of view, achieving autonomy represented the fulfillment of more than a decade of struggles for autonomy and stable support. From the point of view of the government, the agreement that gave financial autonomy to the universities was a price to pay to stop the increasing political costs created by the constant tensions between universities and government, usually escalated by the intense coverage they received by the media.

6. In earlier 2000s, the government launched the program "University for All" (PROUNI), which exchanged tax for tuition exemption for children from low-income families. In 2007, the federal government greatly expanded the old program for financial assistance to low-income students (FIES). Together, PROUNI and FIES solved the biggest problem for expanding access through the private sector, which is the tuition costs and the high level of tuition default.

7. The three universities are USP, UNICAMP, and UNESP.

8. *Privatdozent* (or PD, for short) is both a title and a position in the German tradition. In Germany, PD-ship is conferred to academics with a PhD degree. In order to achieve the PD title, candidates must write another dissertation as well as give a number of lectures, a procedure that takes, in all, about six more years after finishing the doctoral training. In the German system, the PD is a necessary step for access to the rank of full professor. In the state of São Paulo system, the procedures are similar: the academic is supposed to present a new dissertation and to pass through a number of exams, which includes a written examination, an open defense of the dissertation, an open lecture, and an open inquiry of the academic's curriculum vitae by a committee of senior academics.

9. CAP—Changing Academic Profession—was an international research network comprising research teams from 19 countries that was held between 2005 and 2013. The research produced a survey with academics from all countries participating in the network, inquiring on their work conditions. For more details of this research network, see "Changing Academic Profession (CAP)—An International Research Project: The Situation in Germany," Universität Kassel, http://www.uni-kassel.de/einrichtungen/en/incher/research/research-area-change-of-knowledge/the-changing-academic-profession-cap.html (accessed September 16, 2018). The author thanks FAPESP for the financial support (contract 2006/03329-0) for the Brazilian survey.

10. This is a Guttman scale with a coefficient of reproducibility of 0.92, which is well above the usual threshold of 0.85. The very possibility of building up such a robust scale is a powerful indication of how well organized is the system for supporting science and technology in Brazil.

11. Until 2012, federal universities were allowed to choose between opening new academic positions at the beginning of the career ladder or at midlevel. In competitions to fill the most junior positions, candidates were not required to hold a graduate degree, whereas openings for midlevel positions required the doctoral degree. The possibility of opening new positions at the midcareer level created a relevant external market in the public sector. Many young academics started their career at a less demanding, teaching-oriented

public university and then moved to a more research-oriented institution after accumulating enough experience and research outputs. The new law regulating the academic career in the federal system (Law 12722/2012) imposed strong restrictions on this "informal" external market. Since December 2012, the only entry position in all federal universities is the lowest level: teacher-assistant.

12. The Brazilian Federal Council for Support of Research (CNPq), for example, classifies researchers in its files using only the information on whether they are or are not an advisor in doctoral programs.

13. One of the most important indicators in CAPES evaluations is the publishing profile of the academics linked to a graduate program. Accepting an academic with a low publishing profile as a full member of a graduate program can jeopardize its evaluation. Since CAPES's support to programs is linked to the evaluation, performing badly in the evaluation process has severe consequences for academics and students.

REFERENCES

Balbachevsky, Elizabeth. 2000. *A profissão acadêmica no Brasil: as múltiplas facetas de nosso sistema de ensino superior.* Brazil: EditoraFunadesp.

———. 2011. "Academic Careers in Brazil: The Legacy of the Past." *Journal of Professoriate* 5, no. 2:95–121.

———. 2013. "Academic Research and Advanced Training: Building Up Research Universities in Brazil." In *Latin America's New Knowledge Economy: Higher Education, Government and International Collaboration,* ed. Jorge Balan, 113–33. Stamford, CT: AIFS Foundation and Institute of International Education.

Balbachevsky, Elizabeth, and Antonio José Botelho. 2015. "Research and Knowledge Production in the Private Sector." In *Private Universities in Latin America: Research and Innovation in the Knowledge Society,* ed. G. Gregoruti and J. E. Delgado, 185–204. New York: Palgrave Macmillan.

Balbachevsky, Elizabeth, and Simon Schwartzman. 2010. "The Graduate Foundations of Brazilian Research." *Higher Education Forum* 7, no. 1:85–100.

———. 2011. "Brazil: Diverse Experiences in Institutional Governance in the Public and Private Sectors." In *Changing Governance and Management in Higher Education,* 35–56. Dordrecht, Netherlands: Springer.

Braun, Dietmar. 2003. "Lasting Tensions in Research Policies: A Delegation Problem." *Science and Public Policy* 30, no. 5:309–21.

CGEE. 2011. *Doutores 2010: Estudo da demografia da base técnico-científica Brasileira.* Brasília: Centro de Gestão e EstudosEstratégicos.

Clark, Burton. R. 1983. *The Higher Education System: Academic Organization in Cross-National Perspective.* Berkeley: University of California Press.

Crane, Diana. 1972. *Invisible Colleges: Diffusion of Knowledge in Scientific Communities.* Chicago: University of Chicago Press.

Kehm, Barbara M. 2006. "Doctoral Education in Europe and North America: A Comparative Analysis." *Wenner Gren International Series* 83:67.

Klein, Lúcia. 1992. *Política e políticas de ensino superior no Brasil: 1970–1990.* Documento de Trabalho NUPES 2/92. São Paulo: Universidade de São Paulo.

Mattos, Pedro L. 1990. "Avaliação e alocação de recursos no ensino superior brasileiro." *Revista Educação Brasileira* 24, no. 1:139–64.

Moore, Kathryn M. 1992. "Faculty Reward and Incentives." In *The Encyclopedia of Higher Education*, ed. B. Clark and G. Neave. Oxford: Pergamon Press.

Polanyi, Michael. 1962. "The Republic of Science: Its Political and Economic Theory." *Minerva* 1:54–73.

Sampaio, Helena. 2000. *Ensino superior no Brasil: O setor privado.* São Paulo: Hucitec/ Fapesp.

———. 2014. "Privatização do ensino superior no Brasil: Velhas e novas questões." In *A Educação Superior na América Latina e os Desafios do Século XXI*, ed. S. Schwartzman. Campinas: Editora Unicamp.

Schwartzman, Jacques. 1993. "Universidades Federais no Brasil: Uma avaliação de suas trajetórias (décadas de 70 e 80)." *Documentos de Trabalhos NUPES* 4:93.

Schwartzman, Simon. 1992. "Brazil." In *The Encyclopedia of Higher Education*, ed. B. R. Clark and G. Neave, 82–92. Oxford: Pergamon Press.

———. 2010. *Space for Science: The Development of the Scientific Community in Brazil.* State College: Pennsylvania State University Press.

Schwartzman, Simon, and Elizabeth Balbachevsky. 1997. "The Academic Profession in Brazil." In *The International Academic Profession: Portraits of Fourteen Countries*, ed. Philip G. Altabach, 231–78. Princeton, NJ: Carnegie Foundation for the Advancement of Teaching.

———. 2013. "Research and Teaching in a Diverse Environment: Converging Values and Diverging Practices in Brazil." In *Teaching and Research in Contemporary Higher Education: Systems, Activities and Rewards*, ed. Jung Cheol Shin, Akira Arimoto, William K. Cummings, and Ulrich Teichler, 221–36. Dordrecht, Netherlands: Springer.

Silva, Nelson do Valle. 1990. *Introdução à análise de dados qualitativos.* Rio de Janeiro: Vértice Universitária.

Velloso, Jacques. 1987. "Política educacional e recursos para o ensino: o salário educação e a universidade federal." *Caderno de Pesquisa* 17, no. 1:3–28.

7 | India

The Challenge of Change

N. JAYARAM

The current system of higher education in India was originally implanted by the British colonial regime in the mid-nineteenth century in pursuit of its economic, political, and administrative interests (see Ashby & Anderson, 1966: 54–146). It was inherited by the ruling elite of independent India as a colonial legacy in 1947 and has expanded phenomenally since then. Between 1950 and 1990, the number of universities increased from 30 to 190, and the number of colleges from 695 to 7,346. By the mid-1980s, the system had become an "immobile colossus—insensitive to the changing contexts of contemporary life, unresponsive to the challenges of today and tomorrow" (Dube, 1988: 46). The economic crisis of the 1980s, characterized by the debt crisis and a sluggish annual average growth rate of 3.6 percent (1.5 percent in per capita terms), forced the ruling elite to rethink their economic options, to embrace, though not wholeheartedly, neoliberal ideology and to engage with the larger process of globalization and introduce economic reforms, including deregulation in the key sectors, encouragement of the private sector, inviting foreign direct investment, and so on. This inevitably impacted the higher education system and the career and work of academics.

However, given the uncertainties inherent in coalition politics during the last three decades, the changes in higher education have neither been directed nor regulated.[1] Many important legislative bills relating to higher education—including those on research universities, private universities, and foreign education institutions—have remained on the back burner, and the system has been gradually drifting. It is in this context of the state losing its grip on the economy, the assertion by market forces, and the constraints of coalition politics resulting in a drift in the higher education system that academics in India now live and work. This chapter elucidates the trends in the career and work organization of academics in response to the changing national context.[2]

This chapter is divided into two sections: the first focuses broadly on the national higher education context (the organization of higher education, its expansion, the typology of higher education institutions, and the mounting demand for college teachers), and the second more narrowly on the professoriate itself (including the varieties of teaching positions, the standardization of the professoriate, and service and working conditions of the professoriate).

National Higher Education Context
BASIC ORGANIZATION OF HIGHER EDUCATION

India is a federal constitutional republic consisting of 29 states and seven union territories (administered by the central government). Higher education in the country is the responsibility of both the central and the state governments.[3] At the central level, the Ministry of Human Resource Development (MHRD) oversees higher education matters; it even directly funds some higher education institutions. The states have their own ministries of education, and some even have a separate ministry for higher education.

The functioning of universities as degree-awarding institutions is overseen by the University Grants Commission (UGC); technical education and medical education are overseen by the All India Council for Technical Education (AICTE) and the Medical Council of India, respectively.[4] Considering the inordinate number of institutions they are required to oversee, these regulatory bodies are finding it difficult to enforce their regulations and recommendations.

The central government assumes the full cost of all new initiatives and programs in higher education at those institutions it directly sponsors, but only 85 percent of the costs, for a maximum period of five years, at institutions sponsored by the state governments. The responsibility for continuing with initiatives and programs beyond the first five years rests with the state governments. Given the competing demands for scarce financial resources, the state governments find it extremely difficult to sustain new initiatives and programs beyond the first five years. This explains the immense differences in the quality of education between centrally funded institutions and those funded by the states.

Complicating the situation further is the diarchy in university education. With the UGC exercising oversight, but with the state governments regulating it in practice, higher education has virtually remained an unbridled horse. The compulsions of democratic politics often make the state governments ignore quality considerations in higher education. Over the decades, the UGC has been reduced to a mere fund-disbursement agency. Thus, it was not surprising that, in its first report to the nation, submitted in 2006, the National Knowledge Commission (NKC) appointed by the Government of India emphasized the need to make the regulatory structure "more robust, flexible, transparent and dynamic" (NKC, 2007: 42).[5] However, nothing has changed during the last decade.

EXPANSION OF HIGHER EDUCATION
Scope

Prior to the adoption of structural reforms by the Government of India in the 1990s, that is, in the 40 years between 1950–51 and 1990–91, the system expanded steadily under state patronage: the number of universities increased from 30 to 190, and the number of colleges from 695 to 7,346. However, in the next 20 years (between 1990–91 and 2010–11), the system expanded rapidly both under the state aegis and under private entrepreneurship, which found in higher education a lucrative investment proposition. By 2014–15, the number of universities had risen

Table 7.1.   Growth of Higher Education in India, 1950–51 to 2010–11

	1950–51	1960–61	1970–71	1980–81	1990–91	2000–2001	2010–11
Universities	30	55	103	133	190	256	564*
		(83.33)	(87.27)	(29.13)	(42.86)	(34.74)	(120.21)
Colleges	695	1,542	3,604	4,722	7,346	12,806	33,023**
		(121.87)	(133.72)	(31.02)	(55.57)	(74.33)	(157.87)
Teachers	23,549	59,673	128,876	193,341	263,125	411,628	816,966[†]
		(153.39)	(115.97)	(50.02)	(36.09)	(56.44)	(157.87)
Students[††]	397	1,050	1,954	2,752	4,925	8,399	16,975
		(823.25)	(86.10)	(40.84)	(78.96)	(70.54)	(102.11)

Source: Computed from charts in UGC (2012).
    Note: Figures in parentheses refer to the decadal percentage increase.
    *711 in 2014–15.
    **40,760 in 2014–15.
    [†]Includes all categories of teachers, including part-time, ad hoc, contract, and visiting teachers.
    [††]Enrollment in 2000s.

Table 7.2.   Number of Higher Education Institutions in India, 2014–15
(in absolute numbers)

University-Level Institutions	
Established by Parliament and Funded by Central Government	
Central university	46
Central open university	1
Institution of national importance	68
Established by State Assemblies and Funded by State Governments	
State public university	329
State open university	13
Institutions under state legislature act	3
Established by Parliament / State Assemblies with or without Government Funding	
Deemed university	128
Established by State Assemblies without Government Funding	
State private university	205
Others	3
Total (university-level institutions)	796
Colleges	40,760
Stand-Alone (Nonuniversity Level) Institutions	
Diploma-level technical	3,541
Postgraduate diploma in management	392
Diploma-level nursing	2,674
Diploma-level teacher training	4,706
Institute under ministries	132
Total (stand-alone institutions)	11,445

Source: Adapted from Government of India (2014: 3) and UGC (2015: 4).

to 711, that of the colleges to 40,760, and that of stand-alone (nonuniversity level) institutions to 11,445.[6] With 1,261,000 teachers (excluding those in stand-alone institutions) and 26,585,000 students, India today has one of the three largest higher education systems (with the United States and China). See tables 7.1 and 7.2 for the growth of India's higher education system.

Drivers of Expansion

While both public and private initiatives are driving the growth of higher education in the country, the underlying motives differ—substantially. The central government has been keen to boost the Gross Enrollment Ratio (GER) in higher education for the age cohort of 18–23 years, which was at an abysmal 8.1 percent in 2001–2.[7] This keenness is due to the state's eagerness to take advantage of what is called the "demographic dividend."[8] According to the Census of India, the proportion of population in the age group 15–59 increased from 53.3 percent in 1961 to 56.9 percent in 2001 (that is, by 3.6 percentage points). In absolute numbers, the increase in the 15–34 age-group population is even more dramatic: from 174.26 million (31.79 percent) in 1970 to 354.15 million (34.43 percent) in 2000. The youth segment of the population is projected to peak at 484.86 million in 2030 (see Altbach & Jayaram, 2012). With the exception of China, no other country has such a massive youth population. However, the state has not been able to invest adequately in higher education. To boost GER, it has found it easier to expand the conventional universities and colleges rather than invest in research universities and innovative institutions of higher education. Not surprisingly, about 71 percent of all enrollment in undergraduate programs in 2014–15 was in conventional areas such as arts, humanities, and social sciences (37.41 percent); science (17.59 percent); and commerce and management (16.39 percent), programs that require little financial and infrastructural investment (UGC, 2015: 8).

It is in the context of the growing demand for higher education in such fields as technology, medicine, and management—and the state's inability to meet this demand—that private entrepreneurship has found in higher education a lucrative option for investment. Private colleges supported by the state, known in Indian educational parlance as "grant-in-aid colleges," have been in existence since colonial times. What are new in the field of higher education in India are the private and mostly for-profit colleges and universities. Much of the enrollment outside the conventional areas of higher education has been taking place in these private institutions.

Obviously, the orientation of the private sector in higher education is different from that of the public sector. In establishing and funding public institutions, the state views higher education as a national good and students as prospective enlightened citizens and a human power asset. Private entrepreneurs investing in higher education view higher education essentially as a commodity and students as customers or clientele. For the state, return on investment in higher education is primarily in terms of the socioeconomic good; for the private enterprise, it is a cost-benefit and rate-of-profit proposition.

Many universities and colleges established or funded by the state governments, however, are of very poor quality. There has been a general decline of the university as a public institution in India (see Jayaram, 2013b). While most of the private universities and colleges are no more than "teaching shops," a few of them, mostly established by the trusts and foundations of successful multinational corporate houses such as the Tatas, Azim Premji (Wipro [Western India Products] Limited),

and Shiv Nadar (HCL [Hindustan Computers Ltd.] Technologies Ltd.), are note-
worthy exceptions that are aiming to become centers of excellence in higher
education.

TYPOLOGY OF HIGHER EDUCATION INSTITUTIONS

This massive and growing system of higher education, encompassing the entire spectrum of postsecondary education beyond 12 years of formal schooling (see
FICCI, 2012: 9–13), is highly diversified: institutions vary in terms of their degree-
granting authority, legislative origin, functions, and funding (see table 7.3). And
their governance involves a myriad of overlapping centers of authority and
regulation.

Broadly speaking, we can delineate five types of educational institutions, forming an informal hierarchy: (1) institutions of national importance, (2) central
universities, (3) state universities, (4) grant-in-aid colleges that are constituent of
or affiliated with a university, and (5) unaided (purely private) universities/
colleges. Besides their objectives (stated or unstated), the differences are also
reflected in the academic preparation, ability, motivation, and commitment of
their teachers and students (Jayaram, 2014: 196–97).

Institutions of national importance, which include the reputed Indian Institutes
of Technology (IITs), are university-level institutions that enjoy special status ac-
corded them by the Indian Parliament, and they are funded directly by the MHRD.
They are empowered to award degrees, which, according to the UGC Act of 1956,
can be granted only by a university. While the institutions of national importance

Table 7.3.   Typology of Higher Education Institutions

Dimension	Type of Institution
Degree-granting powers	Institutions of national importance
	University—unitary
	University—affiliating
	College
	Stand-alone (nonuniversity)
Legislative origin	Central
	State
	Deemed-to-be university (under UGC Act)
Funding	Public—government
	Public—grant-in-aid
	Private—unaided (de jure not-for-profit, de facto for-profit)

Source: Adapted from Agarwal, 2009: 2.

are academically and administratively autonomous, they are governed by the rules and regulations of the central government. These institutions are national, that is, all-India in their orientation, lay greater emphasis on research in addition to teaching, spend more per student, and offer better remuneration and working conditions compared to all other universities.

Central universities are established or incorporated by an act of Parliament and are financed by the MHRD through the UGC. They are multidisciplinary in their spread, combining postgraduate teaching (mainly) with research (secondarily). They do not have colleges affiliated with them, the notable exception being the University of Delhi, which has constituent colleges. Besides these, the central government has recognized many institutions—other than universities, working at a very high standard in a specific area of study—as "deemed-to-be universities" under section 3 of the UGC Act of 1956. These deemed-to-be universities enjoy the academic status and privileges of a university; some of these institutions are funded by the Government of India and others are private enterprises. While these central universities and centrally funded deemed-to-be universities are academically and administratively autonomous, they are governed by the rules and regulations of the central government. They, like the institutions of national importance, are all-India in their orientation, have a better academic reputation, a greater research orientation, better remuneration and working conditions, and spend more per student compared to state universities.

State universities are established or incorporated through legislation by the 29 states constituting the Indian federation. They receive financial assistance (up to 85 percent) for five years for all development initiatives (including teaching positions) from the UGC; thereafter, they need to be funded by the respective state governments. They have a central campus, housing schools and departments of study that offer instruction largely at the graduate level, and undertake research. Most state universities have colleges affiliated with them whose academic work they regulate and oversee. While state universities are academically and administratively autonomous, like the two types of educational institutions above, state universities are governed by the rules and regulations of the state government, not the central government.

Grant-in-aid colleges, established with private resources, are funded to the tune of 85–90 percent by the state governments concerned—a practice going back to colonial times. They generally offer first-degree-level education and are affiliated with the state universities. The academic standards of these colleges are determined and overseen by the university to which they are affiliated, which also conducts centralized examinations for the students enrolled in them. These colleges may be dispersed geographically but they are under the jurisdiction of a university as determined by law. These colleges may be run either by the state government, through its department of higher education, or by private management bodies, many of them established by religious minorities.

Unaided (purely private) universities and colleges are privately run institutions; they do not receive any financial support from the government, except perhaps land at concessional rates. They rely almost entirely on funding from tuition fees and donations (often made as a consideration for admission into the institution). As universities, they are either deemed-to-be, so under the UGC Act of 1956, or they were established by an act of a state legislative assembly.[9] Compared to the central and state universities, private universities enjoy greater freedom in the appointment of faculty and staff as well as in their day-to-day management. They are nevertheless governed by a broader framework of rules and regulations of the government. For example, because they are established and managed by private trusts, trust laws govern their administration and finance, and their academic programs are determined and overseen by the university to which they are affiliated. Since they raise their own funds, the purely private universities and colleges mostly offer programs like computer science, biotechnology, management studies, and so on, which are in high demand and are financially lucrative.

The bulk of the expansion in student enrollments in higher education has taken place in affiliated colleges in state universities in first-degree courses (about 88.26 percent) and in general education (arts, science, and commerce) (about 71 percent) (UGC, 2015: 8). Most of the teachers (84.7 percent) are also working in these institutions (ibid., 4), and their work almost exclusively entails teaching and examining candidates at the undergraduate level.

Among degree-awarding higher education institutions, research is only a priority in the institutions of national importance, central universities, and select departments in state universities. That is, the university system has largely concentrated on dissemination of knowledge rather than creating and refining knowledge—a function assigned to specialist institutes treated as institutions of national importance and laboratories outside the university system. This peculiar disjunction between universities and research institutes, a legacy of the colonial era, explains the paradox that the large and experienced system of higher education in India is hardly known for its excellence in research (see Jayaram, 2007).

The Professoriate

NUMERICAL GROWTH

Table 7.4 documents the decadal increase in the number of teachers relative to the number of universities, colleges, and students, revealing interesting facts. The average number of teachers per university increased from 785 in 1950–51 to 1,608 in 2000–2001, but declined to 1,449 in 2010–11. The average number of teachers in colleges (where most students in higher education are enrolled) has decreased from 34 in 1950–51 to 32 in 2000–2001 to 25 in 2010–11. Meanwhile, the average number of students per teacher increased from 16.86 in 1950–51 to 20.40 in 2000–2001 to 20.78 in 2010–11.

Thus, the growth in the number of teachers has not kept pace with the increase in the number of universities and colleges and the expansion of student enroll-ment. Partly, this relatively slow rate of growth in faculty was caused by the mor-atorium imposed by the central and the state governments in the 1980s to curtail public spending in an effort to manage the economic crisis. The rapid expansion of universities and colleges since 2000–2001 has only exacerbated this teacher shortage. According to the MHRD's task force report, the then-current corps of college and university faculty was estimated to be around 54 percent of originally approved strength (Times News Network, 2011).

VARIETIES OF TEACHING APPOINTMENTS

Given the diversity of the system of higher education, on the one hand, and the arrangements that have evolved to address the shortage of teachers, on the other, the teachers in higher education in India do not constitute a homogenous category.

Table 7.4.   Number of Teachers Relative to Number of Universities, Colleges, and Students, 1950–51 to 2010–11

Average number	Year						
	1950–51	1960–61	1970–71	1980–81	1990–91	2000–2001	2010–11
Teachers per university	784.97	1,084.97	1,251.22	1,453.69	1,384.87	1,607.92	1,448.52
Teachers per college	33.88	38.70	35.76	40.94	35.82	32.14	24.74
Students per teacher	16.86	17.60	15.16	14.23	18.71	20.40	20.78

Source: Computed from charts in UGC, 2012.

There are different types of teaching positions depending upon the duration of employment and the privileges that go with them. The most coveted is the *permanent* (tenured) teaching position in a publicly funded university or college. Appointees to these positions are placed on probation for a period of two years. The appointees who successfully complete the period of probation are confirmed in the post, and they remain in the employment of the institution until they reach the age of superannuation, which varies from 60–62 years (in state universities and grant-in-aid colleges) to 65 years (in central universities and centrally funded institutions).

Thus, a candidate entering the academic position in a college with only a master's degree at around 24 years of age, or in a university with a doctorate at around 27 years of age can theoretically work for anywhere between 36 to 38 years depending upon whether the institution is a state university / affiliated college or a centrally funded one. Permanent positions are nonexistent in purely private universities and colleges. Appointment to teaching positions in such institutions is contractual in nature. The duration of the contract may vary from about five months (one semester) to five years. The *terms of contract* may vary from case to case and they are specifically spelled out in each case, unlike the *terms of appointment* to permanent positions, which are uniform and stipulated in the statutes and ordinances governing the publicly funded institutions and which are enforceable in a court of law. Given the shortage of well-qualified and experienced teachers, retired teachers often find opportunities for contractual appointments in purely private institutions. Since contractual appointments offer greater flexibility in human resource management and involve limited long-run financial commitments, even publicly funded institutions are now turning to such appointments.

Both permanent and contractual teaching positions involve full-time engagement in teaching in the institution. In India, the concepts of *part-time teachers* (who teach for a specified number of teaching hours in a week) and *guest faculty* (who help the college/department to complete portions of the syllabus) originated as a result of the unmet demand for teachers in particular disciplines. For some positions, full-time teachers were either not available (in narrow fields of specializations), or it was not viable to appoint full-time teachers (as they would not have sufficient workload, defined as number of classroom teaching hours). Typically, part-time teachers and guest faculty are paid a consolidated sum by way of remuneration for the number of hours of teaching work they are assigned. Their monthly remuneration is nowhere near that of a permanent teacher. Furthermore, they are not entitled to any statutory employment benefits, such as leave, medical insurance, pension, gratuity, and so on.[10] Unsurprisingly, they are looked down upon in the system and are considered "daily wage workers." Guest lecturers, if they are professionals (medical doctors, lawyers, chartered accountants, etc.), receive better emoluments and status than those who are underemployed master's degree holders.

What was introduced as an interim solution to a practical problem in academic administration has gradually become a modality for appointment of teachers, especially in private colleges, who do not receive governmental support. State universities too depend on part-time teachers. From the college or university's point of view, it is obviously more economical to employ part-time teachers than permanent teachers. There is also greater flexibility in hiring and firing part-time teachers.

From the prospective candidates' perspective, part-time teaching offers *some* employment opportunity as well as the possibility of gaining experience, which may be useful as and when opportunities for more stable or full-time permanent or contractual employment arise. Periodically, part-time teachers with 10 or more years of service have successfully brought political pressure to bear on the state governments to "regularize" their appointments on humanitarian grounds. Courts of law have also been sympathetic to their cause. To overcome the administrative and financial problems resulting from such "backdoor entry" into the academic profession—mostly encouraged by grant-in-aid private colleges—some state governments have abolished the post of part-time teachers and suggested the reappointment of retired teachers on a contract or hourly basis (see Jayaram, 2003).

To meet faculty shortages in specific subjects in a limited way and for a short duration, some universities are assigning teaching work to PhD scholars receiving research fellowships awarded by the UGC. Some state universities, which have few or no such awardees, have instituted their own fellowships for PhD scholars who are assigned teaching work (*India Education Review*, 2012). Similarly, some institutions have introduced the informal position of teaching assistants who, in fact, function as teachers.

Thus, the diversity of higher education institutions and the shortage of teachers have resulted in heterogeneity in the Indian professoriate, precluding any blanket generalization about either the academic profession or those entering it. As difficult as the task is, while revising the salary and service conditions of teachers in higher education in 2006, the UGC attempted to standardize the qualifications of various categories of teachers, the procedures for recruiting them, the requirements and process of their career advancement, and the salaries and nonsalary benefits to which they are entitled. The following sections present various aspects of this standardization in the academic profession and examine what they mean to those entering the academic profession today.

STANDARDIZATION OF THE PROFESSORIATE
Academic Ranks and Recruitment Criteria

Since January 2006, a three-tier hierarchy of academic ranks—professor, associate professor, and assistant professor—has been standardized in publicly funded higher education institutions across the country. In most cases, entry into the academic profession is at the assistant professor level, both in university departments and in colleges.[11] For appointment to the post of an assistant professor in arts, commerce, education, humanities, journalism and mass communication, languages, law, sciences, and social sciences in a college, university, or university-level institution, a candidate must have obtained a score of 5.5 on a 10-point scale at the master's level examination in the relevant subject.[12] Furthermore, the candidates must have qualified in either the National Eligibility Test (NET) or an accredited State Eligibility Test (SET).

The NET as an eligibility criterion for entry into the academic profession is perhaps unique to India. It was introduced by the UGC following the recommendation of the New Education Policy in 1986. In order to ensure minimum standards for entry into the teaching profession and research, the UGC introduced an eligibility test. Those qualifying in this test become eligible for an entry-level teaching position (assistant professorship) in universities or colleges; in addition, those with "higher merit" become eligible for a Junior Research Fellowship (JRF) to pursue doctoral research in any UGC-recognized institution for a period of five years (UGC, 2010–11: 180). The UGC conducts this test twice a year (in June and December) in 84 subjects and at 89 centers spread across the country (UGC, 2013).[13] The eligibility test for five core science subjects—chemical sciences, life sciences, physical sciences, mathematical sciences, and earth/atmospheric/ocean/planetary sciences—is also conducted twice a year by the Council of Scientific and Industrial Research (CSIR) under the Joint CSIR-UGC NET. There is no time bar on the eligibility certificates issued by the UGC.

In recognition of the fact that many candidates who had obtained the PhD degree had not registered for the NET/SET, the UGC, in 2009, exempted such candidates from the requirement of a NET/SET qualification for recruitment for an assistant professorship. (A similar exemption exists for applicants with master's degrees in disciplines for which the NET is not conducted.). This not only sparked a debate in academia but also resulted in litigation. Those critical of this exemption believe that it will pave the way for backdoor entry into the academic profession and adversely affect the quality of higher education. Those supportive of it argue that it will ease the faculty shortage problem (see Anand, 2010).

The percentage of candidates successfully qualifying at the NET to enter the academic profession is miniscule. This partly reflects the poor quality of education and the liberal standards of evaluation at the master's level in Indian universities. To increase the number of candidates qualifying at the NET, from June 2010 onward, the UGC abolished negative marking (i.e., deducting marks for wrong answers) in the tick-marking type of examination papers.

In the NET conducted in June 2013, of the 738,955 candidates who registered, 574,448 (or 78.74 percent) appeared for the test. Of the 574,448 who appeared for the test, 27,402 (4.77 percent) qualified for both an assistant professorship and a JRF, and 3,684 (0.64 percent) qualified for an assistant professorship only. That is, in all, 31,086 (5.41 percent) qualified to enter the academic profession (UGC, 2013).

However, eligibility is only a necessary condition; qualified candidates must still go through the process of recruitment and prove their suitability before they formally enter the academic profession. To address regional specificities, many state governments had been permitted by the UGC to conduct a SET, which was treated as equivalent to the NET, for assistant professorships. In some states, the standard of the SET had been so appallingly diluted and the norms so brazenly flouted that the UGC had to withdraw the permission granted to them to conduct the SET (Jayaram, 2003). The UGC has since introduced a system of accrediting the SET conducted by state governments to ensure that the pattern and standard of SET is the same as that of the NET. The accreditation is renewed periodically based on a review by an expert committee. Moreover, since June 2002, the candidates qualifying in the SET are eligible for an assistant professorship only in the universities and colleges in the respective states, not throughout the country as earlier.

Unlike for higher-level teaching positions like professor or associate professor, for an assistant professorship, no additional qualifications in the form of research publications or work experience are prescribed as essential. However, candidates with such qualifications are preferred, especially in university departments. For this reason, many candidates accept contract appointments or appointments as part-time, ad hoc, or guest lecturers, even if they are paid on an hourly basis, for they can cash in on such work experience as, and when, vacancies arise.

A majority of assistant professors in the universities now possess doctorates. In colleges, the percentage of assistant professors with doctorates is very low; those with a doctorate seek entry into university at the associate professor level (or even as an assistant professor). As a rule of thumb, if not as a formal guideline, a doctorate from an internationally renowned university is valued more than a doctorate from a state university or unknown foreign university.

In publicly funded institutions, the regulations governing minimum qualifications can hardly be flouted. There are far too many applicants with minimum eligibility requirements vis-à-vis the number of posts available, and the slightest doubt that an appointment is made by disregarding a regulation is challenged in a court of law, and such appointments are struck down by the courts. These institutions have also become more careful after the enactment of the Right to Information Act of 2005 whose provisions will invariably be invoked by unsuccessful applicants.

The purely private universities and colleges have greater flexibility in the matter of teachers' qualifications. However, they too would like to ensure the minimum as regards the academic qualification of the faculty, such as the grade in the culminating master's level examination and receipt of the doctorate. As for unaided private colleges, the university to which they are affiliated acts as the watchdog.

While the elaborate guidelines suggested by the UGC underline the importance of transparency and credibility of recruitment to teaching positions, in actual practice rules are bent and appointments are often manipulated and fixed. Not infrequently, complaints of favoritism, nepotism, and corruption are heard, even as most institutions go through the process of recruitment with a veneer of legality and fairness. In many institutions, there is backdoor entry into the academic profession for candidates who cannot face competition. Such candidates are first appointed as ad hoc / temporary assistant professors and given an opportunity to gain experience. At the interview, the chairperson of the selection committee (the vice-chancellor, director, or the president of the governing body) pleads their case, and generally the external experts are very obliging. The selection of candidates on extraneous considerations or through dubious methods often results in charges of nepotism and corruption in publicly funded institutions. On this, however, data are hard to come by.

By law, appointment to teaching positions in publicly funded institutions is open to all citizens of the country. While there is provision for inclusion through reservation of posts for traditionally oppressed caste groups (Scheduled Castes), ethnically isolated groups (Scheduled Tribes), and socioeconomically backward groups (Backward Castes) under the policy of protective discrimination, no candidate can be excluded on sociocultural or regional considerations. However, most state universities and colleges affiliated with them make knowledge of the regional language a desirable qualification, effectively showing preference to candidates from the state. This has had the inadvertent consequence of limiting mobility among teachers and results in a deleterious inbreeding within the institutions.

The private universities and unaided private colleges are not bound by any formal guidelines for recruitment to teaching positions. They are not obliged to advertise their vacancies, and their advertisements are frugal on details. Their recruitment procedures are not transparent. Given the type of resources that some of the private universities have been able to mobilize, they seem to have greater elbow room in the matter of scouting for talent and the selection of high-quality teaching faculty. Incidentally, as private enterprises, they are not encumbered by the policy of protective discrimination referred to earlier.

TEACHING AND PROFESSIONAL DEVELOPMENT

Starting in 1987, the UGC established at least one academic staff college (ASC) in each state with the mandate to improve standards of teaching through "orientation courses" for the new entrants to the profession (focusing on pedagogy and on the social relevance of education) and "refresher courses" for those already in it (providing up-to-date information on the contents of various disciplines). In 2014–15, there were 66 ASCs spread across the country. The duration of the orientation course is 24 working days and involves 144 contact hours, and that of the refresher course is 18 working days and involves 108 contact hours. Attending an orientation course is mandatory for confirmation of an assistant professor, and attending two refresher courses is required before an assistant professor can become eligible for promotion to the next stage in the academic career. To build an element of seriousness, UGC introduced an end-course assessment. Part-time teachers and guest faculty are not required to attend the orientation or refresher courses.

As with all such well-intentioned innovations by the UGC, the orientation and refresher courses are now trivialized at the ASCs (Jayaram, 2003: 209–11). Recognizing this, the National Assessment and Accreditation Council (NAAC) has advised that the ASCs be renamed Human Resource Development Centers, which should make induction training mandatory for all entrants into the academic profession, including those appointed in private institutions and on a temporary basis (*Times of India*, 2012). It is doubtful if the NAAC's advice will be heeded and, if heeded, also will be trivialized.

PERFORMANCE APPRAISAL AND PROMOTION

For several decades, the job performance of teachers in higher education institutions remained unevaluated, and any attempt at evaluation was either resisted or done perfunctorily. Only in state government-run colleges were confidential reports of teachers written by their principals and filed in their personnel files, called "service registers." In universities and institutes, teachers on probation were confirmed generally on the basis of confidential reports by the head/chairperson of the department, or the dean if the teacher was the head/chairperson of the department. However, as part of the package of pay revision and increases, performance evaluation of teachers in all publicly funded universities and colleges was introduced in 2010.

The UGC (2010: 103–7) has listed three categories of teacher's performance for appraisal, namely, (1) teaching, learning, and evaluation-related activities; (2) curricular, extension, and professional development-related activities; and (3) research and academic contributions. For each category, indicators and weights are specified. To suit their specific requirements, the institutions have been advised to adapt the template provided by the UGC or devise their own self-assessment-cum-performance-appraisal forms for teachers, in compliance with the UGC prescriptions. Purely private institutions do not have a mandatory or standardized self-appraisal system.

The Indian professoriate is pyramidal in structure: there are fewer positions of professor than that of associate professor, and fewer positions of associate professor than that of assistant professor; and this is more so in the affiliated colleges. To improve the opportunities of teachers for moving up in the career ladder, and as an incentive to performance, the UGC introduced a six-stage Career Advancement Scheme (CAS). How soon an entry-level assistant professor can move to stage 2 depends on whether he or she possesses a PhD degree (four years), an MPhil degree (five years), or only a master's degree in the subject (six years). An assistant professor who has completed five years of service in stage 2 is eligible to move to stage 3. After completing three years of service in stage 3, the assistant professor will be eligible to move to stage 4 and be designated as an associate professor; and after three years of service in stage 4, an associate professor can move up to stage 5 and become a professor. After ten years of service in stage 5, one can become eligible for promotion to the highest level, professor, stage 6. Promotion under the

CAS is based on the performance appraisal of teachers referred to earlier. It is not possible for a teacher to jump stages under the CAS, but a candidate who is eligible for associate professorship can compete for that position under direct recruitment.

The UGC has formulated guidelines for promotions under CAS. The process of promotion has to be initiated by the teacher through an application. Candidates who fail the selection process can be reassessed only after one year. Promotion under the CAS being specific to the individual teacher, the position will be restored at the original rank upon the incumbent's retirement from active service. Incidentally, student feedback is not taken into consideration in the performance appraisal of teachers for the CAS. Some centrally funded deemed-to-be universities and institutions of national importance obtain student feedback on curriculum and teaching, but such feedback is not a formal part of the performance appraisal of teachers.

Private universities being new in India, very little is known about their performance appraisal practices. However, student feedback apparently influences the renewal of teachers' contracts in these universities.

Service and Working Conditions of the Professoriate

The terms of appointment in publicly funded institutions are specified in the *appointment order* issued to a teacher, and they are enforceable in a court of law. Among other things, the order specifies the pay in the pay band (salary scale) and other admissible allowances and benefits. Generally, in the universities, there is no negotiation on salary or other benefits. But during the interview the candidate can make a case for a higher starting pay, and, if convinced, the selection committee may recommend, with reason, up to five increments, that is, a maximum of 15 percent higher basic pay.

In private universities, theoretically, the terms of appointment are negotiable. In reality, however, such negotiations take place only in the case of faculty of very high caliber or faculty in narrow fields of specialization. That is, private institutions have the autonomy to compete for faculty and can use better salaries, fringe benefits, reduced teaching obligations, research subsidies, etc., to make an offer that is more attractive than one by other similar institutions or publicly funded institutions. Apparently, the publicly funded institutions are, on occasion, at a disadvantage. However, the private institutions can hardly match the employment security, career advancement, and graduated increase in salary and other statutory benefits that are offered by publicly funded institutions. Not surprisingly, publicly funded institutions, especially those funded directly by the MHRD/ UGC, are the best bet for aspirants to the academic profession.

SALARIES AND REMUNERATION

The implementation of new pay bands by the UGC since January 2006 has made teaching an extraordinarily attractive option for master's degree holders and doctorates in the job market. The gross monthly salary of a new entrant now consists of five components: (1) pay in the pay band, (2) academic grade pay, (3) transport allowance, (4) dearness allowance,[14] and (5) house rent allowance. The gross salary drawn by assistant professors at the bottom, middle, and top of the pay band are shown in table 7.5.

Being in higher ranges of income, all assistant professors now pay graduated income tax (10 or 20 percent)—deducted from their salaries by their employing institutions—depending upon the range in which their gross income falls after availing tax concessions and incentives for saving.

In publicly funded institutions, irrespective of the academic field, all assistant professors are paid similarly. However, in private institutions, teachers are paid varyingly depending upon the demand and supply of teachers in particular disciplines. Assistant professors in the institutions of national importance are paid marginally better salaries. Even among publicly funded institutions, those in centrally funded institutions get relatively higher gross salaries than those in state-funded institutions, since in many states a transport allowance is not paid and the house rent allowance is fixed as per state government rates, which are invariably lower than the central government rates.

Table 7.5.   Monthly Salary of Assistant Professor as of September 1, 2012

Pay Details	Bottom of Pay Band	Middle of Pay Band	Top of Pay Band
(Basic) Pay	15,600	27,350	39,100
Grade Pay*	6,000	7,000	8,000
Transport Allowance	3,200	3,200	3,200
Dearness Allowance	14,040	22,328	30,615
House Rent Allowance	6,480	10,005	11,910
Gross Salary	45,320	69,883	92,825

Source: Adapted from UGC (2010).
   Note: All figures in Indian rupees; approximately, $1 = Rs 67 in February 2017.
   *Apart from the (basic) pay, the teachers receive grade pay, which depends on their position in the six-grade Career Advancement Scheme.

Over the decades, the gap in salaries at the entry level between academic and other professions has narrowed considerably. Nevertheless, those entering in the management, ICT (information and communication technology), and biotechnology sectors earn considerably more than teachers. However, in India, as regards teachers' salaries, the general comparison is with those of civil servants,[15] and the salaries of these two are now more or less comparable, though the bureaucrats get better perquisites. The minimum gross salary of assistant professors varies marginally between centrally funded institutions and state-funded institutions, and between universities in general and the institutions of national importance. In fact, the UGC has fixed the remuneration even for part-time teachers and guest faculty. To ensure transparency and avoid cheating by grant-in-aid private institutions, the teachers' salaries are credited to their bank accounts. In contrast, there is no minimum pay in purely private universities and colleges. Seldom are their salary scales and allowances advertised. Most of them are evasive on pay matters; many of them pay their teachers in cash.

In all publicly funded institutions, all teachers, including assistant professors, are entitled to an annual increase of 3 percent in their basic pay (that is, pay in the pay band plus academic grade pay). Apart from this, teachers get a bigger hike in salary if they are promoted under the CAS. There is, however, no negotiation on salary size or service conditions. In purely private institutions, negotiation is possible; most often, such negotiations are to the advantage of the management.

Overall, those entering the academic profession in publicly funded universities and colleges now lead comfortable, middle-class lifestyles based on their salaries. Housing and transportation are additional components of the salary. Inflation in the economy, that is, the rise in cost of living, is also addressed through biannual revision of the "dearness allowance," as noted earlier. And there is no difference in pay scales among academics in different faculties: those teaching English or mathematics get paid the same as their counterparts teaching Urdu or history. Since the pay scales are now uniform across the country, though with minor interstate differences, the quality of life of academics living in small towns has also improved. For teachers in purely private universities and colleges, the story is different; market conditions rule here, and there are large salary differentials in terms of the disciplines and the qualifications of the teachers. In some private institutions, the salaries are exploitative. In all institutions, the part-time teachers are invariably worse off.

For those seeking entry into the professoriate, job security and statutorily guaranteed salary are the key attractions. The location of the university/college, reputation of the institution, availability of facilities for research, and the like could also be influential for the few who have a choice. The nonsalary benefits for teachers are all as per the government provisions, and they have no bearing on the choice of teaching as a career or of a particular institution.

Those appointed to permanent teaching positions in publicly funded institutions after January 2004 have to contribute 10 percent of their basic pay to the pension fund, and the government makes a matching contribution. They are eligible for a variety of paid leave, but none of them can be availed as a matter of right. Every academic year, a teacher can avail themselves of 8 days of *casual leave* (to meet exigencies) and this leave cannot be accumulated. The teacher can get one day of *earned/privilege leave* for 11 days of work and this leave can be accumulated to a maximum of 300 days. This leave can be exchanged for additional pay at retirement. The most attractive part of the academic profession is the fully paid *vacation leave* of eight weeks in a year.

Female teachers get a maximum of one year of fully paid *maternity leave* during their career, and their spouses get a maximum of 15 days of fully paid *paternity leave* for each child born (and for not more than two children). Besides maternity leave, female teachers are entitled to two years of fully paid *childcare leave* provided they have exhausted all other leaves to their credit. They can take this leave anytime until the child attains 18 years of age; it can be split between two children.

Teachers can take advantage of the "leave travel concession" benefit (return fare for self and dependents) once every two years by using their vacation or applying for leave to go on a holiday in India. In lieu of this, teachers hailing from outside their place of work can avail "home travel concession" to visit their "home town" (as declared at the time of joining the service). The amount paid by the university or college toward such travel is taxable.

Teachers are eligible for medical leave and medical assistance both for themselves and for their dependents. They are entitled to the use of central or state government health service facilities. In lieu of this, some institutions have extended medical insurance coverage to teachers or they reimburse medical expenses up to a particular amount. To check misuse of this benefit (by the hospitals, insurance companies, and teachers alike), there are elaborate norms governing medical assistance.

As part of their salary, teachers are given a percentage of their basic pay (pay in the pay band, the grade pay and transport allowance) as house rent allowance depending upon the location of the university/college. According to the Government of India's classification, those in Category A cities (e.g., Bengaluru, Chennai,

Delhi, Hyderabad, Mumbai, and Kolkata) get 30 percent; those in Category B cities (e.g., Ahmedabad, Chandigarh, Jaipur, Lucknow, and Patna), 20 percent; and those elsewhere, 10 percent. In case the university provides housing (no college does that), teachers will not get the house rent allowance; they will have to pay a small sum as "license fees" and maintenance charges, and the electricity and water charges are payable as per consumption.

Housing provided by the university is in great demand, as it provides residential security and obviates commutation to work. However, some teachers prefer to stay away from campus, especially if they can get cheaper accommodation, as they would save some money from the house rent allowance. Furthermore, with income tax rebates given to those who build houses or buy apartments, it is doubly advantageous to stay off campus. This choice is especially exercised by those teachers who have decided to settle down in the city in which they work. Besides house rent allowance, there are special categories of allowances such as tribal area allowance, hardship area allowance, island special pay, and so on, but these are applicable to a very limited number of institutions. Before the liberalization of lending by banks, until the mid-1990s universities that had surplus funds advanced loans at concessional rates to teachers for buying or building houses and buying cars.

As an incentive for promoting the small family norm, male teachers undergoing a vasectomy or female teachers undergoing a hysterectomy are given one increment in pay upon the production of a certificate from a medical authority. Such teachers must have one surviving child and not more than two children. To be eligible for this incentive, the male teacher must not be over 50 years of age and his wife must be between 20 and 45 years of age. Similarly, the female teacher must not be over 45 years of age and her husband must not be over 50 years of age.

The foregoing nonsalary and service benefits are statutory entitlements in publicly funded institutions. That is why, once in a permanent job, generally no teacher would voluntarily retire. These benefits are, however, a matter of contractual agreement in purely private educational institutions; in very rare cases will they offer a more attractive package than publicly funded educational institutions.

There are very few opportunities for supplementary employment for new entrants into the academic profession. Those occupying a permanent position in a publicly funded university or college are prohibited from taking up supplementary employment. However, with the permission of the institution, they can undertake a teaching assignment in another university/college as visiting/guest faculty for a brief period (by availing up to 30 days of duty leave to which they are entitled in a year). The remuneration received for this work is called an honorarium (not salary) and is liable to be taxed. Generally, teachers collect the honorarium in cash and do not disclose this in tax returns.

The restriction on working in more than one institution does not apply to part-time teachers. In purely private institutions, this may be part of the contract. Incidentally, young faculty doing consultancy or moonlighting is very rare. But some of them (mostly college teachers and rarely university teachers) earn additional income by giving private tuition or writing guidebooks (in a question-answer format) for students appearing for university examinations.

WORKLOAD

While announcing the revised pay scales in 2008, the UGC (UGC, 2010: 60) prescribed a workload of 40 hours a week for 30 working weeks (180 teaching days) in an academic year for teachers with full-time appointments. Moreover, teachers are required to be available in the university department/center or college, as the case may be, for at least 5 hours daily. The number of classroom contact hours for an assistant professor is 16. This heavy teaching load hardly leaves any time for research by teachers, especially those in colleges.

Since the grant-in-aid colleges are dependent on government funds, they enforce workload norms strictly, and teachers with an inadequate workload are required to teach in another college to complete it. If in any subject the workload falls well below the prescribed 16 hours, it is farmed out to part-time teachers. For paucity of financial resources, especially since the introduction of new pay scales, many state governments across the country have imposed an embargo on recruitment to teaching positions in the universities. The state universities are permitted to recruit teachers only if they justify the need in terms of unmet workload.

Central universities, centrally funded deemed-to-be universities, and the institutions of national importance, however, do not observe the UGC prescriptions because of the special status they enjoy as institutions of repute in higher education. There is no standardized workload in private universities, and workload in private colleges is exploitatively higher than in grant-in-aid colleges.

The main responsibility of college teachers is to teach the prescribed curriculum to the students and prepare them for examinations conducted by the university. Besides teaching, university teachers are also required to engage in research. Only in a few university departments/centers and institutions of national importance is the primary emphasis on research. As such, publication as an academic activity is more characteristic of university teachers than college teachers, and a college teacher being engaged in research and publication is commendable indeed. Often this enables the college teacher to move to a university, pursue her or his research interests, and improve career prospects. In private universities, the emphasis is almost exclusively on teaching. In all universities and colleges, teachers are expected to assist the university/college in such administrative activities as processing applications for admission, counseling students, assisting in the conduct of examinations (supervision and evaluation) and participating in extension, cocurricular, and extracurricular activities. Some teachers perform nonteaching work as a matter of duty; most teachers avoid it, if they can.

Conclusion

Overall, the academic profession in India today is an attractive option for those graduating from universities. Many of those completing their master's degree, who would not have thought of teaching as a career a decade or so ago, are now appearing for the UGC-NET with the intention of getting employment at a college or university. This also explains the steady increase in the enrollment of candidates in doctoral programs. This generalization, however, needs to be qualified, as the system of higher education in the country is diverse.

The institutions of national importance (like the IITs and the Indian Institutes of Management) pay higher gross salaries and offer better service conditions. Closely following them are the well-established central universities and centrally funded university-level institutes, which come under the umbrella of the UGC. But the vast majority of teaching positions are in the state universities and grant-in-aid colleges affiliated with them. For teachers working in these universities and colleges, the salary and allied benefits could not be better.

As regards the purely private universities and colleges, the vagaries of the market for higher education will continue to mediate their recruitment practices and remuneration packages. But, if the private universities hope to carve a niche for themselves in higher education, they will have to improve upon what is already offered in centrally funded institutions. Only then will they be able to attract the best of teaching and research talents. This is what some private institutions—backed by leading industrial houses and committed academic administrators—aim to achieve. But it will take some time before their efforts bear fruit.

Paradoxically, however, at a time when the university system is undergoing rapid expansion and the salary and working conditions of the professoriate have improved remarkably, the system is facing an acute shortage of faculty. On the one hand, the number of aspirants who are *formally qualified* for teaching positions by virtue of a master's degree is growing. On the other hand, the universities and colleges have been finding it difficult to recruit *suitable* candidates (i.e., with an aptitude for teaching) for the vacant positions either because such candidates are hard to come by, reflecting the lax standards of graduate education, or because of impedimental statutory/regulatory requirements in the form of protective discrimination quotas, domiciliary restrictions, and the like. With the imminent entry of foreign educational establishments into the country, the competition for well-qualified and experienced faculty is sure to increase. Only institutions offering the best remuneration and service conditions can expect to get the best teaching talents. Viewed in this light, the prospects for state universities and grant-in-aid colleges, which constitute the largest segment of the higher education system in the country, do not appear to be bright.

For the MHRD, the faculty shortage is a serious challenge. It wants to triple enrollment in higher education from around 13 million to 40 million to reach its ambitious target of 30 percent GER by 2020. And it wants to achieve this by expanding the university system even if it means throwing caution to the wind. But the planning commission (disbanded in 2014), which appeared to understand the problem better, wanted the MHRD to consolidate the expansion that had already taken place before expanding further.

In this context, many options have come up for addressing the faculty shortage. The MHRD has now permitted the centrally funded institutions to reemploy retired teachers for one year at a time for up to five years. Such reemployment is subject to the evaluation of the teacher and the teaching requirements of the institution. Reemployment is entirely at the discretion of the institution, and it cannot be claimed as a matter of right by the retired teacher. Reemployed teachers continue to receive all their prior benefits. In some universities, the retired teachers are invited as visiting faculty.

Some vice-chancellors and educational managers feel that the retirement age should be uniformly raised to 65 years, as with those retiring at 60–62 years in some state universities and colleges, the faculty shortage will soon become acute. Others argue that this is only a makeshift arrangement and will negatively affect the prospect of young people wanting to enter the teaching profession (see Anand, 2011). Since the available vacancies are high, the argument against raising the age of retirement does not seem to hold water. But it must be conceded that raising the retirement age by itself will not serve the purpose as the faculty should also be competent to hold the position. Making the academic profession an attractive option for those graduating from the university system is no longer a problem; filling the vacancies with competent young faculty is. In an age of internationalization of higher education and global ranking regimes, appointing competent and committed faculty remains a challenge for those engaged in formulating and implementing higher education policy in India.

NOTES

1. All but one of the governments formed at the federal level in India since March 1977 have been coalitions of various parties, often with contradictory ideologies (Chakrabarty, 2014).

2. In writing this chapter, I have drawn on my earlier work on higher education and the academic profession in India (see Jayaram, 2003, 2007, 2013b) and have reproduced portions from my recent work (2012, 2013a, 2014).

3. According to the Constitution of India, the union parliament legislates on 100 items (Union List), the state legislative assemblies legislate on 61 items (State List), and both the union and state governments legislate on 52 items (Concurrent List).

4. The University Grants Commission was set up by an act of Parliament in 1956. The All India Council for Technical Education was set up in 1945 as an advisory body but came to be vested with regulatory authority by an act of Parliament in 1987. The Medical Council of India was set up by an act of Parliament in 1956.

5. The NKC observed, "The present regulatory system in higher education is flawed in some important respects. The barriers to entry are too high. The system of authorizing entry is cumbersome. There is a multiplicity of regulatory agencies where mandates are both confusing and overlapping. The system, as a whole, is over-regulated but under-governed. NKC perceives a clear need to establish an Independent Regulatory Authority for Higher Education (IRAHE). The IRAHE must be at an arm's length from the Government and independent of all stakeholders including the concerned Ministries of the Government" (NKC, 2007: 43).

6. Thus, between 1950–51 and 2014–15, there was a 24.7-fold increase in the number of degree-awarding universities/institutions and a 58-fold increase in the number of colleges. In addition, there was a 52-fold increase in the number of teachers and a 67-fold increase in student enrollment.

7. By 2011–12, the GER for the 18–23 age-cohort had increased to 20.8 percent (Government of India, 2014: 24).

8. "Demographic dividend," which is also termed "demographic bonus," "demographic gift," or "demographic window," refers to the rise in the rate of economic growth due to an increase in the share of working-age people in a population. The working-age (15–59 years) population, as of now, largely consists of youth (15–34 years). Given the nature of the age structure transition in China and India, the two most populous countries in the world, this dividend is expected to largely accrue to these two countries.

9. The Indian Parliament has yet to legislate on private universities. Meanwhile, invoking the existing legal provisions (e.g., the UGC Act of 1956), several private institutions of higher education have been given the deemed-to-be university status. The controversy resulting from this is now before the Supreme Court of India. Also, considering that higher

education is a concurrent subject under their constitution, some states have enacted legislations for establishing private universities sponsored by a society registered under the Societies Registration Act of 1860 (or any other corresponding law for the time being in force in a state), or a public trust or a company registered under section 25 of the Companies Act of 1956.

10. Gratuity is a lump sum that an employer pays an employee (as gratitude) as one of the retirement benefits. The basic requirements for gratuity are set out under the Payment of Gratuity Act of 1972.

11. In institutions of national importance such as the Indian Institute of Science (Bangalore) and the IITs, a fourth level, namely, assistant professor (to be recruited on a contractual basis), was introduced in September 2009. This position is not part of the regular faculty cadres in these institutes, and appointment to this position is made on a contractual basis to enable bright, young doctorate degree holders to teach and earn experience in premier institutions. It is stipulated that at least 10 percent of the total faculty strength should be recruited at this level.

12. In academic fields such as engineering and technology, medicine and pharmacy, management / business administration, occupational therapy and physiotherapy, physical education, music and performing arts, etc., special qualifications are prescribed for different levels of teaching staff (see UGC, 2010: 4–36).

13. Taking effect in June 2015, on behalf of the UGC, the Central Board of Secondary Education headquartered in New Delhi conducts the NET.

14. The "dearness [expensiveness, in British English] allowance" is intended to compensate for inflation and is revised twice a year (on 1st of January and July, respectively) based on the price index (100 points as of January 1, 2006). As of July 1, 2016, it was 132 percent of pay (that is, pay in the pay band plus academic grade pay plus transport allowance).

15. Although teachers are not civil servants, they are both governed by the same civil service conduct rules.

REFERENCES

Agarwal, Pawan. 2009. *Indian Higher Education: Envisioning the Future.* New Delhi: Sage.
Altbach, Philip G., and N. Jayaram 2012. "Can India Garner the Demographic Dividend?," in *Permanent Transition: A Half-Century of Indian Higher Education (Essays by Philip G. Altbach),* ed. P. Agarwal, 97–99. New Delhi: Sage.
Anand, Abhay. 2010. "UGC Announces NET Exemption Cut-Off Date for MPhil Holders." *India Education Review,* November 9, 2010. http://www.indiaeducationreview.com /features/impact-ugc-regulationexempting-net-mphil-holders. Accessed July 7, 2012.
Ashby, Eric, and Mary Anderson. 1966. *Universities: British, Indian, and African.* London: Weidenfeld and Nicolson.
Chakrabarty, Bidyut. 2014. *Coalition Politics in India: Oxford India Short Introductions.* New Delhi: Oxford University Press.
Dube, S. C. 1988. "Higher Education and Social Change." In *Higher Education in India: The Social Context,* ed. A. Singh and G. D. Sharma, 46–53. Delhi: Konark.

FICCI (Federation of Indian Chambers of Commerce and Industry). 2012. *Higher Education in India: Twelfth Five Year Plan (2010–2017) and Beyond (FICCI Higher Education Summit 2012)*. New Delhi: FICCI.

Government of India. 2014. *Educational Statistics at a Glance*. New Delhi: Bureau of Planning, Monitoring and Statistics, Ministry of Human Resource Development. http://mhrd .gov.in/sites/upload_files/mhrd/files/statistics/EAG2014.pdf. Accessed April 8, 2015.

India Education Review. 2012. "On Shortage of Faculty at Universities (Comments)." http:// www.indiaeducationreview.com/vc-desk/shortage-faculty-universities-0. Accessed August 28, 2012.

Jayaram, N. 2003. "The Fall of the Guru: The Decline of the Academic Profession in India." In *The Decline of the Guru: The Academic Profession in Developing and Middle-Income Countries*, ed. Philip G. Altbach, 199–230. New York: Palgrave Macmillan.

———. 2007. "Beyond Retailing Knowledge: Prospect of Research-Oriented Universities in India." In *World Class Worldwide: Transforming Research Universities in Asia and Latin America*, ed. P. G. Altbach and J. Balán, 70–94. Baltimore: Johns Hopkins University Press.

———. 2012. "Academic Salaries and Career Advancement: Tuning the Professoriate for a Knowledge Economy in India." In *Paying the Professoriate: A Global Comparison of Compensation and Contracts*, ed. P. G. Altbach, L. Reisberg, M. Yudkevich, G. Androushchak, and I. F. Pacheco, 155–65. New York: Routledge.

———. 2013a. "India: Streamlining the Academic Profession for a Knowledge Economy." In *The Global Future of Higher Education and the Academic Profession*, ed. P. G. Altbach, G. Androushchak, Y. Kuzminov, M. Yudkevich, and L. Reisberg, 93–125. Basingstoke: Palgrave Macmillan.

———. 2013b. "The Decline of the University as a Public Institution in India." In *Education, Religion and Creativity: Essays in Honour of Professor Yogendra Singh*, ed. I. Modi, 23–40. Jaipur: Rawat.

———. 2014. "Whither Innovations in Higher Education in India?" In *The Forefront of International Higher Education: A Festschrift in Honor of Philip G. Altbach*, ed. A. Maldonado and R. M. Bassett, 195–205. Dordrecht, Netherlands: Springer.

National Knowledge Commission (NKC). 2007. *Report to the Nation—2006*. New Delhi: National Knowledge Commission, Government of India.

Times News Network. 2011. "Higher Edu Short of 54% Teachers." *Times of India* (Mumbai), August 10, 2011, 15.

University Grants Commission (UGC). 2010. *UGC Regulations on Minimum Qualifications for Appointment of Teachers and Other Academic Staff in Universities and Colleges and Measures for the Maintenance of Standards in Higher Education*. New Delhi: UGC.

———. 2012. *Higher Education in India at a Glance*. New Delhi: UGC. www.ugc.ac.in. Accessed July 7, 2012.

———. 2013. *Press Release: Result of NET held on 30th June, 2013*. http://www.ugcnetonline .in/Press%20Release%20UGC%20NET%20June%2020 13%20_1_.pdf. Accessed June 30, 2015.

———. 2015. *Annual Report, 2014–15*. New Delhi: UGC. http://www.ugc.ac.in/pdfnews /2465555_Annual-Report-2014-15.pdf. Accessed November 1, 2016.

8 | China

The Changing Relationship among Academics, Institutions, and the State

FENGQIAO YAN and DAN MAO

The modern Chinese university system and academic profession were formed during the late nineteenth and early twentieth centuries when the last Qing Dynasty was forced to open up to the outside world by imperial invasion and to learn from Western knowledge for self-defense. Since then, the Chinese university and the academic profession have evolved through several sovereignties, including the Republic of China, Mao's planned economic system, and Deng's market economic system in the People's Republic of China.

In the process of creation and development of the higher education system, China was influenced by different foreign models. Generally speaking, in the modernizing process, starting from the late nineteenth century and early twentieth century, Western university models apparently made imprints on the Chinese university system. In retrospect, China first learned from the German, French, and British university models to create its own contemporary university system. Missionary universities, like St. John's University (1879), the University of Nanking (1888), Soochow University (1900), and Yenching University (1919), are typical modern universities in China. Then, due to the short geographic distance and similarity in culture and language, it learned from the Japanese university system, which was largely based on the German university model. Later, Tsinghua Academy (predecessor of Tsinghua University) was founded in 1911 by the Boxer Indemnity from America. The university was a preparatory institution and was supposed to select Chinese students for American universities. As more and more Chinese students studied in the United States and returned to serve China, the American university model became widely recognized.

After the People's Republic of China was founded in 1949, the Russian university model dominated the Chinese university system, for political and ideological reasons. In 1952, China adopted the Russian university model and transformed its higher education system completely. All missionary and private universities were either transformed into public institutions or closed down. During the Cold War period between 1949 and 1978, China closed its gateway to Western systems because of ideological confrontation.

The Russian university model had two important features: the system was centralized and specialized alignments between government ministries controlled specific industries and universities that addressed the human resource needs of those industries. This led China to a difficult situation: the system was constrained and lacked vitality. Universities lost direct linkages with society, and their graduates could not meet demands from business. Eventually, China rejected the Russian model and since the late 1970s has shifted to American and European models (Hayhoe, 1996; Yan, 2013a). This time, instead of being forced, China voluntarily opened up to the outside world for the sake of self-improvement and prosperity.

Higher education and the academic profession are deeply embedded in Chinese society. Even today, we can observe a historical imprint on the subject of this study. Most contemporary histories of Chinese higher education have noted that China began to get rid of its out-of-date system beginning in 1978, that is, its planned and rigid economic model. This is the period of focus of this chapter.

Since the 1978 reforms, China has been involved in a process of globalization. New products, technology, managerial systems, values, and viewpoints from Western countries have been introduced into China. Of course, this process is also painful in the sense of the contradiction between Chinese and Western value systems, conflict among interest groups, stratification of social classes, and an enlarged economic gap. But overall this trend overcame previous issues and has changed society and the higher education system positively.

The dynamism of contemporary Chinese society reflects itself in higher education and the academic profession. The remarkable changes in the past 40 years can be summarized into two kinds of fundamental shifts: the shift from a planned system to a market system on the one hand, and the shift from a closed system to an open system on the other. These shifts have been widely accepted by both the academic community and by the population at large.

The market system brought rapid economic growth over the last four decades. Chinese gross domestic product (GDP) increased from RMB 365.02 billion in 1978 to RMB 68,905.21 billion in 2015, with an average growth rate above 9 percent.[1] In 2010, China's GDP surpassed Japan's and ranked second in the world, only after the United States. This economic growth brought a greater demand for university graduates, and economic prosperity in return contributed to higher education development in terms of more resources (Cai & Yan, 2015). The market became an increasingly powerful force, which changed the traditional relationship betweens state higher education institutions (HEIs) and the academic profession, which we will elaborate upon in the following section.

China's higher education system has changed significantly. This has attracted a lot of research efforts both domestically and internationally. Interestingly, both positive and negative judgments about China's higher education reform can be found. In Chinese literature and mass media, authors tend to criticize some phenomena, such as institutional mergers and the dramatic expansion of scale. In this essay, we adopt a neutral stand related to reforms, and the changes in higher education are summarized as five transformations: massification, decentralization, marketization, differentiation, and internationalization. Such a dynamic context has complicated the scenario of the Chinese academic profession. Before coming to the focus of this study, however, we will give a general picture of China's higher education system as well as the practices and rationale of the academic profession.

General Characteristics of China's Higher Education System and the Academic Profession
Commonalities and Particularities

The general characteristics of China's higher education system can be captured by static and dynamic analyses. The static analyses will be based on theoretical frameworks constructed in the first chapter of this book. Ben-David (1977), Burton Clark (1983), and Christine Musselin (2010) articulated several analytical concepts and models based on the comparative study of higher education systems in developed countries. State authority, academic oligarchy, and market are three pillars in a triangle pattern in Clark's work (1983). His model has been widely used for the comparative study of higher education systems. Any particular country can be positioned in his triangle. Can this static model fit in the study of China's higher education system and academic profession? The answer is both yes and no. The positive answer is due to the interpretative power of the model. Specifically, before 1978, China's higher education system could be categorized as a state authority type. Afterward, it implemented a number of reforms, and components of the market system and academic oligarchy were introduced and interacted with state authority. Consequently, China's higher education system shifted its position from a previous state authority pillar to somewhere in between. The negative answer results from particularities in the Chinese higher education structure and process that the existing model cannot interpret well (Hayhoe, Li, Lin & Zha, 2011).

Particularities deserve more attention academically, and they can be studied from a dynamic perspective. China is now a dynamic hybrid of the three imperatives mentioned above. For example, if we explore organizations in general and the academic organization in particular at the micro level, special features can be discovered, namely the *danwei* system. *Danwei* is a Chinese word, which refers to work units or organizations. However, they are not the same. Scholars explored work units using different approaches. Some scholars explored its historical heritage from old feudal society. Others argued that the current work unit is quite different from its predecessor. Walder, a sociologist, negated the above legacy proposition and identified certain features embedded in the Communist society after 1949. In his book, Walder employed the *danwei* concept to delineate a unique arrangement under the Communist Party and bureaucratic authority (Walder, 1986). It involves a parallel structure of administrative bureaucracy and Communist Party, soft financial budgets, low mobility of workforces, and low productivity. Some similar features can also be found in universities, such as low faculty mobility (Yan, 2013b). Zhao studied a Chinese university and found collective elitism and *Danwei* as two kinds of uniqueness that Western academic organizations do not have (Zhao, 2006). In this regard, sociological and economic theories, such as institutional theory, can be usefully employed, and different models can be developed in the study of Chinese higher education.[2] However, this is beyond the focus of this essay.

The Higher Education Institutions

First, we need to identify the legal specificities of public and private (*minban*) HEIs in Chinese society. China has four legal entities: government agencies, business firms, public enterprises, and social organizations.[3] Public HEIs are considered public enterprises while private HEIs belong to social organizations (Yan, 2010b). There are important distinctions between these two categories. Public universities depend largely on government budgets, while private universities get most of their revenue from students' tuition. Correspondingly, the status of workers in the four types of organization is different in terms of their salaries, benefits, and social standing. We can identify civil servants as those who work for Chinese governmental agencies, and employees as those who work for business firms. A member of the academic profession, employed in either the public sector or the private sector, is neither a civil servant nor an employee. In other words, members of the academic profession are independent actors and have connections with both the state and the market.[4] Comparatively speaking, an academic position in the public sector is more secure and regulated by the government. To the contrary, an academic position in the private sector is less safeguarded and regulated by the government. In this dynamic and transforming context, significant differences in terms of criteria for recruitment, promotion and tenure, and working conditions (i.e., compensation and benefits, academic freedom, administrative participation) can be observed between the public and private sectors, between central and provincial affiliations, across geographical locations, and across academic professions. Statistical data and empirical study can identify the nuances among them.

Again, to borrow the analytical concepts and frameworks introduced in chapter 1, China's higher education system is neither unitary nor federated; it is mixed. Both the central government and the provincial governments administer some proportion of HEIs in the public sector. In 2014, of the 2,529 regular HEIs, 113 HEIs were under central governmental jurisdiction and 1,689 were under a provincial one.[5] In addition to public HEIs, China has 727 private higher education institutions (Ministry of Education, 2015a).[6]

In terms of institutional type, China has a highly differentiated higher education system, with both academic and vocational subsectors. In 2014, of a total of 2,529 HEIs, 1,202 HEIs could be categorized as academic and 1,327 as vocational (Ministry of Education, 2015a). In terms of quality or status, China's higher education system can be arbitrarily divided into four tiers: "Project 985" institutions, "Project 211" institutions, teaching institutions, and application-oriented institutions (see fig. 8.1) (Cai & Yan, 2017). In the first tier, the 39 "Project 985" universities are typically research-oriented universities.[7] The second tier comprises 73 "Project 211" institutions,[8] which are oriented toward both research and teaching. In the third tier, there are around 600 (mainly provincial) HEIs that mostly engage in teaching activities but also perform research to a small extent. The rest of the over 1,000 HEIs (often tertiary vocational colleges) are in the bottom tier, providing mainly two-to-three-year undergraduate programs (associate degrees).

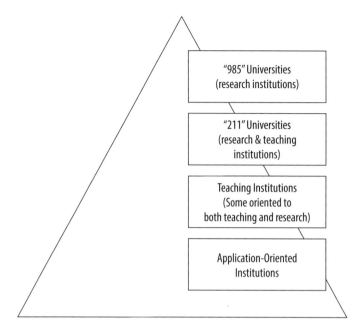

Figure 8.1. Pyramid of Chinese higher education institutions.
Source: Cai & Yan, 2017.

The Academic Profession

The Chinese higher education system is complex and diverse. Efforts are made below to describe general patterns and practices based on a review of relevant legal and policy documents.

Qualifications of university teachers are stipulated in both the *Teacher's Law* (1993) and the *Higher Education Law* (1998, revised in 2015). Regulations specify that university teachers are supposed to have a bachelor's degree or higher (i.e., master's and doctoral degrees). If applicants to the academic profession have not obtained a bachelor's degree, which occurs only in rare cases, they have to pass a qualification examination organized by the state's professional agencies.

National legislation, therefore, provides a minimum qualification standard for university faculty. In practice, however, universities and colleges set up their own reasonable standards, above the minimum standard, according to their specific circumstances, especially supply and demand in the academic labor market. In the spectrum of qualifications for the academic profession, a doctoral degree is a necessity for all national and research universities, while a master's degree is an expected standard for third-tier public and private universities, and a bachelor's degree for bottom-tier three-year vocational colleges (see fig. 8.1). Table 8.1 compares the evolution of highest degree attainment by academic staff in China in 1990 and 2014. The majority of academic staff had only a bachelor's degree (83.79 percent) in 1990, compared to less than half (43.57 percent) in 2014. This scenario was shaped by past practice, as mentioned earlier.[9] With the expansion of graduate education, faculty credentials have risen dramatically.

With regard to recruitment to the academic profession, there is no uniform national procedure; it is currently determined by individual institutions. After getting quotas from the government agency for a public university (private universities usually do not need quotas), the recruiting university usually makes an open announcement on its website, stipulating qualifications, requirements, benefits

Table 8.1.   Faculty's Rank, Academic Degree, and Age in Chinese Regular Higher Education Institutions in 1990 and 2014

| | 1990 | | 2014 | | Change* |
Category	Number	Percent	Number	Percent	Percent
Rank					
Professor	15,052	3.81	189,136	12.33	1,157
Assoc. prof.	84,150	21.33	448,625	29.24	433
Lecturer	148,428	37.62	613,729	40.00	313
Assist. prof.	134,730	34.15	195,763	12.76	45
No rank	12,207	3.09	87,257	5.67	615
Highest Degree					
Doctorate	3,882	0.98	313,136	20.40	7,966
Master's	60,105	15.23	552,854	36.03	820
Below Master's	330,580	83.79	668,520	43.57	102
Age					
<30	141,319	35.82	221,992	14.47	57
31–35	50,804	12.88	357,884	23.32	604
36–40	28,486	7.22	292,771	19.08	928
41–45	27,775	7.04	226,865	14.78	717
46–50	38,460	9.75	186,599	12.16	385
51–55	64,588	16.37	149,982	9.77	132
56–60	34,538	8.75	69,700	4.54	102
>61	8,597	2.17	28,757	1.88	235
Total	394,567		1,534,510		289

Source: Ministry of Education, 1991, 2015.
    *Change = (data in 2014 – data in 1990) / data in 1990 × 100 percent.

and hiring procedures, and so on. Usually one open position in a decent institution can attract dozens or even hundreds of applicants. The academic labor market is highly competitive, especially for HEIs located in large municipalities. The recruiting university selects a short list of applicants for interview on the basis of applicants' paper files. The hiring decision is made mostly on the basis of applicants' merit even though informal connections and social ties, or *guanxi* in Chinese, cannot be denied completely.

In China, there are commonly four academic ranks for university faculty: assistant professor, lecturer, associate professor, and full professor. The promotion of faculty is based on seniority and performance. For a typical national or provincial university, a doctoral degree holder can skip the rank of assistant professor and be granted a lecturer title (which is regarded as a higher rank than assistant professor) upon his or her recruitment. He or she can then apply to become an associate professor after a minimum of two years as a lecturer. An associate professor can apply to become a full professor after a minimum of five years of service. If an applicant is excellent and has an outstanding record of academic productivity, he or she can apply to be promoted to the rank of associate professor or professor before the specified two- and five-year minimum periods. However, for most applicants, the actual period for promotion is longer than the minimum period because a rigorous tenure system is now becoming a more common practice. The introduction of a tenure system at some universities caused tension between faculty and their institutions.[10] Applicants' merits are measured jointly by teaching and research performance, but research productivity measured by publications is usually assigned a higher value than teaching performance. The particular procedure for promotion varies from one institution to another, but common components include a quota provided by the university administration, the applicant's dossier, international and domestic peer reviews, a vote by the academic committee at the school or departmental level, and a final decision from the university central committee or university president.[11]

Most faculty members conduct three tasks: teaching, research, and service. There are no national requirements or statistics in terms of workload in these three areas. It is hard to provide a general pattern in this regard, but a distinction can be made in prioritizing teaching or research between a provincial and a national university because the latter has a smaller student-faculty ratio (i.e., a proxy for teaching load) than its provincial counterpart. In addition to teaching and research, faculty are supposed to engage in service activities. However, only a small number of them are involved in university governance. Senior faculty can be involved in institutional governance to a varying extent at school and departmental levels, but junior faculty have fewer opportunities.

In sum, the academic profession in China follows some common practices with its international counterparts and has its own unique domestic practices, showing disparity within the system. The uniqueness of China's case is that the national political governing party, that is, the Communist Party, is involved in university governance. Specifically, Chinese universities have a parallel governing structure with both the party and the administration. The party secretary and the president are top leaders in a university. Major policy decisions concerning major personnel, financial, and academic issues, are made by a party committee. An administrative committee, under the president's leadership, makes routine decisions. This statement is also true at the school level. Decisions on school deans and department heads are made by a department named *Zuzhi Bu*, under the Community Party. Quite a few academics take double or even triple responsibilities—academic, administrative, and political.

Institutional Autonomy and Academic Freedom

In terms of institutional autonomy and academic freedom, China lacked them but intended to enlarge both of them. For example, before the 1980s, governments controlled the entire process of faculty promotion. An exception emerged when a few national institutions were given the authority to make their own decisions on faculty promotion, and the governments only reviewed the institutional decisions. With more recent reforms, institutions have been delegated more power to make their own decisions on faculty promotion. The *Decision on Advancing the Reform of the Personnel System of Higher Education Institutions* issued in 2000 by the Ministry of Personnel states that: "The objectives of personnel system reform in higher education are as follows: Define and clarify the authority and responsibility of HEIs and governments; create a good environment for the reform and development of HEIs; build a new personnel system in which HEIs can recruit their employees freely; faculty members can choose their jobs freely; and the government will only supervise the process based on laws." Since then, universities have started to build their faculty committees for academic decision making, including faculty recruitment and promotion. However, governments are still involved in certain important decisions on the academic profession, such as research and teaching evaluation, especially for provincial universities.

The 1998 Higher Education Law revised in 2015 stipulates autonomy for HEIs. It states: "based on their own teaching needs, HEIs take the initiative in proposing and checking admission numbers, making admission plans, adjusting admission across programs within the university (Article 32), determining and adjusting disciplines and programs (Article 33), designing their own teaching plans, selecting textbooks and organising teaching activities (Article 34), and conducting scientific research, technological development, and social service (Article 35)."[12] However, implementing the law has been challenging, and autonomy is restricted in practice. For example, a university cannot independently determine its personnel quota, program blueprint, or size of doctoral enrollment. Furthermore, it does not have total autonomy to select its president and vice presidents, it has to follow the guideline designated for its financial budget, and students have to learn some courses designated by the national government (just to mention a few of the restrictions and interference).

The term "academic freedom" does not appear in China's official documents. In the Teacher's Law, there are six rights for all teachers, including university teachers: (1) teach and conduct teaching reform and experimentation; (2) do research and academic exchange, join professional and academic communities, express ideas and opinions; (3) instruct students, guide their development, judge their performance; (4) get timely compensation, enjoy welfare and vacation and sabbatical; (5) provide proposals and suggestions to improve teaching and administration, and be involved in the institutional governance through teacher and staff congresses; (6) participate in all training and development programs. The limit on academic freedom comes from orthodoxy or official ideology stipulated by the ruling party, and this limit can be felt more by some academics in certain fields than others. Specifically, members of the academic profession in the natural sciences and engineering generally enjoy more freedom than those in the social sciences and humanities.

Five Transformations and Their Impact on the Academic Profession

Drawing on the generalizations described above, this section will look at major transformations that are taking place within Chinese higher education and the impacts of these changes on the academic profession. We identify and describe five transformations: massification, decentralization, marketization, differentiation, and internationalization.

Massification

The Chinese government resumed college entrance examinations in 1977 just after the Cultural Revolution (1966–76). Since then, universities and colleges have

Table 8.2.   Higher Education Development in China (1998–2010)

Year	No. of institutions	No. of undergraduates and junior college students (10 thousand)	Annual growth of no. of undergraduate and junior college students		Scale of the institutions (students per institution)	Gross enrollment rate (%)
			Quantity (10 thousand)	Ratio (%)		
1998	1,022	340.87	23.43	7.38	3,335	9.8
1999	1,071	413.42	72.55	21.28	3,815	10.5
2000	1,041	556.09	142.67	34.51	5,289	12.5
2001	1,225	719.07	162.98	29.31	5,870	13.3
2002	1,396	903.36	184.29	25.63	6,471	15.0
2003	1,552	1,108.56	205.20	22.72	7,143	17.0
2004	1,731	1,333.50	224.94	20.29	7,704	19.0
2005	1,792	1,561.78	228.28	17.12	7,666	21.0
2006	1,867	1,738.84	177.07	11.34	8,148	22.0
2007	1,908	1,884.90	146.06	8.40	8,571	23.0
2008	2,263	2,021.00	136.10	7.22	8,931	23.3
2009	2,305	2,144.66	123.66	6.12	9,086	24.2
2010	2,358	2,231.79	87.13	4.06	9,298	26.5

Source: Yan, 2014.

gradually expanded their admission. As a result, more and more graduates from senior high schools have opportunities to go to college. In 1999, the government launched a blueprint for higher education massification targeting a higher-education enrollment rate of 15 percent for each age group cohort by 2010. Consequently, university enrollment increased dramatically. In 1998, the number of undergraduates and junior college students was 3,408,700, whereas in 2010 the number reached 22,317,900 (see table 8.2).

Several striking changes can be observed during the 24-year period from 1990 to 2014, when China's higher education system transitioned from elite to mass. First, the number of institutions, student enrollment, and faculty and staff numbers increased dramatically (e.g., student enrollment increased 11.35-fold).

Second, massification deeply changed the higher education system in China, not only in terms of the enrollment rate but also in its mission and structure. Different from the elite system, which trains scientists, researchers, and high-ranking administrators for the next generation, producing a well-prepared workforce has instead become one of the practical missions of higher education. Subsequently, advanced vocational education and the nonuniversity sector have gained an increasing share in the higher education system. In 1998, the ratio between three-year colleges and four-year universities and colleges was 1:1.37 (431:591), and the ratio between enrollments in the two sectors was 1:3.56 (733,310:2,611,259).[13] In 2012, they were 1.13:1 (1,297:1,145) and 1:1.48 (9,642,267:14,270,888), respectively.[14]

Third, structural changes went along with these quantitative increases, with the pendulum swinging from specialized institutions to comprehensive ones, from central jurisdiction authority to a provincial one, and from bachelor's degree institutions to associate's degree ones, and the private higher education sector emerged from scratch in the 1990s.

Fourth, there were efficiency gains in terms of student-to-faculty ratio. In the 1990s, the ratio was about 5:1; in 2014, it was about 20:1. This implies that the academic profession had to adapt itself to this new situation.[15] Table 8.3 provides basic data from 1990 and 2014 and makes a comparison between the two. Accordingly, the number of faculty members in universities and colleges has also increased greatly. In 1998, there were about 407,000 faculty members in China, whereas in 2010 that number reached 1,343,000, which is about a threefold increase (see fig. 8.2).

Table 8.3. Basic Data on Chinese Regular Higher Education Institutions in 1990 and 2014

Category	1990		2014		Change* (%)
	Number	Percent	Number	Percent	
Institutions	1,075		2,529		135
Comprehensive	50	4.65	603	23.84	1,106
Noncomprehensive	1,025	95.35	1,929	76.16	88
Central	354	32.93	113	4.46	−68
Provincial	721	67.07	1,689	66.79	134
Private	NA	NA	727	28.75	
Bachelor	620	57.67	1,202	47.53	94
Associate	455	42.33	1,327	52.47	192
Enrollment	2,062,695		25,476,999		1,135
Central	902,295	43.74	1,823,234	7.16	102
Provincial	1,160,400	56.26	17,908,279	92.84	1,443
Faculty & staff	830,988		2,218,556		167
Central	422,093	50.79	327,293	14.75	−22
Provincial	408,895	49.21	1,481,319	66.77	262
Private	NA	NA	409,944	18.48	

Source: Ministry of Education,1991, 2015.
    *Change = (data in 2014 − data in 1990) / data in 1990 × 100 percent.

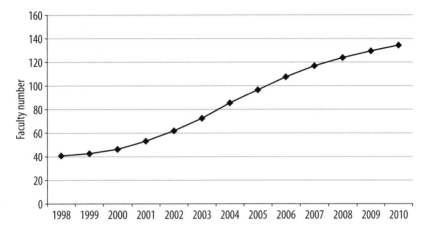

Figure 8.2. Number of faculty members in China (1998–2010) (unit: 10 thousands). *Source:* Authors' own calculations based on *Zhong guo jiao yu shi ye fa zhan tong ji gong bao* [*Report on Education Development Statistics of China*], http://www.moe.edu.cn/publicfiles/business/htmlfiles/moe/moe_335/index.html (accessed May 2014).

During this same time period, the proportion of senior titles (professor and associate professor) increased while the proportion of junior titles (assistant professor) shrunk. This change was largely due to the end of a freeze on promotions before 1977 and a return to normal starting in the 1980s. Additionally, an increasing number of faculty members began to hold doctoral and master's degrees due to enhanced requirements for faculty recruitment and the expansion of graduate education. Finally, the share of young faculty (under the age of 40) increased, for when student admission expanded, many young master's and doctorate holders were hired as fresh faculty upon their graduation. According to many universities' policies, new faculty with a doctoral degree are automatically entitled to commence employment as lecturers upon graduation and can be promoted to associate professor two years later. The promotion process is easy. It is one of the reasons there is an increasing share of young faculty but fewer at the rank of junior faculty. It is more difficult to be promoted from associate professor to full professor. Recently some Chinese universities adopted the tenure system, which originated from American universities. But full professor instead of associate professor is the threshold for tenure in China. Table 8.1 provides general data on faculty ranks, academic degrees and age ranges in 1990 and 2014, and makes a comparison between the two. The student-faculty ratio increased significantly as well during this time period, going from 8.37:1 in 1998 to 17.33:1 in 2010.[16]

The rapid growth of enrollment, faculty and the student-faculty ratio brought about great challenges. First, there was a concern that the actual quality of faculty members (not as measured by ranks or degrees) would decline. A survey conducted by Peking University in 2012[17] on the academic profession in China showed that, compared with faculty members who were recruited before the enrollment expansion, those recruited after the expansion gave lower scores to their training on both teaching and research in their graduate education. This is one of the signals indicating the worsened situation of scholarly quality.

Second, new faculty members have insufficient academic support and development opportunities. At the phase of elite higher education, there was a tradition that each junior faculty member was under the mentorship of a senior faculty member, as an assistant instructor, before delivering lectures independently. This one-on-one mechanism functioned as a training and quality assurance system, which gave junior faculty some teaching preparation in advance. However, with the rapid growth of the number of faculty members, the traditional one-on-one mechanism did not work anymore because there were not enough senior faculty members to mentor incoming colleagues.

Third, in the mass system, faculties have been challenged by a large and diverse student pool, as Martin Trow (1973) predicted. Under the high student-faculty ratio, big classes became the dominant way of teaching, and less faculty and student contact was expected.

DECENTRALIZATION

In Mao Tse-tung's era, centralization was the distinguishing feature of China's higher education administration, where most universities and colleges were under the jurisdiction of the central government (Min, 2002). In 1985, the central government issued a policy, "Decision of Educational Reform," which was intended to change the previous centralized system. Although there were some attempts to decentralize the administrative system, there was no real change until 1993, when the "Outline for Education Reform and Development" was stipulated and implemented. It stated, "According to the fundamental policies and macroscopic planning of the central government, provinces (autonomous regions and municipalities) will take responsibilities for local universities. Accordingly, the central government should delegate the power of decision-making to provinces (autonomous regions and municipalities) and extend the latter's jurisdiction to coordinate those universities administered by the central government but located in their territories" (cited from Yan et al., 2014).

The Higher Education Law (1998) insisted upon the same idea. Based on this principle, mechanisms for reform can be categorized into four maneuvers or approaches: joint jurisdiction, adjustment of jurisdiction, cooperation between central and provincial governments, and institutional mergers (Li, 2003; Yan, 2000; Yan et al., 2014).

Along with the reform of government structure, some industrial ministries were dissolved and universities that had been under the jurisdiction of these dissolved ministries had to change their affiliations from central government to provincial government. The change in institutional ownership has reflected itself in both student and faculty shares in two subsectors. By 2010, 84.17 percent of faculty members were located in the provincial higher education subsector.[18] But the percentage was only 48.60 percent in 1992.[19]

In a decentralized administrative system, local governments have greater authority regarding higher education planning and coordination. After 1999, provincial governments obtained full rights to establish and approve vocational colleges in their jurisdictions. This policy unleashed the aspiration of higher education supply and led to a mushrooming of vocational colleges nationwide.

This structural change was combined with large-scale institutional mergers. More than 600 higher education institutions were involved in mergers. Through mergers and the broadening of institutional missions/scopes, many HEIs transformed from specialized institutions into comprehensive universities.

During the process of decentralization, the revenue gap between universities under the jurisdiction of the central government (national universities) and those under the jurisdiction of provincial governments (provincial universities) grew. Compared with national universities, the percentage of tuition in the total revenue of provincial universities was larger. In 2001, tuition in provincial universities accounted for 33.2 percent of total revenue whereas in national universities it was only 13.4 percent (Guo, 2004). This is because national universities receive more appropriations from government than provincial universities. In other words, provincial institutions have to rely more on tuition revenue than their national counterparts (Yan, 2010a). Consequently, a gap can be found for expenditure per student between national universities and provincial universities. In 2015, the statistical data is 45,926.54 yuan at national universities, and 22,399.13 yuan at provincial universities. The ratio between them is 2.05:1 (45,926.54/22,399.13).[20]

As for expenditure on research, the situation is similar. In national universities, research expenditure has increased since 1998 and reached 8 percent of the total revenue in 2001 while it was only 1 percent at provincial universities in the same year (Guo, 2004). If we compare the indexes of research funds per faculty between national universities and provincial universities, the two indexes are calculated as 64,407.17 yuan (12,687,826,000/196,994) and 3,400.49 yuan (3,640,616,000/1,070,754). The ratio between the two is 18.94 (64,407.17/3,400.49).[21] This shows that faculty in national university get much more research funding than their counterparts in provincial universities. Furthermore, faculty in national universities have more privileges than faculty in provincial ones in terms of development opportunities, office facilities, library collections, laboratory conditions, domestic and international exchanges, promotions, and the like.

MARKETIZATION

The marketization of higher education in China was a part of societal change. Several changes indicated the emergence of marketization of higher education in China, including a shift from a tuition-free to a fee-charging system and the development of private HEIs (Mok, 2000). Before 1997, college students were not charged tuition, except for a small number of commissioned training programs. Consequently, almost all the revenues for HEIs came from the government. Facing insufficient revenue, the central government started to transfer the cost burden from the public purse to families and individuals. The "Interim Regulations on Fee-Charging in Higher Education Institutions," issued in December 1996, proposed the fee-charging policy. Since then, the percentage of tuition in total revenue has increased greatly. In 1990, only 0.5 percent of revenue came from tuition, while in 2001 that figure increased to 24.7 percent (see table 8.4).

In addition to seeking increased funding through tuition, more and more HEIs participated in business and commercial activities to get more resources. They established university-affiliated corporations, ran short-term courses, and provided adult education and evening courses (Mok, 2002).

The decline in the share of total institutional revenue from government appropriations and the increase in the share of total revenue from tuition and other channels has changed the behavior of HEIs. The market has now become an important consideration when making decisions on programs and courses. Disciplines that are applied, practically oriented, or closer to the market receive more funds and have become more influential in decision making at the institutional level. The income gap among faculty in different disciplines has also grown.

As a result of the income gap between disciplines, some faculty have been lured or forced to be involved in market activities, either voluntarily or involuntarily. To

Table 8.4. Share of Revenue (by Percent) by Source of Regular Higher Education Institutions in China, 1990–2001

Year	Fiscal funding				Educational revenue				Other
	Budgeted	Education Tax	Transfer	Subtotal	Tuition	Other	Subtotal	Endowment	
1990	83.4	–	10.1	93.5	0.5	2.3	2.8	–	3.7
1991	75.1	–	15.4	90.6	2.8	2.8	5.6	–	3.8
1992	75.1	–	15.4	90.6	2.8	2.8	5.6	–	3.8
1993	82.4	0.1	8.6	91.8	6.1	–	6.1	0.7	1.3
1994	72.6	0.3	8.9	82.2	11.8	–	11.8	1.3	4.7
1995	69.6	0.3	9.7	80.5	13.6	–	13.6	1.6	4.3
1996	67.8	0.9	8.7	78.8	14.4	–	14.4	1.7	5.2
1997	65	1	8.7	76.4	15.7	–	15.7	2.3	5.6
1998	49.6	1.4	2.1	64.9	13.4	13.2	26.6	2.1	6.4
1999	49.4	1	1.8	62.8	17.2	12.7	29.9	2.3	5
2000	47.9	0.9	1.8	58.5	21.3	13.4	34.7	1.7	5.1
2001	46.7	0.6	1.4	55	24.7	13.3	38	1.5	5.5

Source: Zha, 2008.

increase their income, some faculty members were willing to participate in some commercial activities, including providing consultancy to corporations, selling their patents, or setting up their own businesses. Others even misused research funds as a way to increase their personal incomes. This behavior is punished whenever exposed.

Another remarkable change is the emergence and growth of private higher education. Obvious differences exist between public and private HEIs. With regard to academic quality, the private sector is inferior to its public counterpart even though exceptions exist. According to college admission policy and procedure, public universities can admit top-tier faculty and students, and private ones admit bottom-tier faculty and students. The work pattern and campus climate of private HEIs are also quite different from those of public universities. Because they get little funds from the government, private HEIs have to depend heavily on tuition fees. As for faculty, the teaching load is heavier in the private sector than in the public sector. Faculty members in the private sector are less loyal to their institutions, are more likely to leave to pursue other opportunities, and their performance is more likely to be evaluated by administrators instead of the academic community (Yan, 2009; Cai & Yan, 2011; Yan & Lin, 2011).

DIFFERENTIATION

China's economy benefits from a collapsed egalitarian policy, which means that a few high-performing people are initially advantaged and these benefits gradually become more dispersed. This rationale was applied to the higher education system. In the past few decades, the central government of China launched several projects, such as Project 211, Project 985, and the Double World-Class Project, as well as the Yangtze River Scholar and Thousand Talent personnel programs to improve the academic quality of a few top universities and top disciplines, and promote their development as world-class institutions and disciplines.

The 211 Project, first announced in 1995 by the Ministry of Education, aimed to build 100 high-level universities in the twenty-first century. Now, 112 universities are included in this project—69 are national universities, and 43 are provincial universities.[22] Currently, one-quarter of all doctoral students, two-thirds of all graduate students, and one-third of all undergraduates are enrolled in Project 211 institutions. Approximately 96 percent of China's key laboratories are located in these institutions, and researchers at these institutions are responsible for 70 percent of scientific research findings.[23]

A world-class university blueprint (the origin of the 985 Project) was first announced at the hundredth anniversary of Peking University in May 1998. The objective of the 985 Project is to promote in the world the standing and reputation of a few Chinese universities. Funds are raised jointly by the central government, local government, and institutions. Resources are mainly used on facilities, talent, and international networking opportunities. In the first wave of implementation, nine elite universities were selected for the project. Both Peking University and Tsinghua University (the top two universities in China) were granted 225 million each over three years, while Nanjing University and Shanghai Jiaotong University each received 150 million US dollars.[24] By the end of the second wave, a total of 39 universities were selected and sponsored.

Some developed provinces and municipalities such as Beijing, Shanghai, Shenzhen, Guangdong, Zhejiang, and Jiangsu competed to improve higher education in the region. They invested considerable sums of money on HEIs in their geographical areas.

The differentiation policies mentioned above built a pyramid-shaped higher education system in China (fig. 8.1). The pyramid-shaped higher education system legitimated and ensured elite universities would have excellent investment from the central government.

According to resource dependence theory (Pfeffer & Salancik, 1978) and institutional theory (DiMaggio & Powell, 1983), organizations tend to simulate successful organizations in their fields to get more resources or legitimacy. In recent years, there has been a trend for some bachelor's degree-granting universities to simulate the research universities—for example, by transforming from specialized universities to comprehensive universities to grant master's or doctoral degrees. This phenomenon is very similar to the "academic drift" that occurred in Britain and elsewhere (Zhang, 2006).

These bachelor's degree-granting institutions set strict quantitative standards for publications (especially those indexed by Science Citation Index, Engineering Index, and Index to Scientific and Technical Proceedings) and research funds in faculty promotion policy. Below is an example of the criteria used in the promotion process to the rank of full professor (science, technology, engineering, and math [STEM] only) in a public teaching-type university with regard to research funds and publications (see table 8.5).

However, overemphasizing the quantity of publications, especially in teaching universities, may cause some problems. First, the strict requirement on publications brings high stress to faculty members. Second, based on the fact that

Table 8.5.   Promotion Criteria Related to Research Funds and Publications in a
Teaching University

Research funds and projects (meet one of the two criteria)	1. Take charge of two provincial research projects or work as a key member of a national research project. 2. Get RMB 200,000 research funds in total.
Publications (meet one of the three criteria)	1. Publish 8 journal papers (first author or only author). 2. Publish 1 book (the candidate should write at least 80,000 words) and publish 5 journal papers. 3. Publish 3 journal papers that are indexed by SCI, EI, or ISTP.

Source: Website of an anonymous university.

teaching universities have less access to research funds than research universities, it's unfair to require faculty members in teaching universities to publish as many papers as their counterparts in research universities. Finally, the overemphasis on the quantity of publications may have negative effects on teaching quality.

Academic drift destroyed diversity in the higher education system. Recently, the Ministry of Education noticed this problem and decided to change the mission of 600 institutions from academic to vocational.[25] This reform will be a great challenge for faculties in these institutions, as they have to change their work pattern in the next couple of years.

INTERNATIONALIZATION

As mentioned before, China was open to and studied higher education models that originated from developed countries years ago. But this is different from the so-called internationalization of higher education that goes along with the globalization of the economy. Internationalization of higher education is a global trend in which "a country responds to the impact of globalization, yet at the same time respects the individuality of the nation" (Zha, 2003). In recent years, internationalization of higher education has attracted more and more research attention. We will analyze internationalization in Chinese HEIs from three aspects: policy, activities, and faculty's values.

Policy

To promote internationalization and attract talent from abroad, the Chinese government has launched several policies in recent years, including two famous programs: the Chang Jiang (Yangtze River) Scholars Program and the Recruitment Program of Global Experts.

In August 1998, the Ministry of Education launched the Chang Jiang Scholars Program. There were two waves to this program. The first wave started in 1998 and ended in 2003. In this wave, between 500 and 1,000 distinguished professors were selected both at home and abroad for a three-year period. Each professor was given RMB 100,000 every year. Talented scholars, who worked abroad and could not work full time for China's institutions, could be recruited as chair professors. The program established a competitive fellowship called the Chang Jiang Honorary Scholar Fellowship, and the winners received either one or a half million RMB, respectively, for first and second place.[26]

The second wave of the Chang Jiang Scholars Program started in 2004 and ended in 2007. There were several changes in this wave. First, talents from the humanities and social sciences were included in the program. Second, the quantity of chair professors was increased from 10 to 100 each year. Finally, HEIs were required to provide research funds to the professors (two million each for STEM, half a million each for humanities and social sciences).[27]

The program recruited 1,308 professors in ten years: 905 of them were from China, and the others were from abroad. 941 were Chinese, and 367 were foreigners. More than 90 percent of them have worked or studied abroad. Two hundred and fifty-nine distinguished professors and all the chair professors were recruited directly from world-class universities[28] such as Princeton, Harvard, and MIT. These international professors worked as a bridge to connect Chinese universities to institutions around the world, and they have contributed to the internationalization of Chinese higher education.

In December 2008, the general office of the Party Central Committee issued the "Decision of the Party Central Committee on Recruiting Outstanding Talents from Abroad." The Recruitment Program of Global Experts planned to recruit outstanding talent from abroad to work on key national scientific research projects, in key disciplines and labs, or to set up their own business five to ten years after their arrival in China.[29]

To attract talent from abroad, the government offered favorable conditions. For example, each candidate was given one million RMB yuan by the central government (the local government also provided some money). They were offered tax privileges, medical insurance, medical treatment, start-up funds for research, spousal work, and so on, and housing and salary (to maintain a standard of living similar to what they would have obtained abroad) were provided by the institutions.

In addition to the central government, most provincial governments also launched their own Thousand Talents Plan (see table 8.6). For example, Jiangsu

Table 8.6.   Recruitment Program of Global Experts in Provinces

Launch Year	Province
2008	Liaoning, Jilin
2009	Beijing, Tianjin, Shandong, Guangdong, Shanxi, Anhui, Henan, Hubei, Hunan, Chongqing, Sichuan, Qinghai, Ningxia, Shannxi, Yunnan
2010	Hebei, Shanghai, Zhejiang, Fujian, Jiangxi, Neimenggu, Guangxi
Number of experts recruited	Province
100	Hebei, Shanxi, Anhui, Hunan, Guangxi, Chongqing, Qinghai, Yunnan
120	Henan
200	Beijing, Shandong, Hubei, Sichuan, Ningxia, Shanxi
300	Zhejiang, Fujian, Jilin
500	Guangdong, Jiangxi, Jiangsu
1000	Tianjin, Liaoning
2000	Shanghai

Source: Shen & Zhu, 2013.

Province planned to recruit 500 experts within five years. Initially, the provincial governments intended to invest one billion Yuan into this program; in 2008, the provincial governments increased the funds from one billion to two billion Yuan. However, these policies were criticized for two main reasons. First, the experts recruited from abroad earned a much higher salary than their local colleagues at the host institution. Second, it took a long time for international experts to get used to the research climate and evaluation system in China.

Activities

In recent years, more and more activities were held to promote the internationalization of higher education in China, including recruiting foreign academics and holding international conferences. The national government, provincial governments, and HEIs provide funds for overseas exchange programs, the duration of which varies from a few months to one year. The purpose of this program is to improve academic excellence and international involvement.

Faculty Values and Behaviors

During the process of internationalization, an increasing number of faculty members realized that it was important to communicate with scholars abroad, attend international meetings, and publish their research findings abroad. They started to include international perspectives in courses. Research universities are more involved in international exchanges than teaching universities. This may enlarge the gap between the two. Many faculty members hold positive attitudes toward internationalization.

However, the extent of internationalization in the academic profession differs from institution to institution, and from discipline to discipline. For natural sciences and engineering, international and national standards are compatible, and publication in a journal published in English is quite popular. But internationalization is intertwined with localization for the humanities and social sciences. Academics in these fields focus on local issues and Chinese classics. Consequently, most publications are in Chinese. In this regard, it is hard to make an international comparison for academic excellence.

Concluding Remarks

China has made efforts to modernize its higher education system in the past century. The process can be viewed as a rational one in which the state played a pivotal role. According to Clark's (1983) taxonomy, the Chinese higher education system can be classified as a state-control type. Numerous phenomena can be interpreted from this perspective. Over the last three decades, the Chinese higher education system and the academic profession have experienced dramatic reform and change that have gradually brought in market professionalization forces. A new higher education system has evolved, shaped by a new social environment featuring marketization and internationalization.

Five transformations in higher education and their impact on the academic profession were summarized in this essay: massification, decentralization, marketization, differentiation, and internationalization. Each of these seems to be a double-edge sword providing both opportunities and challenges for the academic profession. Massification has changed the academic market and the research and teaching climate of institutions. A faculty development system is needed to meet the changing student population. The decentralization process provides provincial governments and institutions more authorities, allows institutions to make their own decisions on faculty policies, and faculty members have more freedom than before. However, the gap in research resources between national and provincial universities has grown in the process. Marketization has changed the composition of revenue. As a result, faculty are lured or forced to be involved in market activities. The differentiation policy has formed a pyramidal structure in higher education. The value and behavior of research universities have influenced those in teaching universities, which may result in decreased emphasis on teaching and publication inflation. The internationalization process has changed the research and teaching pattern of faculty members, for better or for worse. The positive aspect is that open and diverse ideas and rigorous standards and norms have been introduced into China, and Chinese academics can learn from their international counterparts in many ways; the negative aspect is that traditional fields of Chinese studies have suffered.

The change is still in process. The driving forces come from the top or the bottom, or from both. The transformation is difficult, and the new system is challenged by tensions between, for example, an emphasis on a service orientation or traditional academic authority, or between local or international standards, and there is growing resistance from lower-status institutions that are not benefiting from new government investments.

NOTES

1. See National Bureau of Statistics of China, http://data.stats.gov.cn/search.htm?s=2016 GDP (accessed February 2017).

2. We argue that China is transitioning from a traditional to a modern society. This involves institutional changes. From institutional theory, three elements of institutions are rules, norms, and cultural recognition (Scott, 2008). It can be hypothesized that cultural recognition is the most difficult to change; norms and rules follow.

3. Obviously, government agencies cover all kinds of governmental bodies at both the national level and the local level, such as the Ministry of Education. Business firms refer to factories, stores, banks, and so forth, which seek profits. Public research institutes, public universities, public schools, etc., are under the category of public enterprises, which can get financial revenue from taxation. Social organizations include private, not-for-profit organizations, such as voluntary bodies, foundations, private schools, and private universities.

4. The differences are both apparent and subtle. Civil servants get their salaries and benefits (medical care and pension) from the government budget. Employees are paid by their firms and get their benefits from the market (medical insurance). Faculty and staff in public universities get partial payment and benefits from the government budget, and partially from their universities, which have the capacity to get revenue from both public and private sources, such as research funds. Faculty and staff in private universities are more similar to employees than their counterparts in public universities.

5. Regular HEIs and adult HEIs are two types of public higher education institutions in China. Regular HEIs admit students from the traditional age cohort. In contrast, adult HEIs admit adult students. The former takes a dominant share. In this chapter, only the former is considered. In statistics, regular HEIs also cover 275 independent universities, which are private.

6. Some data are available for 2017. There are 2,631 regular HEIs (including 265 independent universities), 1,243 of them are academic oriented and 1,388 are vocational. The

number of private universities is 747, which also covers 265 independent universities. In addition, the number of adult universities is 282. See Ministry of Education, China. http://www.moe.edu.cn/jyb_sjzl/sjzl_fztjgb/201807/t20180719_343508.html (accessed August 2018).

7. Project 985 is a national effort to create world-class universities for the twenty-first century, launched on May 4, 1998.

8. All "985 Project" institutions enjoy "211 Project" status. To differentiate between them in this essay, 211 Project institutions exclude those that enjoy 985 Project status.

9. China has had the three-level degree system and postgraduate programs since 1981.

10. Peking University is a typical case that one author of this essay has experienced and was familiar with. In 2003, the administration of Peking University initiated an ambitious tenure proposal. The proposal borrowed and intended to apply a rational "up or out" scheme, meaning that an associate professor had two chances to apply for a full professor title. If he or she failed to achieve this target, he or she would be fired. This radical scheme was controversial and unpopular among some faculty members, especially those in the humanities. This led to a major adjustment of the original plan. In 2014, the university started a new reform scheme, which seemed to be milder and more incremental. This is still going on. Any fair judgment seems to be too early.

11. A typical Chinese university comprises three levels: the university center, a school or college, and the department. In some universities, department and school are at the same level. In addition, some institutes and centers are created for research. Usually the teaching unit and the research unit are intertwined.

12. Ministry of Education, http://www.moe.gov.cn/s78/A02/zfs__left/s5911/moe_619/201512/t20151228_226196.html (accessed February 2017).

13. China Ministry of Education, http://www.moe.edu.cn/publicfiles/business/htmlfiles/moe/moe_573/200505/7679.html (accessed May 2014).

14. China Ministry of Education, http://www.moe.edu.cn/publicfiles/business/htmlfiles/moe/s7567/201309/156873.html (accessed May 2014).

15. In the 1990s, efficiency was a hot topic in higher education research; quality is the current issue.

16. China Ministry of Education, http://www.moe.edu.cn/publicfiles/business/htmlfiles/moe/moe_633/201203/132634.html (accessed May 2014).

17. The survey is a part of a comparative research project called "The Changing Academic Profession of Asia" led by Hiroshima University. The survey was conducted by the Graduate School of Education, Peking University in 2012 and investigated faculty members in 28 four-year universities; the total sample size was 2,474. All the survey data mentioned in this article are from this project.

18. China Ministry of Education, http://old.moe.gov.cn/publicfiles/business/htmlfiles/moe/s8492/list.html (accessed August 2015).

19. Calculated by raw data (470,339/967,778)*100 (Ministry of Education, China, 1992).

20. *China Educational Finance Statistical Yearbook 2015* (Beijing: China Statistics Press).

21. Source: *China Educational Finance Statistical Yearbook 2015* (Beijing: China Statistics Press). *Educational Statistics Yearbook of China 2015* (Beijing: People's Education Press).

22. Name list of 211 Project universities, Ministry of Education, http://www.moe.gov
.cn/publicfiles/business/htmlfiles/moe/moe_1680/201002/xxgk_82762.html (accessed
May 2014).

23. Over 10 billion yuan to be invested in 211 Project, http://english.people.com.cn
/90001/6381319.html (accessed May 2014).

24. International Rankings and Chinese Higher Education Reform, WENR World Education News + Reviews, Oct. 1, 2016, http://www.wes.org/ewenr/06oct/practical.htm
(accessed May 2014).

25. Ma Xiaoqian, "More than 600 Higher Education Institutions Have Been Transformed to Vocational Education," sohu, March 22, 2014, http://learning.sohu.com
/20140322/n397039059.shtml (accessed August 2015).

26. A document for the tenth annual meeting for Chang Jiang Honorary Scholar Fellowship, by Xuelinhua, Ministry of Education, China, http://www.moe.gov.cn/publicfiles
/business/htmlfiles/moe/moe_2566/200812/42137.html (accessed May 2014).

27. Ibid.

28. Build a team with outstanding talents in higher education institutions: the talk of
state councilors Zhili Chen on the meeting of Chang Jiang scholars, website of Ministry
of Education, China, March 28, 2005, http://www.moe.gov.cn/publicfiles/business
/htmlfiles/moe/moe_694/200506/9812.html (accessed May 2014).

29. The introduction to the Recruitment Program of Global Experts, 1000 Talents plan,
December 2008, http://www.1000plan.org/qrjh/section/2?m=rcrd (accessed May 2014).

REFERENCES

Altbach, Philip G., and Jane Knight. 2007. "The Internationalization of Higher Education: Motivations and Realities." *Journal of Studies in International Education* 11,
no. 3–4:290–305.
Ben-David, Joseph. 1977. *Centers of Learning: Britain, France, Germany, United States.* New
York: McGraw-Hill.
Cai, Yuzhuo, and Fengqiao Yan. 2011. "Organizational Diversity in Chinese Private Higher
Education." In *Public Vices, Private Virtues? Assessing the Effects of Marketization in Higher
Education,* ed. Pedro N. Teixeira and David D. Dill, 47–66. Rotterdam: Sense
Publishers.
———. 2015. "Demands and Responses in Chinese Higher Education." In *Higher Education in the BRICS Countries: Investigating the Pact between Higher Education and Society,*
ed. Simon Schwarzman, Romulo Pinheiro, and Pundy Pillay, 149–70. Dordrecht, Netherlands: Springer Science and Business Media.
———. F. 2017. "Universities and Higher Education." In *Handbook of Education in China,*
ed. W. John Morgan. Cheltenham, UK: Edward Elgar.
Clark, Burton R. 1983. *The Higher Education System: Academic Organization in Cross-National
Perspective.* Berkeley: University of California Press.
DiMaggio, Paul J., and Walter W. Powell. 1983. "The Iron Cage Revisited: Institutional Isomorphism and Collective Rationality. *American Sociological Review* 42, no. 2:147–60.
Educational Statistic Yearbook of China. 2010. Beijing: People's Education Press.

Guo, H. 2004. 20 shiji 90 niandai zhongguo gaodeng jiaoyu jingfei de laiyuan goucheng bianhua qushi [The tendency of changes of funding sources of Chinese higher education in 1990s]. *Economics of Education Research* 2, no. 2. http://www.gse.pku.edu.cn /BeidaEER/pdf/040207.pdf.

Hayhoe, Ruth. 1996. *China's Universities, 1895–1995: A Century of Cultural Conflict*. New York: Garland.

Hayhoe, Ruth, Jun Li, Jing Lin, and Qiang Zha. 2011. *Portraits of 21st Century Chinese Universities: In the Move to Mass Higher Education*. Dordrecht, Netherlands: Springer Science and Business Media.

Huo, B. Z 1993. Fang quan jian kong zhuan xing gao xiao jiao shi zhi wu pin ren zhi hong guan guan li zhi tan tao [Decentralization, oversight and transformation: The discussion on macroscopic management mechanism of faculty promotion and appointment in higher education]. *Jiangsu Higher Education* 2: 27–30.

Li, L. Q. 2003. *Li lan qing jiao yu fang tan lu [On education: Interview with Li Langqing]*. Beijing: People's Education Press.

Li, Li Xu. 2004. "China's Higher Education Reform 1998–2003: A Summary." *Asia Pacific Education Review* 5, no. 1:14–22.

Mazzolini, Elizabeth. 2003. Review of *Academic Capitalism: Politics, Policies and the Entrepreneurial University. Workplace: A Journal for Academic Labor* 10:196–97.

Min, W. F. 2002. *Gao deng jiao yu yun xing ji zhi yan jiu [The study of higher education mechanism]*. Beijing: People's Education Press.

Ministry of Education, China. 1991. *Educational Statistics Yearbook of China 1990*. Beijing: People's Press.

———. 1992. *Educational Statistics Yearbook of China, 1991–1992*. Beijing: People's Education Press.

———. 2015a. *Educational Statistics Yearbook of China 2014*. Beijing: People's Press.

———. 2015b. *China Educational Finance Statistical Yearbook 2015*. Beijing: China Statistics Press.

Mok, Ka Ho. 1996. "Marketization and Decentralization: Development of Education and Paradigm Shift in Social Policy." *Hong Kong Public Administration* 5, no. 1:35–56.

———. 1997a. Privation or Marketization: Educational Development in Post-Mao China. *International Review of Education* 43, nos. 5–6:547–67.

———. 1997b. "Professional Autonomy and Private Education in Guangdong Province." Leeds East Asia Papers 41.

———. 2000. "Marketizing Higher Education in Post-Mao China." *International Journal of Educational Development* 20, no. 2:109–26.

———. 2002. "Policy of Decentralization and Changing Governance of Higher Education in Post-Mao China." *Public Administration and Development* 22, no. 3:261–73.

Musselin, Christine. 2010. *The Market for Academics*. New York: Routledge.

Pfeffer, Jeffrey, and Gerald R. Salancik. 1978. *The External Control of Organizations*. New York: Harper and Row.

Scott, W. Richard. 2008. *Institutions and Organizations: Ideas and Interests*. 3rd ed. Thousand Oaks, CA: Sage.

Shen, Yue Qing, and Jun Wen Zhu. 2013. "The Provincial Comparative Analysis of Global Experts Import Policies in China." www.scgti.org/zyx/shenyue.pdf.

Trow, Martin A. 1973. *Problems in the Transition from Elite to Mass Higher Education*. Berkeley, CA: McGraw-Hill.

Walder, Andrew G. 1986. *Communist Neo-Traditionalism: Work and Authority in Chinese Industry*. Berkeley: University of California Press.

Yan, Fengqiao. 2000. "The Theory of Transaction Cost and Choosing Appropriate Reform Models for the Higher Education Administrative System in China." *Current Issues in Chinese Higher Education*. Institutional Management in Higher Education, OECD, 45–54.

———. 2009. "Policies on Private Education: An Economics Analysis." *Chinese Education and Society* 42, no. 6:30–39.

———. 2010a. "The Academic Profession in China in the Context of Social Transition: An Institutional Perspective." *European Review* 18, supp. 1:99–116.

———. 2010b. "The Academic Profession in China in the Context of Social Transition: An Institutional Perspective." *European Review* 18, no. 1:99–116.

———. 2013a. "The Spread of Western Learning to the East and the Formation of the Modern Chinese Academic Profession." In *The Changing Academic Profession in Asia: Teaching, Research, Governance and Management*, report of the International Conference on the Changing Academic Profession Project, 37–50. Hiroshima: Research Institute for Higher Education, Hiroshima University.

———. 2013b. "The Same Term but Different Connotations: Cultural and Historical Perspectives on Studying the Academic Profession in China and Other Asian Countries." *Frontiers of Education in China* 8, no 2:198–213.

Yan, Fengqiao, and Jing Lin. 2010. "Commercial Civil Society: A Perspective on Private Higher Education in China." *Frontiers of Education in China* 5, no. 4:558–78.

Yan, Fengqiao, Dan Mao, and Qiang Zha. 2014. "Institutional Transformation and Aggregate Expansion of Chinese Higher Education System." In *Spotlight on China: Changes in Education under China's Market Economy*, ed. S. B. Guo, 191–213. Rotterdam: SensePublishers.

Zha, Qiang. 2003. "Internationalization of Higher Education: Towards a Conceptual Framework." *Policy Futures in Education* 1, no. 2:248–70.

———. 2009. "Diversification or Homogenization: How Governments and Markets Have Combined to (Re)shape Chinese Higher Education in Its Recent Massification Process." *Higher Education* 58, no. 1:41–58.

Zhang, J. 2006. *Gao Deng Jiao Yu Ti Zhi Yan Jiu* [The study of higher education system]. Beijing: Education Science Press.

Zhao, Juming. 2006. "Jingying Zhuyi yu Danwei Zhidu: Dui Zhongguo Daxue zuzhi yu Guanli de Anli Yanjiu" [Collective elitism and Danwei: A case study of Chinese university]. *Peking University Education Review* 1:173–91.

9 | Japan

Opening Up the Academic Labor Market

AKIYOSHI YONEZAWA

The history of the modern higher education system in Japan is relatively short, at least compared with that in North America and Europe. However, Japan has established academic communities with a strong sense of decentralized and research-oriented autonomy and collegiality (Ehara, 1998). From the point of view of Japanese academics, the current global trends toward managerialism, corporatization, and marketization are largely perceived as a threat to the existing autonomous culture protected at the school and department levels (Hirota, 2013). At the same time, new opportunities are opening up for academics from more diverse backgrounds assuming more diverse roles. The pace of academic internationalization is posing adjustment challenges to traditional modes of operation in historically closed academic communities (Poole, 2010). However, it is also evident that the working environment of especially young academics at universities in Japan is changing rapidly (Horta, Sato & Yonezawa, 2011).

In 2016, Japan had 86 national, 91 local public, and 600 private universities. The share of students enrolled in private universities differs, from 77.6 percent at the undergraduate level, 34.3 percent at the master level, and 25 percent at the doctoral level. This symbolizes the general characteristics of the private university sector that absorbs the market demand for higher learning. While a few prestigious private universities are active in research, especially in social sciences and applied sciences, most of the high-level research activities and research training are implemented at around 10 prestigious national universities, including 7 former imperial universities. Adding to the universities, 341 junior colleges (324 are private), 57 colleges of technology (3 are private), and 2,817 professional training colleges (2,622 are private) provide tertiary education programs (i.e., associate degrees and diplomas).

This chapter examines the national context of the academic profession in Japan. Fiscal limits (and an impending demographic decline) are constraining the growth of the academic profession; at the same time, work pressures are also increasing with new demands for attention to teaching. The basic organization of this chapter involves four major components: (a) Historical development, pre-1980, (including pre-World War II national universities and private-sector and American-imposed reforms after World War II); (b) liberal reforms pushed in the 1980s during Japan's economic boom, but largely not implemented until the 1990s (e.g., emergence of graduate education, modification of the chair system, criticism of inbreeding, and an effort to open up the academic marketplace, including a contract system and granting corporate status to national universities); (c) current challenges, including demographic changes in aging, declining international competitiveness in research, and a declining academic opportunity structure; and (d) most recent reforms, especially the push for top universities by the government to open up the academic labor market to international competition. As a conclusion, the author recommends a deeper examination of the well-being of the academic profession and institutional autonomy through links with the international academic community.

Historical Legacy

The traditional identity of the academic in Japan is based on the historical legacy of the academic profession before and just after World War II. This historical context is still influential among current university professors, partly due to the high-level dominance of the national academic labor market by alumni networks from the small group of universities with long histories and high prestige. However, the gap between these historical images of the academic profession and current self-image is increasing through the emergence of nontraditional types of academics and the rapidly changing work environment.

The history of modern Japanese universities started with the establishment of the University of Tokyo, the first national university, in 1877. The University of Tokyo first employed experts from overseas as university teachers but replaced them around ten years later with Japanese academics who had been sent to study in North America and Europe (Nakayama, 1989). The second university, Kyoto

University, was founded in 1897, and its professors were mainly appointed from among the alumni of the University of Tokyo (Yonezawa, 2015). In 1919, the Japanese government officially authorized private universities. However, several private higher education institutions, such as Keio University, claim that their origin in 1858 goes back before the national universities were established. At private universities, alumni often took leading roles as stewards of the institutional missions set by the founders.

The first presidents of the University of Tokyo, as well as the professors, were appointed by the Japanese government. However, gradually, the national universities gained autonomy in recruiting academic staff, appointing deans by school-level election at the level of academic unit known as the "faculty," and finally electing university presidents, starting at Kyoto University in 1919. Through this process, the faculties at universities acquired strong collegial decision-making power, not only in academic affairs but also in the recruitment and promotion of faculty members (Terasaki, 2000)—effectively resembling the German universities on which they were modeled. At private universities, governance patterns were highly diversified because private universities, in general, were more independent from government control than national universities.

Autonomy of the Professoriate Established by the Post–World War II Regime

During the Second Sino-Japanese War and World War II (1937–45), Japanese universities gradually strengthened their collaborative relations with the wartime government. As a result, some academics were forced to leave universities because freedom of speech was not assured during the war (Shogimen, 2014). Even students were drafted into the army and forced to support the wartime regime.

After World War II, comprehensive educational reform occurred under the supervision of the General Headquarters of the Supreme Commander for the Allied Powers (GHQ/SCAP). Through this reform, Japanese universities were given strong autonomy to "democratize" Japanese society and the education system (Shibata, 2005). Notably, the then-enacted School Education Law required universities to set *Kyojukai* (school-level faculty meetings) to examine important items in the school, faculty, and even university (Yonezawa, 2014a). The deans of schools and the presidents of all national universities were elected mainly by faculty members. While the election of the deans and presidents had been in practice before World War II, the legal authorization of decision-making power by *Kyojukai* after the war was an important change in protecting collegial autonomy by the professoriate. This legal framework continued until all national universities transitioned by law into corporate bodies in 2004. Even today, most national universities continue to implement voting to "refer" the candidates preferred by faculty members; however, sometimes, presidential selection committees make decisions that differ from the voting results. Many private universities, especially the prestigious ones, also follow the custom of the election of deans and presidents (Poole, 2010).

University academics also enjoyed a very stable employment status from after World War II until almost the end of the twentieth century. Faculty members of national universities and local public universities possessed a highly protected civil servant status until it changed in 2004 to employees of national or local public university corporations (Newby, Weko, Breneman, Johanneson & Maassen, 2009).

Faculty members of private universities possessed the employee status of non-profit "school corporations." In general, however, the status of faculty members at private universities was equally stable. Private universities in Japan developed as safety valves for preserving the public sector by absorbing the excess demand for higher education. Especially after the mid-1970s, the government strengthened its support and control of private universities as part of its national higher education planning (Yonezawa, 2013). Until around the mid-1990s, it was very rare that private universities closed, as the higher education market faced excess demand (Kitamura, 1997).

DIVERSIFICATION AND MASSIFICATION AFTER WORLD WAR II

After World War II, the new university system moved in the direction of the model of the US system, and the number of universities increased significantly from 48 in 1945 under the old system to 201 in 1950 under the new system to 777 in 2016. Accordingly, the number of university faculty members also increased from 12,859 in 1945 to 19,332 in 1950 and 184,264 in 2016, according to the School Basic Survey by the Ministry of Education, Culture, Sports, Science and Technology (MEXT). During this time period, the diverse characteristics of the academic profession became apparent (Cummings & Amano, 1977).

First, through the postwar reform, various types of public and private polytechnics and high schools that offered pre-university general education (gymnasium) were upgraded and merged into universities. Therefore, the teaching staff of these nonuniversity institutions were also upgraded to university professors. Especially among the newly established and upgraded private universities, the image of universities and the academic profession on the part of the university managers and staff was frequently quite different from the image of the highly respected profession at the universities established before World War II.

Second, through the transformation into a system that emulated the United States, the government required that universities introduce general education as part of undergraduate education. At national universities, it was common to set up *Kyoyobu* (a division of liberal arts or general education) and assign faculty members to teach general education. At private universities, faculty members of general education typically were assigned to specialized schools; for example, a professor of physical education, as part of general education, could be assigned to the school of law. Especially at the national universities, the distinction was visible and substantial between faculties affiliated with the general education divisions and other faculties who primarily supervised senior and graduate students.

Third, through the rapid economic development in the 1960s, Japanese higher education expanded significantly. Enrollment at many private universities increased, and the university professors' teaching load became heavy (Ogata, 1977). At many national and local public and private universities, especially the leading ones, massive student movements protested not only political issues, such as the United States–Japan Security Treaty and the Vietnam War, but also the improvement of the learning environment by changing policies on university governance, tuition, fees, and so on. Presidents, governing board members, professors, and other academic staff were also involved in these academic conflicts (Osaki, 1999).

Finally, since the mid-1980s, a further mushrooming of new universities occurred, mostly by upgrading and transforming women's junior colleges and special training colleges that offered vocational postsecondary programs into small coeducational universities (Yonezawa, 2014b). These universities tended to have narrow local student markets or niche vocational fields and tended to be financially unstable because of the shortage of enrollments. Faculty members in these universities also tended to have more diverse backgrounds academically and professionally (Ichikawa, 1995).

DOMINANCE OF THE ALUMNI NETWORK AMID MASSIFICATION

The hierarchical structure of Japanese higher education has been dominated by a small number of alumni networks (Shimbori, 1981). Fujimura (2005) points out that half of the academic staff of universities in Japan were the alumni of only five universities out of 250 in 1961 and 12 universities out of 669 in 2001. Since the beginning of the modern university, Japanese universities have tended to recruit alumni to inherit an academic circle based on the German chair system. Even under the new higher education system after World War II, this chair system was passed down from the former imperial universities that had been founded as national flagship higher education institutions before World War II. Cummings (1990) reports that academic "bosses" at the prestigious universities continued to dominate the recruitment of new faculties in respective academic fields without an open search. Shimbori (1981) also points out that alumni networks dominated hiring, not only for their own university graduates but also for positions at other universities. Conversely, the absolute majority of national and local public and private universities established after World War II introduced program-based teaching bodies.

The domination of academic oligarchs and alumni networks has inevitably led to a high proportion of alumni among the faculty members of their alma mater and to the "colonization," monopoly, or oligopoly of faculty who graduated from a specific university at other universities that do not produce researchers.

There are several reasons this domination of university alumni and academic oligarchs was possible (Yonezawa, 2015). First, at least before World War II, universities tended to regard the recruitment of alumni as a sign that the university had the capacity to foster the next generation of researchers under their university identity. Second, only a limited number of universities systematically produced the next generation of researchers. Third, the proportion and influence of Japanese researchers who studied abroad and returned to Japan was limited, compared with other non-Western countries such as South Korea (Yonezawa, Horta & Osawa, 2016). Therefore, the highly limited international academic mobility of Japanese academics maintained the traditional power relationships. Fourth, a very strong autonomous decision-making power for academic personnel decisions was given to the school-level professoriate. The tradition of electing deans through voting by school faculty members also may have strengthened the network-based recruitment and promotion of academic staff. Last, open searches for academics through public announcements of vacant positions spread gradually beginning in the 1970s, but it was not common among prestigious universities until the end of the 1980s (Yamanoi, 1998). For those outside a specific academic network, it was impossible to learn about available jobs, especially at prestigious universities that had strong alumni networks.

The alumni networks at the prestigious research universities that produce the next generation of researchers have infiltrated the non-elite universities as well (which function as colonies of these prestigious universities) through the "closed" hiring process, thus contributing to academic underperformance. Individual-level competition does not exist due to the closed networks. At the same time, the dominance of the graduates of prestigious research universities in the academic labor market in effect spread the research-oriented culture toward a wide range of academics at various types of universities. An analysis of international surveys showed that, in the balance of teaching and research, academics in Japan maintained a strong research preference compared with those of other countries (Shin, Arimoto, Cummings & Teichler, 2014).

The Academic Profession after University Reforms of the 1980s and 1990s

In the 1980s, a series of reforms in Japanese higher education were initiated by the government and universities. These reforms, many of which were not fully implemented until the 1990s, included a new focus on graduate education, modification of the chair system, constraints on growth (experienced primarily at the bottom of the rank hierarchy in terms of entry-level opportunity or lack thereof), establishment of a contract system (intended as much to "open up" the academic marketplace as to reduce inbreeding and dominance of the elite national universities), development of open search mechanisms for faculty positions, establishment of entry-level research positions, and efforts to support internationalization and university-industry linkages.

First, in 1984, the Nakasone Cabinet started the Provisional Council of Educational Reform to seek a vision of the future of education (Hood, 2003). By the mid-1980s, Japan had become a leading economy, and the country's economic and social development were directed at catching up with the industrial countries in North America and Europe. Consequently, the government and universities focused on a post-catch-up agenda that included the education system.

Second, the development of information and communication technology transformed the global economy to one based on knowledge. Since the success of the Japanese economy was based on science and technology, universities needed to take a more active role in basic and applied sciences, beyond the commitment of individual professors (Branscomb, Kodama & Florida, 1999).

Third, the Cold War ended with the dissolution of the Soviet Union in 1991. China started economic reforms by introducing a market economy in 1978, and the political influence of the Japanese teachers' union, which had had strong links with communist and socialist parties, weakened. In this context, the ideas of neoliberalism and new public management drew great attention in policy dialogues in higher education (Schoppa, 2002); however, the results of these discussions translating into substantial policy change only came about much later.

Lastly, demographic factors influenced educational reforms. Since the end of the 1980s, the first Baby Boomers—those who had been born during the latter half of the 1940s—became the leading generation in the policy making and management of universities. The academics, administrators, and policy makers of this generation had participated in student movements as university students around 1970 and tended to be the parents of the second Baby Boomer university students. Compared with the previous generation, the first Baby Boomers tended to have critical views of the traditional image of universities as ivory towers and were committed more actively to university reforms (Amano, 2001).

EXPANSION AND TRANSFORMATION OF GRADUATE EDUCATION

As a part of the university reforms, the tradition of academic oligarchs and university alumni dominating the academic profession was questioned. Until the reforms, the chair system, which was based on the German tradition and which was still operative among the former imperial universities, and their alumni continued to dominate the academic labor market. The academics of those former imperial universities were affiliated with *Gakubu*, the undergraduate school, as full-time faculty. The de facto final decisions for recruiting new faculty members and promoting existing faculty and deans were made by voting at faculty meetings, though they are officially appointed by the presidents. Only full professors were official members of faculty meetings, but many other schools allowed or required associate professors and other junior faculty members to attend and vote.

In the traditional chair system, each chair has one full professor, one or two associate professors, and research associates. The full professor tends to have absolute power in the personnel decisions regarding the junior faculty in his or her chair. The students usually belong to the same chair from their undergraduate through their doctorate programs and dream of being selected as a research associate of the same chair, being promoted to associate professor of the same chair, and then inheriting the chair as a full professor. Otherwise, academics wait for suggestions or arrangements made by the full professor of their alma mater ("academic oligarch") about where to work. If an academic does not obey the decision of the academic oligarch, the academic may make countless enemies in his or her academic circle and even within the alumni circle in a wide range of academic fields. If an academic votes against the personnel decisions of other chairs at the same school, a similar thing will happen to his or her chair as retaliation.

Through the examination of US universities, the experts of higher education in Japan considered it important to separate undergraduate (college) educational programs and academic organizations (departments) at comprehensive research universities. To create a system that fit the new "global" environment, two major reforms to strengthen graduate education were implemented in the 1990s among the national research universities with chair systems. First, the affiliation of the majority of the faculty members was changed from undergraduate schools to graduate schools. Second, the chair system, with one professor and other junior staff, was transformed into a large chair system that has many full professors and other junior faculty members (Ogawa, 2002).

With the modification of the chair system, graduate education became the core of faculty members' work. Likewise, personnel decisions started to involve faculty members from more diverse fields, which broadened the perspective on hiring decisions. Typically, however, a professor of the former chair system continued to teach undergraduate, graduate, and doctoral candidates. As an unintended consequence of these reforms, at least as viewed by the academics, the number of graduate students per faculty member increased substantially, thus increasing the teaching load of the faculty members even as more diverse graduate students enrolled in the graduate schools. This diversity gradually changed the nature of graduate education into professional education instead of academic training, especially in the fields of science, technology, engineering, and mathematics (STEM). In other words, the government succeeded in expanding graduate education with a relatively small increase in public spending.

General Education Reforms

As previously mentioned, general education began to be a required part of undergraduate education as a legal regulation after World War II, and some faculty members were affiliated with the general education division or assigned to teach mainly general education subjects. Until the 1980s, faculty members who taught general education were in many cases not allowed to supervise senior-year students and graduate students, and those professors' education and research budgets were lower than those of faculty members in specialized schools or subjects.

In 1991, the standards for establishing universities set by the government were amended, and the new guideline abolished the general education requirement (Yoshida, 2002). This amendment gave more flexibility to universities in assigning faculty members, and most universities abolished the official distinction between faculty members who taught general education and those who taught in specific fields. Many faculty members who had previously taught only general education now began supervising senior students and graduate students. The complete abolishment of general education, however, was not realistic since most universities were committed to having some form of general education—in many cases focused more on basic skills development and preparation for individual learning, which are not necessarily taught at the secondary level in Japan. Operationally, many universities required that all faculty members be committed to general education or some type of introductory education for first- and second-year students, typically by rotation.

FIXED-TERM EMPLOYMENT

No clear legal base for fixed-term employment was established until 1997. As mentioned earlier, at national and local public universities, full-time academic staff had civil servant status until 2004, which meant that, technically, all academic staff enjoyed job security until retirement age, which was set at around 60 to 65 years of age, depending on the university. In practice, however, fixed-term appointments were often made based on internal regulation by the universities, especially for junior staff members such as research associates. At private universities, fixed-term appointments were more common, especially among language teachers with non-Japanese citizenship or older professors who were recruited after they had retired from national universities or secondary schools.

Job security from the research-associate level until retirement age often raised serious problems. Especially in the STEM fields, if a chair professor changed, the whole research and education policy often changed. Usually, junior staff members, especially research associates, were encouraged to leave or voluntarily left the university, in many cases by getting new jobs suggested or arranged by academic oligarchs. In some cases, this system did not work. For example, if a research associate had not published for a long time and could not get another job, the university did not promote him or her but could not dismiss him or her either. This also occurred when a chair professor did not give a younger staff member the appropriate environment in which to conduct research. More seriously, some research associates had protested as members of student movements or conducted research that opposed industrial policies, such as pollution, and then stayed for a long period without the possibility of being promoted.

To encourage mobility among academics, the government promoted fixed-term contracts, referring to the US fixed-term contract system that leads to tenure. Open University Japan, established as a government project in 1983, introduced fixed-term contracts for all staff members, including full professors. Some professors sued the university because their contacts were not renewed without clear reasons (Usami & Fukaya, 1989). The Act on Fixed-Term Contracts for Teaching Staff was enacted in 1997, and national and local public and private universities were legally allowed to introduce fixed-term contracts for positions that needed diverse human resources, research associate positions, and positions set up for specific projects with fixed terms. The increase in the 1980s on the reliance of project-based funds for research and education activities also accelerated the use of fixed-term contracts. The *Asahi Shimbun* ("Universities Hire 63%," 2016) pointed out that the share of academic staff at national universities under fixed-term contracts reached 63 percent among those under 40 years old, according to the MEXT. Some warned that, under the fixed-term contract system, researchers would likely lose long-term perspective in their academic activity and the concentration of power among deans and other senior managers would damage academic collegiality.

Obstacles to the Diversification of Academic Staff: Internationalization and Links to Industry

For diverse higher-education functions and stakeholders, the government and universities also felt the need to diversify the profile of higher education. Based on the success of the manufacturing industry, the Japanese government and universities tried to take a leading international role in science and technology. At the beginning of the 1980s, as the main policy for the internationalization of higher education, the government tried to encourage the recruitment of non-Japanese citizens. At national and local public universities, however, it was impossible for non-Japanese citizens who were regular faculty members to become professors or associate professors because faculty members' status as civil servants did not allow the employment of non-Japanese citizens in principle. Before that time, most non-Japanese faculty members were employed as language teachers, and the employment of foreign academics in other fields was limited. Korean and Chinese citizens with permanent residential status had lived in Japan at the time Japan invaded and colonized those countries. These citizens, born and raised in Japan, were not given the opportunity to become senior faculty members at national and local public universities. This situation was criticized as an obstacle to the internationalization of Japanese higher education, and led to a debate for legal amendments (Kitamura, 1983). In 1982, it became legally possible for national and local public universities to employ non-Japanese faculty members as professors, associate professors, and lecturers. After that, the number of non-Japanese faculty members increased significantly, especially in the STEM fields. However, the majority of those who worked in the STEM fields had received advanced degrees at Japanese universities (Yonezawa, Ishida & Horta, 2013). This is partly because the majority of universities implement faculty member meetings and administrative procedures in Japanese. Therefore, non-Japanese citizens must have sufficient communication skills in the Japanese language.

Second, the other major historical issue for the academic profession in Japan was gender balance. The enrollment rate at four-year universities faced a gender gap, partly because junior colleges served as short-term higher education institutions for women. The gender imbalance was evident among senior academics. The hierarchical structure of the chair system was also held up as an obstacle for female researchers (Normile, 2001). Under government policy guidelines, many universities took action to create gender equity. In 2000, the Japan Association of National Universities (JANU) set up numerical targets, such as increasing the percentage of female academics to 20 percent by 2010; however, in 2010, the percentage was 12.7 percent (JANU, 2011). Although the situation is changing gradually, this issue remains a big concern among academics and university managers.

Third, the lack of mobility between the industrial world and the academic world has been a big concern for universities and industry (Cao, Iguchi, Harayama & Nagahira, 2005). Although in Japan the investment in science and technology as a whole is high, the proportion of this investment in universities has been limited. Under the Science and Technology Basic Law enacted in 1995, the government encouraged joint research between universities and industry. Then, the Industrial Technology Enhancement Act, enacted in 2000, enabled faculty members at national universities to take concurrent management positions at private enterprises.

In the wider context, the government had amended the Standard for Establishment of Universities in 1985, allowing the appointment of professors and associate professors based on professional degrees and experience, or without academic degrees and achievement. In 2004, the government established a professional graduate school system (e.g., law schools and teacher-training graduate schools) separate from existing academic graduate schools and required that 30 percent or more of those faculty members have professional experience. In the case of law schools, "practitioner" faculty members could be professionals, such as lawyers or judges, without necessarily having to have written academic publications.

Lastly, various types of university services experts have been hired as faculty members, partly because of the generalist-oriented university administration. For example, Tohoku University, a national comprehensive research university, set up the Institute for Excellence in Higher Education, which employs service experts of institutional research, student exchange, faculty and staff development, student health care, and counseling as professors, associate professors, and other categories of faculty members. Most teach at schools or in general education programs and are allowed to conduct research.

RESEARCH ASSOCIATES TO POSTDOCTORAL FELLOWS

In the traditional chair system at prestigious national universities, each chair professor was supported by one associate professor and one or more research associates who were expected to support the activities of the chair. In the 1980s, because of budget austerity, the government introduced a national plan to decrease the number of national civil servants and workers at government institutions. At the university level, however, the number of professors at national universities actually increased, partly because of newly emerging fields and partly to provide positions to which existing junior faculty members could be promoted. To comply with the national plan, instead of reducing the number of professors, national universities tended to reduce the number of research associates and administrative staff members. This meant that the first job opportunities for young researchers decreased. Even if they did become research associates, the number of senior members those research associates had to support increased significantly, which led to more difficulty in securing time for the research necessary for job promotion.

In 1996, as a policy for promoting science and technology, the government started a scheme to increase the number of postdoctoral fellows from 3,050 in 1995 to 10,000 by 2000. While universities have increased the positions through project funds, most of these postdoctoral fellows have been employed by a government organization called the Japan Society for the Promotion of Science (JSPS), which employs young researchers based on research proposal applications. The JSPS postdoctoral research fellows conduct research under the supervision of faculty members at universities and other research institutes. In this system, young researchers can concentrate on their research and do not have to provide support for senior faculty members. At the same time, however, there is no assurance of getting a faculty position after the postdoctoral fellows' contract ends.

Open Job Searches

Job vacancies were not announced publicly, especially among prestigious universities with a long history, as previously mentioned. However, new universities started to search publicly for candidates by sending letters to other universities through the process of higher education expansion (Yamanoi, 1998). To promote open job searches, the government provided a web-based database of academic job vacancies, beginning in 1997 (Yonezawa, 2015). In 2013, 25,611 job vacancies were announced on the Japan Research Career Information Network (JREC-IN) by the Japanese Science and Technology Agency (JST), a government agency for promoting science and technology, and recorded 18,078 accesses to the database.

This system has had a significant impact on the recruitment of academics in Japan. The influence of alumni networks and academic oligarchs may remain to some degree, but it is becoming more difficult to justify not using the open search system. The JREC-IN web database is provided in English and Japanese. Partly encouraged by the government, many prestigious universities are now implementing open international job searches (Yonezawa, 2015).

Challenges Due to Demographic Changes and Globalization

Challenges

Based on an analysis of the survey data from the Changing Academic Profession, 2007–8, Arimoto, Cummings, Huang, and Shin (2015) reported that the transformation toward a more open and mobile academic market is occurring through various reforms at the policy and institutional levels. Japan has entered the global competition in education and research. At the same time, Japan is facing an aging population, and this phenomenon has a significant impact on the number of students and also the demographics of academics at the universities.

First, it is becoming more difficult to get a regular faculty position at Japanese universities (Horta, Sato & Yonezawa, 2011). The number of undergraduate and graduate students started to decrease in 2012. Although the number of faculty members at the national level is still slightly increasing, the saturation, or even shrinkage, of the higher education market is becoming a reality. At most research universities, the number of academic staff is still increasing. However, many job opportunities are based on fixed-term project funding.

Second, Japan is losing international competitiveness in research productivity at the macro level. Japan's overall share of the world's annual scientific literature has been decreasing since 2000 (Adams, King, Miyairi & Pendlebury, 2010), especially in the research productivity of midrange national universities, which has declined significantly (Toyoda, 2012). The growth of research publications with international coauthors is far behind other leading countries, and this lag has led to substantial obstacles in research performance in Japan (Saka & Kuwahara, 2013). This stagnation or decline in research productivity has been blamed on insufficient financial investment in research conducted at midrange universities and the overconcentration of financial allocation to top universities. The pressure to publish articles and secure research funding is increasing, while systemic guidance and assessment of strategic publication is not well developed.

Third, the teaching and administrative load is heavier and becoming a serious obstacle to research (National Institute of Science and Technology Policy [NISTEP], 2014). Whether the universities are elite, mass, or universal, the universities' and government's emphasis on teaching has increased. By around 2000, quality assurance in higher education was a hot debate internationally, and the Japanese government started to require institution-level accreditation for all universities and colleges. At the same time, the number of secondary education graduates began decreasing at the beginning of the 1990s, and by the end of the 1990s there was an oversupply of university openings. Less prestigious universities faced applicant shortages, and even among elite universities, remedial education and first-year education were needed as they drew deeper into the dwindling applicant pool. Academics in Japan are required to commit more time to teaching activities, such as creating a syllabus and participating in faculty development programs, student recruitment, job placement, and the like. Teaching assistants are allocated by the universities, and computer-based learning assessment systems have been introduced at many universities. However, in general, the expectations for commitment to instructional or teaching activities are higher than before.

Fourth, strengthening the international profiles of universities in Japan, especially in teaching activities, has become an urgent agenda item (Arimoto, Cummings, Huang & Shin, 2015; Ishikawa, 2011). Compared with other leading countries, top universities in Japan have weak international profiles: the proportion of classes offered in English is limited, as is the proportion of international students and faculty members. This is because of a very strong tradition of fostering the next generation of researchers within the country and the influence of alumni networks on academic recruitment. A systematic approach for improving the international profiles of faculty members is required.

Finally, the uncertainty of career prospects for young academics is becoming a social issue (Horta, Sato & Yonezawa, 2011). Although the opportunities for obtaining postdoctoral fellowships have increased, many graduates of these programs face difficulties getting permanent jobs after that. To provide a career path that leads to long-term employment, the government and universities have started to provide a "tenure track" program. In this system, academics are recruited as assistant professors first for a fixed term, and after a performance assessment, tenure-eligible positions are provided. This program is regarded as a strong tool for securing the next generation of research talent in a context of severe competition, not only within the academic world, but also across the various disciplines within the knowledge industry.

THE GOVERNMENT'S PUSH FOR FURTHER REFORMS

In 2014, the government started the Top Global University project and selected 13 comprehensive research universities (Type A) to be globally competitive and 24 universities (Type B) to take leading roles in accelerating the internationalization of Japanese society. This project supports selected universities for 10 years. It also requires and monitors various university reforms, beyond internationalization. Additionally, the project provides detailed performance indicators with strict monitoring mechanisms. Yonezawa and Shimmi (2015) highlight the risk of micromanagement by the government.

First, the project requests that the selected universities strengthen their institution-level governance system so that the president can provide strong leadership based on institutional strategies. In conjunction with the Top Global University project, in 2014 the government enacted a legal amendment to strengthen the decision-making power of presidents and vice presidents and to limit the decision-making power of faculty at the school level who meet to discuss academic affairs. The diminished organizational salience of faculty meetings may lead to a decrease in participation by professors, especially regarding school-level governance. Before the amendment, many argued that faculty had decision-making power over budgets and personnel matters at school-level meetings. Currently, the impact of this governance change on the recruitment and promotion of faculty members is not clear.

Second, the project requests that the selected universities diversify faculty profiles by considering nationality, study and research experience abroad, and gender balance. Universities have published target figures, and achievement will be monitored and assessed against these targets by the government committee.

Finally, the project also requires an increase in the number of classes taught in English and other foreign languages, and the improvement in the administrative capacity to fit the international university profile. This project is expected to open up the Japanese academic labor market to academics who do not have a specific relationship with existing academic communities in Japan. It also requests institutional action plans for introducing the tenure-track system and annual salary contracts based on performance. Universities in Japan are now expected to clarify their personnel strategies for becoming internationally competitive.

Conclusion

University academics in Japan have lost their original status as distinguished intellectuals and have been transformed into a type of knowledge service worker. Various changes are ongoing in the national context of the academic profession. However, the changes are slow, mainly due to the strong autonomy of faculty meetings at the school level and the domination of the alumni networks of prestigious universities. Both of these, however, are losing their power through the reforms being pushed through by the government. Also, the emerging system of fixed-term, often soft-money-based, employment of young academics seems to be posing a long-term risk to the national research and development infrastructure.

The rationale of the government for a series of projects and reforms such as the Top Global University project is the improvement of the international competitiveness of Japanese higher education. It is very difficult for university academics to make a counterargument because the performance of Japanese higher education in education and research is apparently declining and is far behind in terms of global competitiveness.

At the same time, however, there is no clear evidence that the ongoing pressure to transform university governance and change the work environment of university academics will lead to an improvement in international competitiveness. The research environment is not improving, and the necessary support for research, education, and administration is not catching up with the increasing workloads.

Strong doubts had been posed by society about the traditional collegiality of the Japanese university system's governance and faculty centricity. The tradition of collegiality in Japanese higher education is now in crisis. A new history of collegiality, supported by links to international academic communities and university management under institutional autonomy, remains to be written.

REFERENCES

Adams, Jonathan, Christopher King, Nobuko Miyairi, and David Pendlebury. 2010. *Global Research Report: Japan*. Leeds, England: Thompson Reuters.

Amano, Ikuo. 1997. "Structural Changes in Japan's Higher Education System—From a Planning to a Market Model." *Higher Education* 34, no. 2:125–39.

———. 2001. *Daigaku Kaikaku no Yukue* [Direction of university reform]. Tokyo: Tamagawa University Press.

Arimoto, Akira, William K. Cummings, Futao Huang, and Jung Cheol Shin, eds. 2015. *The Changing Academic Profession in Japan*. Dordrecht, Netherlands: Springer.

Branscomb, Lewis M., Fumio Kodama, and Richard L. Florida, eds. 1999. *Industrializing Knowledge: University-Industry Linkages in Japan and the United States*. Boston: MIT Press.

Cao, Yong, Yasutaka Iguchi, Yuko Harayama, and Akio Nagahira. 2005. "University-Industry Cooperation in Japan: Some New Evidence from Universities." In *Technology Management: A Unifying Discipline for Melting the Boundaries*, ed. T. R. Anderson, T. U. Daim, and D. F. Kocaoglu, 75–83. New York: IEEE.

Cummings, William K. 1990. *The Changing Academic Marketplace and University Reform in Japan*. New York: Garland.

Cummings, William K., and Ikuo Amano. 1977. "The Changing Role of the Japanese Professor." *Higher Education* 6, no 2:209–34.

Ehara, Takekazu. 1998. "Faculty Perceptions of University Governance in Japan and the United States." *Comparative Education Review* 42, no. 1:61–72.

Fujimura, Masashi. 2005. "Ryudoka suru Daigaku Kyoin Shijo" [Increasing mobility of academic labor market]. In *Nihon no Daigaku Kyoin Shijo* Saiko [A study of the academic marketplace in Japan], ed. A. Yamanoi. Higashi Hiroshima, Japan: RIHE, Hiroshima University.

Hirota, Teruyuki, ed. 2013. *Soshiki toshiteno Daigaku: Yakuwari ya Kino wo Do Miruka* [University as an organization: Perspectives on its roles and functions]. Tokyo: Iwanami Press.

Hood, Christopher P. 2003. *Japanese Education Reform: Nakasone's Legacy*. London: Routledge.

Horta, Hugo, Machi Sato, and Akiyoshi Yonezawa. 2011. "Academic Inbreeding: Exploring Its Characteristics and Rationale in Japanese Universities Using a Qualitative Perspective." *Asia Pacific Education Review* 12, no. 1:35–44.

Ichikawa, Syogo. 1995. *Daigaku Taishuka no Kozo* [Structure of the massification of universities]. Tokyo: Tamagawa University Press.

Ishikawa, Mayumi. 2011. "Redefining Internationalization in Higher Education: Global 30 and the Making of Global Universities in Japan." In *Reimagining Japanese Education: Borders, Transfers, Circulations, and the Comparative*, ed. D. B. Willis and J. Rappleye, 193–223. Oxford: Symposium Books.

Japan Association of National Universities. 2011. *Kokuritsu Daigaku niokeru Danjo Kyodo Sankaku nitsuite: Action Plan* [On gender equity at national universities: Action plan]. Tokyo: Author.

Kitamura, Kazuyuki. 1983. "Internationalization of Higher Education in Japan." *Law Japan* 16:135.

———. 1997. "Policy Issue in Japanese Higher Education." *Higher Education* 34, no. 2:141–50.

Nakayama, Shigeru. 1989. "Independence and Choice: Western Impacts on Japanese Higher Education." In *From Dependence to Autonomy*, ed. P. G. Altbach and S. Viswanathan, 97–114. Dordrecht, Netherlands: Springer.

National Institute of Science and Technology Policy. 2014. *Kagaku Gijutsu no Jokyo ni kansuru Sogo teki Ishiki Chosa 2013* [Analytical report for 2013 NISTEP expert survey on Japanese S&T and innovation system]. Tokyo: Author.

Newby, Howard, Thomas Weko, David Breneman, Thomas Johanneson, and Peter Maassen. 2009. *OECD Reviews of Tertiary Education: Japan*. Paris: OECD.

Normile, Dennis. 2001. "Women Faculty Battle Japan's Koza System" *Science* 291, no. 5505:817–18.

Ogata, Kikuo. 1977. *Shiritsu Daigaku: "Ari Jigoku" no Naka kara* [Private universities in a "doodlebug's pit"]. Tokyo, Japan: Nikkei.

Ogawa, Yoshikazu. 2002. "Challenging the Traditional Organization of Japanese Universities." *Higher Education* 43, no. 1:85–108.

Osaki, H. 1999. *"Daigaku Funso" wo Kataru* [Talking about university conflict]. Tokyo: Yuhikaku.

Poole, Gregory S. 2010. *The Japanese Professor*. Rotterdam: Sense.

Saka, Ayaka, and Terutaka Kuwahara. 2013. *Kagaku Kenkyu no benchmarking 2012* [Benchmarking research & development capacity of Japanese universities 2012]. Tokyo: NISTEP.

Schoppa, Leonard J. 2002. *Education Reform in Japan: A Case of Immobilist Politics*. Oxford: Routledge.

Shibata, Masako. 2005. *Japan and Germany under the U.S. Occupation: A Comparative Analysis of the Post-War Education Reform*. Lanham, England: Lexington Books.

Shimbori, Michiya. 1981. "The Japanese Academic Profession." *Higher Education* 10, no. 1:75–87.

Shin, Jung Cheol, Akira Arimoto, William K. Cummings, and Ulrich Teichler, eds. 2014. *Teaching and Research in Contemporary Higher Education Systems, Activities and Rewards*. Dordrecht, Netherlands: Springer.

Shogimen, Takashi. 2014. "Censorship, Academic Factionalism, and University Autonomy in Wartime Japan: The Yanaihara Incident Reconsidered." *Journal of Japanese Studies* 40, no. 1:57–85.

Terasaki, Masao. 2000. *Nihon niokeru Daigaku Jichi Seido no Seiritsu* [Establishment of the university autonomy system in Japan]. Tokyo: Hyoronsha.

Toyoda, Nagayasu. 2012. Nihon no Igaku Robun Su no Doko [Medical publication trends in Japan]. *Japanese Journal of Neurosurgery* 21, no. 6:446–51.

"Universities Hire 63% of Young Researchers on Limited Contracts." *Asahi Shimbun*, December 12, 2016.

Usami, H., and M. Fukaya. 1989. *Hoso Daigaku de Naniga Okottaka* [What happened to open university Japan?]. Naogya, Japan: Reimei Shobo.

Yamanoi, Atsunori. 1998. "Daigaku Jinji System toshiteno Kobosei Kenkyu" [Study on the open search system in academic marketplace]. *Daigaku Ronshu (Research in Higher Education)* 27:1–18.

———. 2003. "A Study on the System of Fixed-Term Appointments for Faculty Members: Focusing on the Process from Its Introduction to Legislation." *Higher Education Research in Japan: A COE Publication* 1:21–41.

Yonezawa, Akiyoshi. 2013. "The Development of Private Higher Education in Japan since the 1960s: A Reexamination of a Center-Periphery Paradigm." In *The forefront of international higher education: A Festschrift in honor of Philip G. Altbach,* ed. Alma Maldonado-Maldonado & Roberta Malee Bassett, 189–200. Dordrecht, Netherlands: Springer.

———. 2014a. "The Academic Profession and University Governance Participation in Japan: Focusing on the Role of Kyoju-kai." *Educational Studies in Japan: International Yearbook: ESJ* 8:19–31.

———. 2014b. "The Development of Private Higher Education in Japan since the 1960s: A Reexamination of a Center-Periphery Paradigm." In *The Forefront of International Higher Education,* ed. A. Maldonado-Maldonado and R. M. Bassett, 183–94. Dordrecht, Netherlands: Springer.

———. 2015. Inbreeding in Japanese Higher Education: Inching toward Openness in a Globalized Context. In *Academic Inbreeding and Mobility in Higher Education: Global Perspectives,* ed. M. Yudkevich, P. G. Altbach, and L. E. Rumbley, 99–129. Houndsmill, England: Palgrave Macmillan.

Yonezawa, Akiyoshi, Kenji Ishida, and Hugo Horta. 2013. "The Long-Term Internationalization of Higher Education in Japan." In *Internationalization of Higher Education in East Asia: Trends of Student Mobility and Impact on Education Governance,* ed. K. Mok and K. Yu, 179–91. New York: Routledge.

Yonezawa, Akiyoshi, Hugo Horta, and Aki Osawa. 2016. "Mobility, Formation and Development of the Academic Profession in Science, Technology, Engineering and Mathematics in East and South East Asia." *Comparative Education* 52, no. 1:44–61.

Yonezawa, Akiyoshi, and Yukiko Shimmi. 2015. "Transformation of University Governance through Internationalization: Challenges for Top Universities and Government Policies in Japan." *Higher Education* 70, no. 2:173–86.

Yoshida, Aya. 2002. "The Curriculum Reforms of the 1990s: What Has Changed?" *Higher Education* 43, no. 1:43–63.

10 | United States

A Story of Marketization, Professional Fragmentation, and Declining Opportunity

MARTIN J. FINKELSTEIN

The purpose of this chapter is to provide an overview of the relevant national context factors in the United States—both the character of the higher education system and the larger political, social, and economic context within which the system resides—and how these factors shape academic employment and academic careers in this distinctively American context. We begin with an overview of the organization of the US higher education system per se, including the role of the national disciplinary and professional organizations and the role of the private sector. From there, we move to consider the organization of the national research and innovation system as well as labor and social policy. We then examine how those national context factors interact to yield three distinctive characteristics of academic careers and employment in the United States. Finally, we conclude with a discussion of new developments in the United States that may be modifying the distinctive character of academic work in America.

The Organization of the Higher Education System
INSTITUTIONAL STRUCTURE

The higher education system in the United States, composed of some 4,700 corporately autonomous degree-granting institutions, is distinguished by the twin concepts of *federalism* and the *corporate form* (Duryea & Williams, 2000; Johnstone, 2003). By federalism, we mean that there exists no national ministry in the United States that establishes uniform national policies and practices in education; indeed, jurisdiction of educational policy making for the public sector is largely devolved to government in the 50 states. Within this federated system, the legal basis for individual colleges and universities lies in charters granted by state government to corporately autonomous entities—colleges and universities, whether single- or multicampus—that are governed by lay boards of trustees.

The overall system is bifurcated along two major axes. First, in terms of *mission and degree level*—approximately one-third of the system (~1,600 institutions and 7 million students) is oriented to vocational education or workforce preparation (and offers two-year associate degrees).[1] The other two-thirds provides traditional baccalaureate and graduate degree-level instruction in four-year colleges and universities to a primarily full-time student body (Gumport, 2000). The academic staffs of the vocational sector serve primarily on part-time appointments, while those in the traditional baccalaureate and graduate degree sector serve primarily full time (Slaughter & Leslie, 1997), although that is changing rapidly.[2]

The other axis of institutional differentiation is between *publicly* and *privately* funded institutions. Beyond the appointment method of their respective governing boards (political appointment or election in the public sector; self-perpetuating succession in the private sector), public and private institutions have historically differed principally in terms of their revenue streams—with public institutions typically receiving substantial subventions for their instructional mission from state and local government, allowing them to offer lower tuition prices than the private sector (although still high by the standards of most other nations). Private institutions typically rely on (relatively high) student tuition dollars, other private support (e.g., from alumni, for-profit business corporations, and philanthropic foundations), and government and/or corporate research funding. Within the private sector, there is an increasingly salient distinction between the not-for-profits, whose board of directors are accountable to the original charter, and the growing for-profit sector, wherein institutions are either privately held by individual entrepreneurs or are subsidiaries of global business corporations listed on national stock exchanges and responsible to shareholders for turning a profit or otherwise increasing shareholder value.[3]

In 2013, the institutional landscape of the American postsecondary education appeared as shown in table 10.1. Perhaps most strikingly, table 10.1 shows the relatively small size of the university sector: only 294 institutions, or 16.0 percent of the four-year sector[4] and less than 10 percent of the entire degree-granting postsecondary enterprise (N = 4716). Beyond the 294 research and doctoral universities (two-thirds public; one-third private, not-for profit), just under 40 percent (38.1 percent) of the remaining 4,422 institutions are two-year, associate degree–granting institutions, and the remainder are about evenly divided between master's and free-standing, baccalaureate-granting institutions, the latter of which are disproportionately (two-thirds) private, not-for-profit. At the baccalaureate-granting, special purpose, and master's degree–granting institutions, private in-

Table 10.1.   Number of Degree-Granting Institutions, Full-time and Part-Time Faculty, and Enrollment by Institutional Type and Control (Public, Private), Fall 2013

Type of Institution	Number of Institutions	Enrollment	Full-Time Faculty	Part-Time Faculty
OVERALL TOTAL	4,716	20,375,789	772,464	691,297
Public	1,625	14,745,558	503,436	439,362
Private	3,091	5,630,231	269,028	252,565
Research & doctoral universities				
Public	175	4,258,373	256,821	85,538
Private	119	1,514,065	122,821	60,344
Total	294	5,772,438	379,642	145,882
Master's universities				
Public	273	2,655,967	91,413	69,673
Private	417	1,956,083	61,284	97,975
Total	690	4,612,050	152,697	167,648
Baccalaureate colleges				
Public	198	1,115,474	16,937	15,708
Private	652	954,842	49,193	42,882
Total	850	2,070,316	66,130	58,590
Special-focus institutions				
Public	45	90,603	25,640	7,431
Private	1,153	861,643	25,426	35,075
Total	1,198	952,246	51,066	42,506
Two-year colleges				
Public	934	6,625,141	112,625	261,012
Private	750	343,598	10,304	16,289
Total	1,684	6,968,739	122,929	277,301
OVERALL TOTAL	4,716	20,375,789	772,464	691,297
Public	1,625	14,745,558	503,436	439,362
Private	3,091	5,630,231	269,028	252,565

Source: U.S. Department of Education, National Center for Education Statistics, Integrated Postsecondary Education Data System (IPEDS), Digest of Education Statistics, 2014, "Table 317.40," https://nces.ed.gov/programs/digest/d14/tables/dt14_317.40.asp.

   Note: Excludes 13 institutions that had no enrollment. Special-focus 4-year institutions award degrees primarily in single fields of study, such as medicine, business, fine arts, theology, and engineering.

stitutions outnumber public institutions by nearly 2 to 1, reflecting the dominance of private control. Enrollment in the public sector, however, primarily in research and doctoral universities, outpaces the private sector by 3 to 1.

ORGANIZATION OF THE FACULTY WITHIN THE INSTITUTIONAL STRUCTURE (ACADEMIC ORGANIZATION)

As for faculty, their numbers closely follow student enrollment. The plurality of full-time faculty is located primarily in the public sector, especially in the large public research universities. Part-time faculty, however, are located in larger proportion in the private sector, especially the private for-profit sector as well as the public, two-year, or vocational sector.

Within this federated corporate setting, individual faculty members are considered to be employees of their institutions—even in the public sector—rather than civil servants, that is, government employees, although they may be treated as public employees for the purposes of setting compensation and fringe benefits. Their essentially "at-will" employee status was modified to a greater or lesser extent by a Statement on Academic Freedom and Tenure, promulgated—and subsequently widely adopted—in 1940 by the American Association of University Professors in collaboration with the Association of American Colleges (an institutional membership association representing institutional chief executives). Until the close of the twentieth century, this statement has effectively regulated (albeit voluntarily) "corporate" employment relationships. This has provided an "external" template (set of guidelines) for shaping what are basically organizational careers, including the concept of a fixed probationary period (usually six to seven years), a high-stakes "up or out" evaluation, followed by the offer of a continuous, presumably permanent appointment, subject to dismissal "for cause" only through peer review and due process.

Within institutions, the faculty is organized into multiple levels of relatively self-contained units for the purposes of conducting the instructional and research program. The most essential organizational element (the equivalent of the academic "atom") is the academic department: an aggregation of faculty, usually trained in a specific academic discipline, to form a relatively autonomous unit that controls both undergraduate and graduate instruction in a particular academic field (Clark, 1983). The unit exercises control over academic course offerings as well as research in a particular field, and, most importantly, control over its own membership. Organizationally speaking, American institutions of higher education operate as a collection of "loosely coupled," semiautonomous academic departments that interact with other academic departments only when required to do so by the logic of the broader undergraduate curriculum.

While these relatively self-contained academic units tend to operate with high degrees of autonomy, the individual faculty members within them are expected to form a collegium and to subsume individual choice on at least basic academic policy matters to the "collective (general) will" of the unit, as personified by the department chair. Theoretically, at least, all full-time members of the department—whatever their seniority—are "equal" partners in steering the enterprise. The department form of organization—as opposed to the chair system in Germany, for example—operates as a constraint on the individual autonomy of faculty members in the United States in terms of decisions related to course offerings, teaching assignments, new courses, academic programs in the field, and the like (Clark, 1983).

External Disciplinary and Professional Associations

The individual academic department has its counterpart in the loose array of external disciplinary and professional associations in the United States, many of which now operate globally. The emergence of such disciplinary and professional associations has also modified institutional prerogatives. Unlike those nations in which national disciplinary associations play a formal role in filling faculty vacancies or assessing/certifying faculty qualifications (e.g., France), the US disciplinary associations have historically played an informal role in organizing inquiry in the various academic fields, defining the structure and boundaries of the field, and providing leadership in knowledge production. While the formal, external prestige and rewards they offer practitioners have not infrequently been effectively translated into organizational statuses in colleges and universities via expert testimony in the internal promotion and tenure process and the "signaling" of disciplinary prestige to universities in the hiring process (Musselin, 2010), they have largely played an informal role in the shaping of academic work and careers—with one very important exception. That exception has been the growth of "specialized" accreditation (i.e., discipline- or field-specific quality assurance). Beginning with the American Historical Association in 1884 and the American Psychological Association in 1892, disciplinary associations (and more recently, professional associations) have assumed an increasing role in defining the standards for baccalaureate- and doctoral-level competence in their respective fields and, in short order, have assumed a prominent role in providing ostensibly voluntary

Good Housekeeping seals of approval for specialized areas of study in individual universities—seals that have become virtually required signposts, especially for graduate education and or undergraduate education in the professions, in a very competitive market for educational credentials. In that regard, professional associations have come to play a prominent role in many fields in identifying requisite faculty qualifications for teaching, including minimal levels of scholarly productivity, faculty-student ratios, as well as prescribing the content of academic programs and even courses.[5]

Market Mechanisms That Drive the System

The marketization of American higher education is driven at both the consumer-demand and producer-supply ends. Since at least the passage by the US Congress of the Education Amendments of 1972,[6] the over 4,700 autonomous colleges and universities in the United States have been transformed into a marketplace where students and their parents as "consumers" have shopped around for the best postsecondary education values available, seeking to maximize the prestige of their degree for redemption in the entry-level job market.[7] Thus, over the past 40 years in the United States, a cottage industry of college rankings has sprung up to guide parents and students in their higher education purchases. Beyond such rankings, as we have already discussed, disciplinary and professional associations have stepped up their roles as accreditors of the field-specific degree programs offered by colleges and universities in their areas. Driven by the competition for student tuition and financial aid dollars, colleges and universities have sought to "develop and strengthen their brand" (i.e., deepening and widening their niche) in the education marketplace.

Beyond the competition among institutions for students as consumers, the labor market for faculty, especially in the science, technology, engineering, and math (STEM) fields, is driven by the larger labor market for scientists and researchers—conditioned by the national research and innovation system.[8]

Unlike many other nations, in the United States the industrial sector, and not the university sector, is the driving force behind research in terms of level of overall expenditures. As table 10.2 shows, it was estimated that in 2016 nearly 71 percent of all research and development (R&D) monies in the United States would be spent in the industrial sector, including the oil and gas and chemical and pharmaceutical industries; 14 percent in the academic sector; 4 percent in the private, nonprofit sector; and 7 percent in the government sector. The federal

Table 10.2.   Total Expenditures on US Research and Development, by Sector, in Billions of Dollars

	Monies Spent on Research & Development Activities					
Source of funding	Federal Government	Industry	Academia	FFRDC (Gov't)	Nonprofit	Total
Federal government	43.0	29.0	38.0	15.0	6.3	131.3
Industry		328.4	5.0	3.0	2.0	338.4
Academia			18.0	0.3		18.3
Other government			6.5			6.5
Nonprofit			5.0	0.1	14.4	19.5
Total	43.0	357.4	72.5	18.4	22.7	514.0

Source: Battelle Memorial Institute, "2016 Global R&D Funding Forecast," *R&D Magazine Supplement* (Winter 2016): 7, https://www.iriweb.org/sites/default/files/2016GlobalR%26DFundingForecast_2.pdf (accessed September 26, 2016).

government, as may be expected, has a broader mission: providing funds both for research within its varied internal agencies and awarding grants to academic institutions to support contract research.

Dual appointments, especially between academia and the federal government (occasionally the industrial sector) are possible. Typically, these situations arise from a senior or expert-level scientist at a public or private organization who wishes to also serve as a faculty member at an institution. These "joint" appointments afford the research scientist an opportunity to teach within his or her field of expertise, are temporary in duration, and are generally accompanied by a noncareer ladder rank (e.g., research professor) that does not afford them the possibility of tenure. Conversely, some faculty members may serve as scientists in certain private organizations or government entities on a select basis. Such arrangements are usually made due to the faculty member's expert status in a particular field and are not usually permanent placements (e.g., chief scientist at NASA or director of the Jet Propulsion Laboratory at Caltech).

While academe, then, constitutes just one—and not the largest—component of the US R&D infrastructure, the US university system is clearly an integral part of that R&D infrastructure, broadly speaking. Much of federal research is conducted by direct contract at universities with university personnel or in ostensibly federal laboratories (e.g., Fermi, Livermore, Los Alamos) with university personnel on rotating assignment from their campuses. The critical point here is that the national R&D effort in the United States is larger than, but integrally nested within, the university system, meaning that university faculty play an integral role in the national R&D effort while circulating among sectors on a temporary basis. At the same time, the US economy provides robust opportunities for doctorally prepared individuals outside of academe in both industry and government. Indeed, historically, half of all US doctorates have entered nonacademic employment after receiving their degree, as can be seen in table 10.3.

Moreover, the available evidence suggests that compensation for new doctorates outside academe is typically higher than inside. Table 10.4 shows the entry-level salaries for new doctorates by field in various sectors, including academe. These data suggest that in a number of fields, universities must compete with higher paying opportunities in business, industry—and even government.

Not only are there varied and plentiful nonacademic employment opportunities at entry level, but data from two cohorts of PhD recipients responding to the National Science Foundation's triennial Survey of Doctoral Recipients from 1993 to 2003 and from 2003 to 2013 show that there is somewhat robust and steady outmigration from the academic sector to business/industry and government during the first ten years of a postdoctoral career as well as a steady trickle of senior scholars from academia to business/industry and government (Finkelstein, Conley & Schuster, 2016). This intersectoral mobility between academe and industry/government may be fairly distinctive and, we will argue, influential on academic work and careers in the United States.

The Sociopolitical Environment
National Labor Law and Collective Bargaining

In much of the world, faculty employment in universities—at least in the dominant public sector—is shaped to a considerable extent by either civil service laws and regulations or by collective bargaining agreements negotiated by national (or, in the case of Canada, institutional) unions. This is less so in the United States where no faculty are civil servants and only about one-quarter of all faculty members is represented by a union. While employment by the federal government in the United States is governed at the national level by federal law and civil service regulations, public employment outside the federal government (including employment of faculty at all of the nation's public colleges and universities) is regulated by the individual governments of the 50 states. Several of these states (mostly in the Northeast, Midwest, and West Coast) have passed legislation permitting their public employees, including university faculty, to bargain collectively on compensation and employment conditions. As of the end of 2016, 26 states, most of

Table 10.3. Employment Sector of Doctoral Recipients with Definite Postgraduation Employment Commitments, by Broad Field of Study, 1994–2014

Employment commitment and sector	Total	Life sciences[a]	Physical sciences[b]	Social sciences[c]	Engineering	Education	Humanities	Other[d]
All US employment commitments (number)								
1994	15,141	1,440	1,673	2,843	1,713	3,992	2,067	1,413
1999	16,267	1,681	2,004	2,886	2,265	3,788	2,392	1,251
2004	14,869	1,565	1,540	2,612	1,726	3,697	2,400	1,329
2009	17,179	2,029	2,261	2,894	2,606	3,696	2,154	1,539
2014	14,802	1,905	2,459	2,556	2,710	2,101	1,754	1,317
Academe (%)[e]								
1994	51.2	49.2	39.2	52.7	19.6	44.3	84.4	74.0
1999	48.8	47.5	32.9	51.5	14.1	47.2	81.9	73.5
2004	56.1	52.3	44.3	60.4	22.0	50.2	84.0	76.0
2009	51.8	50.0	34.9	62.7	14.4	50.3	84.9	78.8
2014	49.3	46.7	29.2	60.1	14.9	59.5	82.6	79.1
Government (%)[e]								
1994	8.6	14.9	9.0	12.0	12.8	6.4	2.1	5.3
1999	7.5	12.7	7.7	11.6	9.5	5.3	2.1	4.6
2004	7.4	14.2	8.1	10.8	10.6	4.0	2.3	5.9
2009	6.7	12.3	7.1	10.0	8.5	3.8	1.7	3.6
2014	7.3	10.8	5.7	10.6	10.0	4.7	2.2	4.5
Industry or business (%)[e][f]								
1994	21.1	24.9	47.5	16.1	64.6	6.2	4.4	9.8
1999	27.5	29.8	56.0	20.4	74.2	6.9	6.4	14.0
2004	18.9	23.6	42.0	13.6	61.8	3.9	4.1	10.2
2009	25.7	25.3	52.5	14.8	73.1	4.1	3.4	10.5
2014	32.2	31.0	61.3	16.6	72.2	3.6	4.5	10.5

Nonprofit organization (%)[e]								
1994	6.5	8.3	2.0	12.6	2.0	5.2	5.4	8.8
1999	5.4	7.3	1.9	10.6	1.6	4.4	5.5	6.2
2004	5.7	7.0	3.9	9.6	4.4	4.1	5.0	5.8
2009	4.7	7.8	2.6	7.2	2.1	4.5	4.9	3.8
2014	5.3	9.6	2.3	9.0	2.5	4.4	5.8	4.6
Other or unknown (%)[e,g]								
1994	12.5	2.7	2.3	6.6	1.0	37.8	3.8	2.0
1999	10.8	2.7	1.4	5.9	0.6	36.2	4.1	1.8
2004	11.9	3.0	1.7	5.6	1.2	37.8	4.6	2.2
2009	11.1	4.6	2.9	5.4	1.9	37.3	5.1	3.4
2014	5.9	1.9	1.5	3.7	0.4	27.8	4.9	1.4

Sources: NSF, NIH, USED, USDA, NEH, NASA, Survey of Earned Doctorates, https://www.nsf.gov/statistics/2016/nsf16300/data/tab46.pdf.

Note: Due to rounding, percentages may not sum to 100.

[a]Includes agricultural sciences and natural resources; biological, biomedical sciences; and health sciences.

[b]Includes mathematics and computer and information sciences.

[c]Includes psychology.

[d]Nonscience and engineering fields not shown separately.

[e]Percentages based on number reporting definite employment commitments in the United States.

[f]Includes doctorate recipients who indicated self-employment.

[g]"Other" is mainly composed of elementary and secondary schools.

Table 10.4. Salaries of Postsecondary Teachers (Mean and 25th Percentile) and Nonacademic Professionals in Five Fields and Percent Academic Differential, 2009

Occupation	Private		% Differential: Academic vs. Nonacademic		Public		% Differential: Academic vs. Nonacademic	
	Mean Salary	25th Percentile	Mean Salary	25th Percentile	Mean Salary	25th Percentile	Mean Salary	25th Percentile
Chemistry occupations								
Chemists	77,380	52,850	113.8	105.9	79,650	50,620	108.5	7.8
Chemistry teachers, postsecondary	88,080	55,980			86,400	55,200		
Psychology occupations								
Clinical, counseling, and school psychologist	72,770	45,000	106.1	113.0	72,660	53,050	110.0	-10.9
Industrial-organizational psychologist	92,610	64,200	83.4	79.2	76,160	59,880	105.0	0.7
Psychologists, all other	92,360	54,660	83.6	93.0	86,730	66,960	92.2	82.3
Psychology teachers, postsecondary	77,220	50,860			79,960	55,110		-20.3
Legal occupations								
Lawyers	140,170	77,440	88.7	82.1	102,110	70,600	124.6	22.2
Judges, magistrate judges, and magistrates	N/A	N/A			105,380	56,680	120.7	11.9
Law teachers, postsecondary	124,380	63,580			127,220	74,850		34.4

Source: US Department of Labor, Bureau of Labor Statistics, 2013.

which are politically conservative, have passed right-to-work laws that bar individuals from having to join a union as a condition of employment (National Conference of State Legislatures, 2016, as cited by Finkelstein & Kelchen, 2017).

More liberal states, conversely, have passed legislation permitting their public employees—including university faculty—to bargain collectively on compensation and employment conditions. California and New York accounted for nearly half of the unionized faculty in the United States as of 2012, with other politically liberal states such as Illinois, New Jersey, and Washington having high rates of faculty unionization (Berry & Savarese, 2012). Faculty in the public sectors of those states are protected by union contracts, especially in terms of health and retirement benefits. The trend in recent years—a function largely of the ascendance of the political right in state legislatures and executive offices—is for more states to move toward right-to-work laws that weaken unions' power, with Indiana, Michigan, West Virginia, and Wisconsin all passing right-to-work laws since 2012 (National Conference of State Legislatures, 2015).

The situation in the large private sector of American higher education is quite different. Collective bargaining in the private sector is governed by federal legislation: the National Labor Relations Act of 1935 established regional boards across the country with the legal authority to enforce its provisions. Faculties at individual private institutions can petition the regional National Labor Relations Board (NLRB) to hold a collective bargaining election. Since the famous Yeshiva case of 1980 in which an NLRB regional administrator (backed up subsequently by the US Supreme Court) ruled that faculty at the university were "managerial" employees and therefore not entitled under the NLRB to collective bargaining protections, the pace of unionization in the private sector of US higher education has slowed to a crawl, if not halted[9] (Berry & Savarese, 2012).

The primary purviews of faculty unions are salaries and benefits, basic working conditions (teaching load) and governance rights, that is, prerogatives to participate in certain types of academic decisions. While there is some empirical evidence that unions have improved salaries, especially at the less prestigious institutions and the more junior ranks where faculty have less access to the prestige benefits conferred by disciplinary networks, they have not slowed substantially the marketization of faculty salaries by academic field (Finkelstein, Conley & Schuster, 2016). The fact that institutions of higher education in the United States compete with business, industry, and government for the services of the most able faculty in those fields with the greatest economic value outside the academy, means that the "market value" of one's disciplinary affiliation, in effect, has an important shaping effect on the number of job opportunities, their relative attractiveness in terms of compensation, and the likely pace of landing a tenure-track position and achieving promotion through the faculty ranks.[10]

NATIONAL SOCIAL POLICY AND THE FACULTY RECRUITMENT AND HIRING PROCESS

In the United States, individual universities—even in the public sector—have the autonomy to make decisions on creating faculty positions and to control individual hiring processes. Neither federal nor state government intrudes directly. Once a position is created—either through a vacancy or through a new addition—the search process for full-time academic staff positions, whether in the public or private sector, is typically highly *decentralized:* searches are conducted by individual academic units (departments and even programs) and recommendations are made from the unit to the academic dean supervising the unit in question and ultimately to the campus chief academic officer (Matler, 1991). Two aspects of these searches are particularly important: their scope and the legal parameters within which they operate. Regarding scope, most full-time faculty searches at four-year institutions are national in scope, that is, they seek to identify and recruit the most qualified candidates in the United States in the field or subfield in question. At major research universities, the scope of such searches is increasingly international (Bair, 2003). In reality, searches at lesser institutions and searches for limited-term appointments (even at the research-oriented universities) may be conducted less systematically and may be largely regional or even local in scope.

Beginning with the passage of landmark civil rights legislation in the United States, in the 1960s and 1970s searches for academic staff were conducted within the parameters of United States government antidiscrimination policies reflected in federal legislation protecting against discrimination in employment on the basis of gender, race/ethnicity, age, sexual orientation, and so on. Typically, institutional human resource (personnel) office staffs have prepared recruitment guidelines concerning scope of advertising, strategies for identification of women and minority candidates, permissible questions to ask at interviews, and the like (Twombly, 2005). For example, it is not permissible, according to such guidelines, to ask a prospective female academic staff member if she is pregnant or planning to have children. Nondiscrimination legislation would also require that questions not be asked about an applicant's race or sexual orientation in screening for interviews. While informal collegial sponsorship networks still operate, they do so within the parameters of affirmative action requirements,[11] which include establishing availability pools of minority and women PhDs in the field, mandatory advertising in media designed to reach those nontraditional candidates, mandated reporting on the number of women and minorities included in interviews for a given position, justifications of why a man or nonminority candidate is preferred over a woman or minority candidate, and so on (Goonen & Blechman, 1999).

Overall, a hiring academic unit would recommend several candidates to the academic dean supervising that unit (often in some order of rank), and the dean would make the actual hiring decision, including which candidate should be selected. The dean would also negotiate directly with the candidate terms and conditions of employment, including rank and salary (Twombly, 2005). So, in this sense, while the actual conduct of search and screening processes for academic staff are highly decentralized (albeit quite standardized), actual hiring decisions and negotiations are typically conducted more centrally, and academic deans and chief academic officers, especially in the private sector, would have considerable discretion within basic institutional budgetary constraints.

A second key element of federal social policy that impinges on academic work and careers has been the elimination of mandatory retirement for university professors. The stage was set for the academic labor market to change fundamentally when the federal Age Discrimination in Employment Act (ADEA) was passed in 1967. The legislation prohibits *arbitrary* age discrimination in employment and eventually eliminated mandatory retirement for tenured faculty altogether. It is important to note that drafters of the legislation considered whether it was appropriate to include all professions, and the original legislation included a few exceptions, including "tenured teaching personnel." However, three major amendments followed in 1978, 1986, and 1990. The first amendment in 1978 increased the allowable mandatory retirement age to 70. Mandatory retirement was eliminated altogether in 1986—the year of the second major amendment—with a temporary exemption for "tenured teaching personnel" (i.e., faculty) that was allowed to expire on January 1, 1994. Prior to the passage of the ADEA, and the expiration in 1994 of the exemption for tenured faculty members, most institutions had mandatory retirement ages (Rees & Smith, 1991). This meant that there was a high degree of certainty for both individuals and institutions regarding the timing of retirement. This also meant that staffing plans were much simpler to manage and recruitment efforts could be more targeted. The elimination of mandatory retirement has had a "chilling" effect on the hiring of new faculty, and coincides with the emergence of a revolution in the character of faculty appointments, including a steep decline in the proportion of tenure-eligible appointments and the proliferation of part-time and full-time fixed contract (not tenure eligible) appointments.

The Revolution in Academic Appointments

Between 1979 and 2013, the head count of college and university faculty nearly tripled from 650,000 to almost 1.6 million, largely paralleling in their numbers and distribution the growth and distribution of student enrollment. There were two major shifts in faculty employment over this period: the tremendous growth in part-time faculty to the point where they now outnumber the full-time instructional workforce, and the shift among the full-time faculty from tenured and tenure-eligible to fixed, contract appointments (see fig. 10.1). The surge in part-time appointments is visible across institutional types, although part-time appointments tend to dominate faculty ranks in the two-year college sector (both public and private) and in the for-profit, private sector. In the four-year sector, part-time appointments tend to be clustered in a handful of fields, including those offering general education (mathematics and English), foreign languages, health sciences, business and remedial education.

The shift among full-time faculty away from tenured and tenure-track appointments began abruptly in the late 1980s and grew quickly to the point where more than half of all new, full-time faculty hires in the past 20 years have been off the tenure track (Finkelstein, Conley & Schuster, 2016).

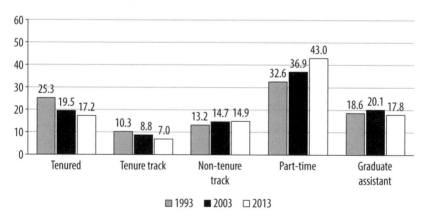

Figure 10.1. Percent distribution of faculty by appointment type, 1993–2013. Figures are for degree-granting institutions only, but the precise category of institutions included has changed over time. Graduate assistants include teaching and research assistants. *Source:* Derived from tabulation by AAUP Research Office, based on data from IPEDS. Released April 2013.

There are several implications for these developments. First, the nontraditional appointments tend to be "specialized," that is, teaching, research, or administration only, which is a departure from the historic, Humboldtian organization of the academic role in the United States involving the integration of teaching, research, and service. Second, off-track, full-time faculty, as well as part-time faculty, tend to assume a marginal role or no role at all in academic governance at the institutional or even the departmental level. Third, career attrition is three times higher for those who begin their careers outside tenure-track or tenured positions (Finkelstein, Conley & Schuster, 2016).

How Do Structural Features of the US Shape Academic Careers and Academic Work?

The Professor as Organizational Employee

The structural features of the US context—the decentralized and corporate organization of the institutional universe; the competitive marketplace fueled by federal student aid policy; the robust nonacademic labor market for PhDs; the internal academic organization of universities into federated department units; the informal role of disciplinary associations as arbiters of prestige and their formal role in specialized accreditation; and the loose, regulatory nature of labor law and social policy—together shape the distinctive features of academic careers and employment in the United States. In its essence, perhaps the defining characteristics of academic life in the United States is its organizational (as opposed to disciplinary or public sector) locus, that is, the fact that academic staff in the United States are, from an organizational and legal perspective, employees of an autonomous corporate entity. They are hired, promoted, and fired by organizational leaders. Their careers are intimately bound to that of their employing institutions. That said, we have noted the emergence historically of a number of forces and entities that have informally imposed constraints on that organizational discretion. Internally, individual faculty are effectively "shielded" from central administration by the relative autonomy of their home academic units/departments. Externally, they are shielded most prominently by the Statement on Academic Freedom and Tenure of the AAUP, which has, paradoxically, given rise to one of the most prominent defining characteristics of academic careers in the United States: their highly defined structure and predictability. The external shield has also come to include the standards and guidelines propounded by specialized subject matter accreditation agencies.

This greater relative dependence on a particular institutional employer and greater vulnerability to institutional administrative controls is confirmed by data from the recent Changing Academic Profession (CAP) survey of 2007–8. While US faculty reported greater autonomy from external, central government control of curriculum, at the institutional level they reported significantly lower levels of decision-making authority in budgeting, administrator selection, and even the establishment of academic programs than faculty in other developed economies, including Germany, Japan, Canada, and the United Kingdom. The only area of internal governance in which they reported comparable decision-making authority was in the area of faculty hiring and promotion (Finkelstein, 2010; Finkelstein and Cummings, 2012).

Despite the fact that, organizationally speaking, faculty in the United States are among the most vulnerable to local, organizational controls, the wide, voluntary acceptance of the academic freedom and tenure policy of the AAUP, has given rise to a widely shared career schedule: a six-year probationary period in the four-year sector (usually three in the two-year sector), a high stakes evaluation, then a continuous appointment subject to good behavior (to which any university hoping to be considered "reputable" must adhere). Adherence to AAUP's policy has been widely considered to be a signal of institutional quality to prospective faculty hires as well as students and their parents insofar as it suggests adherence to standards of faculty employment that characterize the major research universities in the United States. So, quite ironically, in a system where organizational prerogatives of individual campuses are almost absolute and faculty are legally considered to be "employees," institutional behavior is constrained by the competitive nature of the decentralized higher education marketplace where certain signals of what a quality institution is and how it behaves are enforced largely by the marketplace of perceptions—what David Riesman once referred to as the "snakelike academic procession" (Riesman, 1956). That said, the new and increasingly dominant emergence of part-time and fixed-contract appointments means that the majority of the 1.6 million US faculty is no longer protected by the "AAUP shield."

If the tenure system—shrinking as it may be—constrains institutional exploitation of US faculty organizational vulnerabilities, a second set of constraints on exploiting faculty vulnerabilities is primarily external, that is, the disciplinary associations and the broad and deep opportunity structure for PhDs in the United States outside of academe. In their role as "specialized" accreditors for academic programs, disciplinary associations can specify not only the academic qualifications of faculty but also the need for a certain threshold number of full-time faculty as well as student-faculty ratios for certain professional programs in business, nursing, and psychology. Academic disciplines and professional fields, moreover, define the boundaries of the labor market for their practitioners and within which colleges and universities must compete for faculty.

Beyond half of all PhDs who begin their post-PhD employment outside academe (as much as 60–80 percent of PhDs in the physical sciences and engineering), the National Science Foundation's triennial Survey of Doctoral Recipients shows fairly steady and robust out-migration from the higher education to the business sector and, to a lesser extent, to government, throughout the entire course of an academic career—perhaps as much as 10–15 percent of the academic PhD workforce every decade—although that varies a good deal by discipline. Such out-migration trumps any in-migration from business and government by at least 2 to 1 overall. Dissatisfied faculty can leave for other nonacademic opportunities usually at a handsome premium in terms of higher compensation. Moreover, ever mindful of their competitive position in attracting federal research dollars and the best colleagues capable of competing for, and winning, those federal dollars, American universities began to pay "market-driven" faculty salaries following World War II—for example, paying a newly entering professor of engineering or accounting more than a senior professor of literature or philosophy with 30 years of experience (Finkelstein, Conley & Schuster, 2016).

If markets act as a cushion—directly in supporting competition for faculty in the open PhD labor market and indirectly in creating pressures to adapt competitors' faculty-friendly policies, like tenure—they do so, however, only for the those faculty most favored by the market, that is, those in fields with high "market value" outside the academy and those faculty who have received the protections of tenure. Those in nonfavored fields, including nearly all the humanities, many of the social sciences except for economics and possibly political science (in effect, much of the traditional liberal arts fields housed in Colleges of Arts and Sciences on US campuses), are compensated much less well, likely have higher teaching loads, fewer academic resources, and less adequate facilities. The "haves" tend to be in the physical and biological sciences, business, law, and the professional schools.

Much the same bifurcation is observable by tenure status. The vast majority of faculty on American campuses are now full-time fixed contract (not tenure eligible) and part-time faculty (Finkelstein, Conley & Schuster, 2016). Their work role tends to be more specialized, they are less well compensated, and may have very little professional autonomy on the job in terms of what courses they teach and when and what resources are available to them, including office space and secretarial support. In that sense, we are seeing the emergence of a bifurcated workforce within individual institutional employers, based on disciplinary affiliation and type of appointment.

Independence from Government Oversight/Control

While vulnerable—within constraints—to institutional administrative discretion, a second defining characteristic of American faculty members, by way of counterpoint, is the extraordinary degree of professional autonomy they enjoy in their teaching and research from government/state control. We have suggested that such autonomy is reflected especially in curricular matters where individual faculty rather than ministries of education decide on the content of particular courses as well as textbooks, and individual academic departments decide on what academic programs to offer (subject to institutional approval). We have also suggested that such autonomy tends to be highest for tenured and senior faculty and lower for those who are not tenured or full-time staff. In the area of research, faculty are also free to pursue their interests. However, unlike many European universities, American universities do not allocate block funds to academic units or individual faculty for research.[12] Individual faculty are free to pursue their research insofar as they are successful in competing for research funding, primarily from external sources such as government, industry, or private foundations, but even from their own institutions. Generally, with this freedom come organizational expectations for success in research funding and publications, but especially research funding that carries with it offsets for faculty salaries, graduate student assistants, and institutional overhead costs. In the 2007–8 CAP survey, US faculty reported that competition for research funding had increased considerably over the previous decade (Cummings & Finkelstein, 2011).

One of the downsides of the much heralded autonomy of faculty in the United States—at least for those who have it—is that once faculty have achieved tenure, frequently at the age of 40 (or, these days, 45 or 50), they are, from an organizational perspective, largely on their own for what may be, in the absence of mandatory retirement, a very long time. Most human resource departments at American universities steer clear of dealing with faculty members; and most academic administrators are loath to deal with problems that arise, such as normal life problems, including divorce, death, addiction, or major illness of a family member. Since most academics are not trained to deal with personnel issues, they don't. And the vast majority of American campuses have no mechanism, such as post-tenure review, to address challenges that occur in academic careers post-tenure (e.g., past middle age). With an end to mandatory retirement for faculty, and the increased economic uncertainty associated with the recent global recession, a higher proportion of faculty are now choosing to remain in their current positions well past the age of 70 (Finkelstein, Conley & Schuster, 2016). This effectively means that the prospects for a new generation of academics is, to no small extent, stymied or compromised.

Diversity of Background and Work Role

The final characteristic is the enormous diversity of the corps of faculty in the United States—reflective of the diversity of the US higher education system. Earlier, we documented the axes of system differentiation. The vocational sectors, including the two-year community colleges and the for-profit proprietary institutions, primarily hire part-time faculty member who teach exclusively and teach from a syllabus developed by others. Most have no tenure systems and much more limited autonomy for faculty members. Most faculty play little role in institutional or even academic unit governance and likely do not even have an office or a telephone. In the four-year sector, there is enormous variation among the great private research universities, the public comprehensive institutions (former teacher's colleges), the private bachelor's-degree-granting liberal arts colleges that include open access institutions, and the very selective elite colleges. Faculty enter employment at these institutions with very different educational credentials, ranging from no degree to a PhD. They play different roles and have very different careers—many part-time faculty having entered academe from business/industry or government first careers and/or working concurrently outside higher education. Almost nothing can be said about academic work and careers without first answering three preliminary questions concerning type of institution, academic field, and type of appointment.

Indeed, academic careers in the United States are typically pursued within the boundaries established by institutional type, academic field, and appointment types. As we have already suggested, most faculty in part-time and non-tenure-eligible appointments pursue changes in employment within a secondary "contingent" labor market—largely separate from the market for tenured and tenure-track faculty. Among the latter, the "primary" faculty labor market is stratified by both institutional type and academic field. Research universities, especially the elite 150 members of the Association of American Universities that are the leading recipients of federal research dollars, typically hire from within their own orbit. Similarly, other institutional prestige strata hire from within that stratum.

This primary market is further bifurcated by field. In those fields with high opportunity outside academe, movement is easier and institutional competition for talent is more intense; for low opportunity fields, the leverage of faculty inside institutions and in the labor market is severely diminished.

In Closing

The prospects for the academic profession and the conditions of academic work in the United States have entered a period of unprecedented flux, ironically attributable to the increasing popularity of higher education and its salience as a foundation of the "American Dream." As tuition costs—even in the public, let alone the private, sector—have soared (in response largely to declining government subvention), and student indebtedness has come to rival home mortgage debt in magnitude, tremendous political and social pressures have been brought to bear on controlling postsecondary education costs and protecting postsecondary education consumers (students and their parents) as they navigate the very complex postsecondary marketplace. Those pressures have come to be reflected in a broad-based movement to assessing collegiate learning outcomes and putting into place the infrastructure for greater institutional transparency and accountability, especially in regard to student employment outcomes.

Closer to home, they have also been reflected in the reconfiguration of academic work, working conditions, and careers. While the instructional workforce continues to grow, it has been restructured in the direction of non-career-ladder appointments that carry less—and frequently no—job security and that are increasingly specialized in their work pattern: teaching or research or academic program administration. While the influence of the permanent (tenured) academic staff becomes increasingly circumscribed (largely limited now to faculty hiring and promotion), the web of institutional connections between the growing corps of contingent faculty and their home campus remains tenuous indeed. The increasingly fragmented pieces of the academic profession undertake a different scope of work, experience widely divergent working conditions, institutional relations, and support. The fragmentation is accentuated increasingly by marketization, as those disciplines and professions with high economic value outside the academy—who compete with industry and government for faculty—leverage that competitive position in negotiating their institutional status, including salary and influence, while those faculty in fields of marginal outside value languish in their home institutions. And hanging over the entire enterprise is the absence of an endgame: the disappearance of mandatory retirement and the de facto provision of an orderly changing of the guard. Prospects for the future of the academic profession in the United States have not been more fragile in a century.

NOTES

1. As tuition costs in the four-year sector have risen markedly, two-year institutions—with their lower tuitions—have increasingly become the "college of choice" for the first two years of undergraduate education for those students intending to pursue the baccalaureate degree. As this "transfer" (to the baccalaureate sector) function becomes more prominent, some two-year colleges have sought and received state authorization to award baccalaureate degrees in selected fields.

2. The ratio of part-time to full-time appointment among the 1.5 million faculty in the United States is approaching 1:1.

3. In the United States as a matter of law and practical operations, there is a sharp distinction between the not-for-profits and the for-profits as there may not be in other national contexts.

4. That is, the total number of institutions minus the two-year colleges and the special focus institutions equals the four-year sector total.

5. The National Research Council (NRC) is the operational research arm of the National Academy of Sciences (NAS), a private, nonprofit society of distinguished scholars and scientists. NAS was established by the US Congress in 1863 and is charged with providing independent, objective advice to the nation on matters related to science and technology.

6. The amendments created what has become known as the Pell Grant program as the primary vehicle for federal student aid—channeling aid directly to students rather than to institutions as block grants.

7. Prior to 1972, federal government expenditures for student aid were channeled through block grants to individual colleges and universities. The amendments transferred the lion's share of federal student aid dollars directly to individual students and their parents through "portable" Pell Grants that could be used at any college or university—effectively spawning a competitive market to attract students and their federal aid dollars.

8. An earlier version of this discussion appeared in a report submitted as part of the MOREII study by the European Commission.

9. Much of the recent collective bargaining activity in US higher education has been among graduate student teaching assistants and other part-time faculty, rather than among the full-time academics.

10. The available evidence suggests, for example, that the number of tenured faculty appointments has declined in most fields, except for the natural sciences and certain professions, including the health sciences and engineering.

11. Affirmative action (a term borrowed from the text of federal antidiscrimination legislation) refers to the obligation to "take affirmative action" to ensure favorable consideration of members of historically marginalized groups in relation to education and employment vacancies. Favorable "consideration" is distinguished from favorable "outcomes," as would be expected from a pure quota system for marginalized groups as in India.

12. At the time of initial recruitment to a faculty position, especially in the natural science fields, institutions may provide individual faculty with an initial "start-up" subvention for laboratory equipment and other research expenses—usually as a one-time provision.

REFERENCES

American Association of University Professors (AAUP). 2005. "1940 Statement on Academic Freedom and Tenure." https://www.aaup.org/report/1940-statement-principles-academic-freedom-and-tenure. Accessed September 6, 2018.

Bair, Jeffrey H. 2003. "Hiring Practices in Finance Education: Linkages among Top-Ranked Graduate Programs." *Journal of Economics and Sociology* 62, no. 2:429–43.

Ben-Davis, Joseph. 1977. *Centers of Learning: Britain, France, Germany, the United States.* New York: McGraw Hill.

Berry, Joe, and Michelle Savarese. 2012. *Directory of U.S. Faculty Contracts and Bargaining Agents in Institutions of Higher Education.* New York: National Center for the Study of Collective Bargaining in Higher Education and the Professions.

Burke, Delores. 1988. *The Academic Marketplace Revisited.* New York: Basic Books.

Caplow, Theodore, and Richard McGee. 1958. *The Academic Marketplace.* New York: Basic Books.

Clark, Burton R. 1983. *The Higher Education System: Academic Organization in Cross-National Perspective.* Berkeley: University of California Press.

Clark, Robert Louis, and Jennifer Ma, eds. 2005. *Recruitment, Retention, and Retirement in Higher Education: Building and Managing the Faculty of the Future.* Northampton, MA: Edward Elgar.

Conley, Valerie Martin. 2012. "Eroding Retirement and Benefits: The Wrong Response to Fiscal Crises." *NEA 2012 Almanac of Higher Education.* Washington, DC: National Education Association.

Cummings, Williams K., and Martin Finkelstein. 2011. *Scholars in the Changing American Academy: New Contexts, New Rules, and New Roles.* Dordrecht, Netherlands: Springer.

Duryea, Edwin D., and Donald T. Williams. 2000. *The Academic Corporation: A History of College and University Governing Boards.* New York: Routledge Falmer.

Eaton, J. 2012. The Future of Accreditation. *Planning for Higher Education* 40 (April-June).

Finkelstein, M. J. 2010. Diversification in the Academic Workforce: The Case of the US and Implications for Europe. *European Review* 18 (S1), S141-S156.

Finkelstein, Martin, Valerie Martin Conley, and Jack H. Schuster. 2016. *The Faculty Factor.* Baltimore: Johns Hopkins University Press.

Finkelstein, Martin, and William Cummings. 2012. "American Faculty and Their Institutions: The Global View." *Change* 44 (May/June): 48–59.

Finkelstein, Martin, Ming Ju, and William K. Cummings. 2011. "The United States of America: Perspectives on Faculty Governance, 1992–2007." In *Changing Governance and Management in Higher Education*, ed. W. Locke, W. Cummings, and D. Fisher. Dordrecht, Netherlands: Springer.

Finkelstein, M., and R. Kelchen. 2017. "Higher Education Systems and Institutions, United States of America." In *Encyclopedia of International Higher Education Systems and Institutions*, ed. P. N. Texeira and J. Shin. Dordrecht, Netherlands: Springer.

Goonen, Norma M., and Rachel S. Blechman. 1999. *Higher Education Administration: A Guide to Legal, Ethical and Practical Issues.* Westport, CT: Greenwood Press.

Gumport, Patricia J. 2000. Academic Restructuring: Organizational Change and Institutional Imperatives. *Higher Education* 39:67–91.

Johnstone, D. Bruce. 2003. "The International Comparative Study of Higher Education: Lessons from the Contemplation of How Others Might See Us." In *Future Forum 2003: Exploring the Future of Higher Education*, 45–48. http://forum.mit.edu/publications /forum-futures-2003. Accessed September 11, 2018.

Kelchen, Robert. 2018. *Higher Education Accountability.* Baltimore: Johns Hopkins University Press.

Matler, Michael W. 1991. "Recruiting Faculty: Complementary Tales from 2 Campuses." *Research in Higher Education* 32, no. 1:31–44.

Musselin, Christine. 2010. *The Market for Academics.* New York: Routledge.

National Conference of State Legislatures. 2015. *Performance-Based Funding for Higher Education.* July 31, 2015. http://www.ncsl.org/research/education/performance-funding .aspx. Accessed January 23, 2017.

National Science Foundation. 1993. *Survey of Doctoral Recipients.* https://www.nsf.gov /statistics/s0893. Accessed September 11, 2018.

———. 2003. *Survey of Doctoral Recipients.* https://www.nsf.gov/statistics/nsf06320. Accessed September 11, 2018.

———. 2013. *Survey of Doctoral Recipients.* https://ncsesdata.nsf.gov/doctoratework/2013. Accessed September 11, 2018.

Rees, Albert, and Sharon P. Smith. 1991. *Faculty Retirement in the Arts and Sciences.* Princeton, NJ: Princeton University Press.

Riesman, David. 1956. *The Academic Procession: Constraint and Variety in American Higher Education.* New York: Doubleday Anchor.

Slaughter, Sheila, and Larry L. Leslie. 1997. *Academic Capitalism: Politics, Policies, and the Entrepreneurial University.* Baltimore: Johns Hopkins University Press.

Twombly, Susan B. 2005. "Values, Policies and Practices Affecting the Hiring Process for Full-Time Arts and Sciences Faculty in Community Colleges." *Journal of Higher Education* 76:423–47.

Zinner, Darren E., and Eric G. Campbell. 2009. "Life-Science Research within US Academic Medical Centers." *JAMA* 302, no. 9:969–76.

11 | Canada

Decentralization, Unionization, and the Evolution of Academic Career Pathways

GLEN A. JONES

The Development of Higher Education and Academic Careers in Canada

THE EMERGENCE OF PROVINCIAL "SYSTEMS" AND A HOMOGENEOUS UNIVERSITY SECTOR

The Dominion of Canada was created as a federation of British colonies under the British North America Act of 1867. Under this constitutional arrangement, responsibility for education was assigned to the provinces, though it was the federal government that initially led and funded the post–World War II massification of higher education in Canada (Jones, 1996a). When the dust settled following a brief jurisdictional dispute over responsibility for higher education, the provinces emerged as the key players in Canadian higher education policy; the federal government supported higher education through unconditional financial transfers to the provinces, and by assuming a major direct role in related policy sectors, such as student financial support, research and innovation, and the education of Canada's Indigenous peoples (Fisher et al., 2006). Canada remains one of the very few nations on earth without a national ministry of education (or higher education) or national higher education policy. There is no "Canadian system" of higher education; higher education in Canada is best understood as the sum of 10 different provincial and three territorial systems (Jones, 1997).

Given this decentralized arrangement, the provincial governments led the development of higher education systems in the postwar period. The basic structures and coordination arrangements of these provincial systems emerged by the early 1970s, and while there were important differences by province, there were also common elements. All provinces created a binary system with two differentiated sectors: a university sector and a college sector. Universities were relatively autonomous degree-granting institutions. Colleges were generally more tightly regulated by government, offered technical, vocational, and adult education certificate and diploma programs in order to address the labor market needs of the province, and did not have the authority to award degrees; however, the specific role and mandate of these institutional types varied by province. For example, colleges in British Columbia and Alberta offered university transfer programs allowing students to take the first two years of an undergraduate degree program as well as a wide range of technical/vocational programs. Following secondary school, which concludes with grade 11, Quebec students attended a college to complete a two-year pre-university program (required in order to attend university) or a technical/vocational program. Colleges in Ontario, New Brunswick, and Manitoba did not have a university transfer function and operated parallel to the university sector (Dennison & Gallagher, 1986).

While there were major differences among the provincial systems, universities across the country were regarded as a relatively homogeneous institutional type, and one could argue that a common model of a Canadian university had emerged during the transition to mass higher education. Universities were created as private, autonomous, not-for-profit corporations operating under unique legislative charters, but they were considered "public" institutions in that they received provincial operating grants and had been assigned a public monopoly over degree granting (Skolnik, 1987). They were secular institutions, and most were relatively comprehensive, offering some balance of undergraduate, graduate, and professional degree programs. The institutions were largely treated as equals by their provincial governments and there was no formal institutional hierarchy or stratification. All universities had missions that included teaching, research, and public service. Perhaps more importantly, universities generally treated each other as equals; they were all members of the same national "club," the Association of Universities and Colleges of Canada (now rebranded as Universities Canada), and they recognized one another's undergraduate degrees as equivalent in decisions on graduate admission. There were certainly differences between institutions in terms of size, research productivity, language of instruction (English, French, or in some institutions both languages) program offerings, rankings, and so on, but there was little systemic or institutional diversity in the university sector (Jones, 1996b; Skolnik, 1986).

Universities also shared relatively similar governance structures. While provincial governments coordinated higher education systems, they tended to support, or at least tolerate, relatively high levels of university autonomy, especially in contrast to the highly regulated, instrumentalist approach that characterized government-college relations. Provincial governments controlled the major sources of university revenue, government grants, and tuition fees, but universities, operating as distinct, not-for-profit corporations, were relatively free to make their own academic and financial decisions. With few exceptions, the acts that created universities established bicameral governance structures with a division of responsibility between a board of governors and a senate. The board was assigned responsibility for administrative matters, while the senate was assigned responsibility for academic policy, including the creation of degree programs, admissions policy, and academic program requirements. Governance reforms in the 1960s and 1970s led to changes in the composition and functioning of these bodies. Governing boards continued to be composed largely of external members, but almost all were reformed to include both student and faculty members. Academic senates were expanded to include students and, at many universities, other internal constituencies. Board and senate meetings become more open and transparent (Jones, Shanahan & Goyan, 2001).

These governance reforms led to an increased role for faculty in university governance throughout the institution. Faculty already played a key role in academic decisions made at the department, faculty, and central (senate) levels, but the establishment of advisory committees and task forces with faculty representation became commonplace in dealing with almost every major area of university policy, including budgets, planning, and in the selection of senior administrators, including the president (Jones, 1996a).[1]

Academic Career Pathways and Unionization

A common model of academic work and academic career pathways had also emerged in the postwar period. As distinct corporations, universities had the authority to make independent decisions on employment and working conditions, subject to provincial labor laws. Professors were university employees, and decisions related to academic appointments, tenure, promotion, salaries, and working conditions were made at the institutional level.

As Horn (1999) notes, while the structure of academic career ranks (assistant, associate, full professor) had existed for quite some time, few universities had developed detailed policies and procedures on appointments and promotion and most of these decisions involved considerable administrative discretion. Faculty associations had emerged at most universities, and these associations began to play an important role in representing faculty interests in discussions with university management. A national umbrella organization of university-based faculty associations, the Canadian Association of University Teachers (CAUT) was created in 1951 as a forum for discussion of comon issues. In 1958, in response to the Crowe Case,[2] academic freedom and tenure became a major issue for the CAUT; the association created a definition of academic freedom, and began to develop model tenure policies and best practices that could be used to support the work of local faculty associations.

While discussions of unionization can be traced back to the 1950s, the financial uncertainties of the early 1970s spearheaded faculty unionization in Canada. The recession of the early 1970s had a dramatic impact on government revenues, and universities—which had become quite used to large annual increases in government grants—suddenly found themselves facing budget cuts and looking for ways to reduce expenditures in a quite different fiscal environment. Faculty associations began to view unionization as a mechanism for protecting job security, salaries, and working conditions in a context of financial uncertainty. By the middle of the 1980s, faculty associations representing over half of all Canadian university faculty had unionized (Tudiver, 1999). A second wave of unionization took place in the late 1990s in a context of university austerity measures and declining government funding in some provinces.[3]

Unionization had a major impact on university governance and academic work in Canadian higher education. In terms of governance, unionization essentially meant that some decisions that had formerly been left in the hands of the university senate or academic administration were now subject to collective bargaining, and it is frequently observed that unionization weakened the academic senate within the bicameral governance structure of most universities (Penner, 1994; Jones, 1996a; Kool, 2013). In terms of academic work, unionization led to the development of detailed policies and procedures related to academic appointments, tenure, and promotion, and meant that the working conditions of the professoriate were now subject to collective bargaining between the faculty union and management (with final approval given on behalf of the university by the board of governors). Collective agreements essentially defined academic work as including a balance of teaching, research, and service. They described the processes that would be used to appoint new tenure-stream faculty (for example, requiring national advertising and assigning a central role to a search committee composed largely of faculty), the criteria for promotion and tenure, and the process that would be used to make these decisions (i.e., role of faculty committees, role of academic administrators), and they frequently defined academic freedom and the job security of tenure (Jones, Gopaul, Weinrib, Metcalfe et al., 2014). While there are common themes among these agreements, it is also important to note that each is unique. In her analysis of collective agreements across the country, Gravestock (2011) notes that there were major differences in how these agreements defined the criteria for tenure, the processes and mechanisms that were used to determine whether tenure should be awarded, and the role that academic administrators (i.e., department chairs, deans, senior administrators) played in this process.

While collective agreements differed by university and reflected local bargaining between the faculty association and management at each institution, these processes did not take place in isolation. The national umbrella associations of university presidents (the Association of Universities and Colleges of Canada) and faculty associations (the Canadian Association of University Teachers) provided their members with information on collective agreements across the country, identified key issues and trends in collective bargaining, and in some cases provided advice based on the experiences of other institutions. In the larger provincial systems such as Ontario and Quebec, provincial associations of universities as well as provincial faculty associations developed and played a similar role within their respective jurisdictions. The fact that senior university administrators and faculty associations closely monitored changes in collective agreements across the province or nation clearly had a homogenizing effect on how key issues concerning academic work and working conditions were addressed across the country. Even at institutions where faculty were not unionized, the faculty association and the university frequently entered into an agreement on key academic policies, such as appointment, tenure, and promotion procedures that could not be changed unilaterally by either side, and salaries and other working conditions were subject to some form of negotiation. In other words, nonunionized faculty associations entered into agreements with universities that, in many key elements, resembled collective agreements (Anderson & Jones, 1998).

Canadian universities have adopted a relatively common system of academic ranks. Junior initial appointments in the tenure stream are made at the rank of assistant professor. These positions are widely advertised, often both nationally and internationally, and, in identifying the best possible candidate for the position, it is not uncommon for universities to hire professors who are not Canadian citizens (Barbaric & Jones, 2016). Institutional policies specify a maximum probationary time period for a junior appointment before a tenure review, and the review involves a detailed analysis of the candidate's teaching, research, and service activity, though tenure criteria frequently emphasize research and teaching (Gravestock, 2011). Promotion to the rank of associate professor is frequently awarded in parallel with tenure, though at some institutions these review processes are somewhat distinct. Another formal, detailed review of research, teaching, and service takes place in order to make a decision on promotion to the rank of full professor. These processes are not competitive but rather are based on an assessment and determination of whether the performance of the candidate has met the criteria for tenure and promotion established by the collective agreement and/or institutional policies. In other words, while the initial appointment process focuses on obtaining the very best candidate from what is largely an external (and often international) pool of applicants, promotion through the ranks resembles an internal labor market where it is quite common for individuals to spend an entire career at a single university.

In addition to policies concerning appointments, tenure, and promotion, collective agreements between the university and the faculty association play a significant role in determining the working conditions and employment benefits of faculty. While these arrangements vary by institution, collective agreements will often address workload and outline entitlements for professional development funds and research leaves (sabbaticals). Benefits will include health insurance, to supplement the universal health care coverage provided under provincial government programs, and pensions, often funded through contributions from both the employee and the employer. There are differences in salary levels by institution, by region, and by institutional type (Jones & Weinrib, 2012). Comparative international studies of faculty have found that average faculty salaries in Canada are quite high (Altbach et al., 2012).

Collective agreements also frequently define the role and appointment processes for academic administrators, especially department chairs and deans. Department chairs are usually considered members of the union, and the appointment process and job responsibilities of chairs are usually defined within the agreement. Deans, however, are usually considered management and are excluded from the union, but the collective agreement defines the role of the dean in many key academic decisions, such as appointments, tenure, promotion, and the determination of merit pay (in those institutions where merit pay exists) (Boyko & Jones, 2010). While considered management, most deans, like other senior academic administrators in the university, continue to hold academic appointments. These positions have limited terms and individuals will return to the academic ranks after the completion of their administrative appointment.

Unions have a defined membership, and while the faculty association at each Canadian university represents the interests of its full-time tenure-stream faculty (and frequently academic librarians), there are important differences by university in terms of whether the association also represents the interests of other categories of academic workers, such as part-time, limited-term teaching appointments. At some universities, these "other" categories of university teachers are represented by different unions than the full-time, tenure-stream faculty. Of the 20 public universities in the province of Ontario, for example, the associations of full-time faculty at half the universities also represent part-time, sessional university teachers (though frequently through the negotiation of a quite separate and distinct collective agreement), while sessional faculty at each of the other 10 universities are represented by different trade unions than the full-time faculty (Field, Jones, Karram Stephenson & Khoyetsyan, 2014).

Trends and Reforms in Higher Education in Canada

By the early 1970s, the provinces had established the basic institutional forms and structural arrangements that characterized their higher education systems. A common model of the university had emerged; the Canadian university was a public-funded, autonomous, comprehensive institution with a governance structure that included strong faculty participation. Most faculty were unionized, and collective bargaining had emerged as a powerful force in terms of working conditions and career pathways. This relatively homogeneous university sector had emerged across the country, operating alongside a college sector that was, at least from a pan-Canadian perspective, highly diverse in that each province had made distinctive decisions about the characteristics of these non-degree-granting institutions.

The basic structural arrangements that had emerged by the 1970s remained relatively stable for the next two decades. There were modest modifications to provincial policies during this period (see Jones, 1991), but there were no major structural reforms, and the basic division of roles between the federal and provincial governments that had emerged in the postwar period continued until the mid-1990s. Beginning in the early 1990s, however, a number of the structures and assumptions that had underscored provincial higher education systems began to shift, and some of these changes have had important implications for academic work and academic career pathways. These changes will be discussed in terms of three major, and somewhat related, themes: access, funding, and quality; the expansion of degree-granting and the blurring of the binary divide; and an increased emphasis on knowledge, innovation, and university research.

ACCESS, FUNDING, AND QUALITY

In the early 1970s, Canada and the United States were among a very small number of countries that had already made what Trow terms the transition from elite to mass higher education. While participation rates in the United States stabilized, Canadian participation rates continued to increase, and by the mid-1980s Canada had the highest participation rates in higher education in the world.

While it was often difficult to discern anything that might be construed as a multiyear plan for higher education in most provinces, it had become clear that the top priority of provincial governments across the country was to continue to increase access to higher education (Fisher, Rubenson, Shanahan & Trottier, 2014; Jones, 1996a). In the absence of systematic provincial planning, all universities were simply encouraged to expand their enrollment to meet the increasing demand. There continued to be no formal stratification of Canadian universities, and no clear differentiation between elite and mass institutions, as almost all universities continued to open their doors to fulfill their role as "public" institutions. Of course, the government priority of increasing access to higher education did not necessarily imply that universities would be given a blank check. The recession of the early 1970s had already forced governments to apply the brakes on rapidly escalating university and college funding, and most provinces now looked for ways to encourage universities to increase access with stable or modestly increasing government grants. Most provinces had also developed mechanisms for either influencing or directly regulating tuition fees.

The most dramatic shifts in funding occurred in the mid-1990s. The federal government had continued to provide funding for higher education as a component of a broader envelope of transfers to the provinces, but when the government decided to finally address the national deficit in 1995, it made large cuts to the provincial transfers. Most (but not all) provinces made major cuts to university and college operating grants.

There had already been differences in provincial government policies toward tuition fees, and the challenging fiscal environment of the mid-1990s simply exacerbated these differences. In provinces where there was a clear neoliberal agenda, such as Ontario and Alberta, tuition fees increased dramatically, while in others, such as Quebec, tuition fee increases were quite modest.

While it is generally true that students are being asked to pay an increasingly larger share of the costs of their higher education, in the true spirit of the Canadian federation, there are always exceptions. Tuition fee levels in Quebec are less than half the Canadian average, and low tuition has become regarded as a component of the social contract between citizens and the state. Attempts on the part of the Quebec government to substantially increase fees have led to major protests, including, in 2012, the largest and most protracted protest movement in Canadian history, which played an important role in the decision of the government to call an election (which it then lost) (Bégin-Caouette & Jones, 2014). The tuition fee levels in Newfoundland and Labrador have gradually declined over the last decade, and are now less than those in Quebec.

The challenge for universities is that even where there have been modest increases in government grants and tuition fees, operating costs (including faculty salaries) have generally grown at a faster rate than the increases to institutional revenue, and this situation, combined with increasing student enrollment, has forced institutions to look for more efficient ways of teaching this growing undergraduate population.

In many systems, the pressures of access and funding have also led to the development of government-mandated quality assurance mechanisms, but this has not been the case in Canada. The creation of a relatively homogeneous public university sector, where it was assumed that the quality of an undergraduate education was roughly the same across institutions, meant that there was no perceived need for a national accreditation or quality assurance system. While there have been modest experiments in the use of performance indicators and performance funding, the issue of quality has largely been left in the hands of individual institutions. In the two largest provinces, Ontario and Quebec, the provincial university organizations have assumed responsibility for reviewing program quality, in large part to avoid direct government involvement in the assessment of higher education quality. Quality assurance mechanisms have emerged in some provinces, but these have largely focused on the assessment of new degree programs offered by new degree-granting institutions rather than the "traditional" universities (Weinrib & Jones, 2014).

The Expansion of Degree-Granting and the Blurring of the Binary Divide

Provincial governments have tightly controlled and restricted the authority to award degrees. In the structural arrangements associated with the development of provincial higher education systems in the post–World War II era, degree-granting authority was viewed as a public monopoly, and this authority was only awarded to publicly funded institutions. Degree-granting was also a mechanism for differentiating the university and nonuniversity sectors; colleges might offer pre-university or university transfer programs, but they did not have the authority to award degrees.

The expansion of degree-granting authority has provided a new mechanism to expand access to degree programs, especially to populations that might be less likely to attend a university. This policy shift has taken two forms: the expansion of degree-granting authority in the public sector, and the expansion of degree-granting authority to private institutions. Beginning in 1989, British Columbia began to expand the range of publicly supported institutions with the legal authority to grant degrees, and it also repositioned a number of its community colleges as "university colleges" with the authority to grant four-year degrees. The university colleges were later provided with an expanded status as teaching-focused universities. Alberta also expanded degree-granting authority to its community colleges and institutes of technology, and two former colleges were awarded university status. Ontario colleges were provided with the authority to award degrees in applied areas, subject to a detailed review of proposed new degree programs. In total, six provinces and the Yukon Territory have now provided some form of degree-granting authority to the college sector. These changes have clearly blurred what had once been a clear divide between the two sectors of these binary systems (Jones, 2009).

The expansion of degree-granting authority has also led to the emergence of a new, private university sector. Private universities are not a new phenomenon in Canada; in fact, private denominational colleges were the dominant institutional model in the nineteenth and early twentieth century, but for a variety of reasons, provincial governments prioritized the support of public, secular universities, and so most denominational universities either quickly evolved into public, secular

Table 11.1.   Basic Data on Canadian Universities

Type	Number
Public universities	94
Private universities	19
Full-time university students	1,004,652
Part-time university students	301,461
Total university students	1,306,110

Sources: University counts are from Canadian Information Centre for International Credentials. Student counts are from Statistics Canada. Data accessed November 2016.

universities to obtain direct access to funding, or entered into federation or affiliation arrangements with publicly supported secular institutions to expand the educational opportunities of their students and obtain some indirect access to public funding. A number of private denominational colleges continued to exist, though they were generally limited to offering degrees in theology or Bible studies under provincial regulations and were not considered members of the university sector. Many of the new private universities are former religious colleges that have obtained the legal authority to grant degrees and use the name "university" under provincial legislation. However, a number of the new private universities are secular institutions designed to offer students a unique undergraduate experience. There are now approximately 19 private universities in Canada, depending on the precise definition that is applied, almost all of which are primarily undergraduate institutions, though several, such as Trinity Western University in British Columbia, also offer professional and graduate programs (Li & Jones, 2015). Basic data on the Canadian system can be found in table 11.1.

The creation of new types of universities, such as private universities and universities that are former colleges that continue to offer trade and vocational programs in addition to more traditional university offerings, have clearly shattered the view of universities as a homogeneous sector. Universities no longer have a monopoly on degree granting, and there is now some systemic and institutional diversity within the university sector in Canada.

KNOWLEDGE, INNOVATION, AND UNIVERSITY RESEARCH

In the structural arrangements that emerged in the postwar expansion, the Government of Canada (i.e., the federal government) provided funding for postsecondary education through unconditional transfers to the provinces, but it also assumed a major role in supporting student financial assistance (through the Canada Student Loans Program) and university research (through three national granting councils). In the mid-1990s, the federal government decided to tackle its budget deficit, and huge cuts were made to the federal-provincial transfer programs, including both postsecondary education and public health care (Fisher et al., 2006). By the turn of the century, the federal books were balanced, but rather than replace the funds that had been withdrawn from provincial transfers for higher education, the government made major new investments in student financial assistance (through the Canada Millennium Scholarship Foundation) and also research and innovation.

Investments in university research were clearly motivated by notions of the knowledge economy and the desire to ensure that Canada had a strong research infrastructure. There were also concerns that Canadian universities were no longer able to attract world-class professors, and that top university researchers were being enticed to leading universities in the United States as part of a national brain drain.

In addition to increasing support to the national granting councils, the federal government introduced two major national programs designed to strengthen Canada's research and innovation infrastructure. The first was the Canada Research Chairs Program and the second was the Canada Foundation for Innovation.

The Canada Research Chairs (CRC) Program was designed to support 2,000 research chairs in Canadian universities. The allocation of research chairs was largely influenced by the share of research council funding obtained by each university, though each university was allocated at least one chair. Chairs allocations were divided between junior (tier 1 chairs valued at $100,000 per year for a five-year term) and senior (tier 2 chairs valued at $200,000 per year for a seven-year term) appointments, and between new hires (recruiting the best and the brightest) and existing faculty (a retention strategy to reduce brain drain). Chairs were also allocated on the basis of broad categories of knowledge between the social sciences and humanities, the natural sciences and engineering, and health. Universities were free to make their own decisions on the exact descriptions of each research chair in accordance with an institutional research plan, but the files associated with all institutional nominations for chair appointments, including external peer reviews of scholarship, were carefully considered by a national committee to ensure that high standards were maintained by all universities. The program was phased in over a five-year period.

The Canada Foundation for Innovation provides major funding for research infrastructure, such as laboratories, specialized equipment, and other facilities.

Funds are provided on a matching basis, with expectations that the program would support partnerships with private industry, though in some cases it was the provinces that provided matching support to ensure that their provincial universities received a fair share of funding. Foundation programs became linked to the CRC program with an expectation that hiring a new research chair might lead to an application for infrastructure support.

In addition to continuing to support both programs, the federal government has more recently created the Canada Excellence Chairs program, which provides funding of up to $10 million over seven years to a university to support the appointment of leading international scholars and their research teams so that they can engage in ambitious programs of research. Institutions apply for the chairs in a national competition framed around broadly defined areas of research that are viewed as strategically important. There were 27 chairs in place in 2017.

These new investments have clearly strengthened Canada's university research infrastructure, as well as increased the overall importance of research within Canadian higher education. At the same time, there are concerns that the federal government has not been fulfilling its responsibility for funding basic research, and a recent review has called for major new investments in funding through the national research granting councils (Advisory Panel, 2017).

Implications for Academic Work and Academic Career Pathways

The reforms described above have had important implications for academic work and academic career pathways in Canada. They have had implications for the professoriate within what might be viewed as the "traditional" university sector, the network of relatively homogeneous institutions that emerged during postwar massification, and they have had important implications associated with the expansion of degree-granting authorities and the emergence of new types of universities.

Enrollment Growth, Research, and the Canadian Professoriate

Increasing access to higher education has been a major policy in most provinces, though there are important demographic differences by province that indicate the issue has been taken up in slightly different ways in various jurisdictions. From a pan-Canadian perspective, however, the number of students enrolling in universities has increased—in some provinces dramatically—over the last decade, while universities are struggling to deal with additional costs and only modest increases in revenue. An analysis in Ontario suggests that government grant increases have kept pace with enrollment growth and national inflation indices. However, faculty salary costs (and some other university operating costs) have increased faster than inflation (Clark, Moran, Skolnik & Trick, 2009).

Unlike in some other countries, Canadian universities (and, perhaps more importantly, faculty unions) have continued to protect the full-time, tenure-stream professoriate. In fact, the number of tenure stream faculty has increased over the last decade, from 34,000 in 2002 to 46,700 in 2012.[4] Given the financial challenges faced by universities, however, the growth in student enrollment has outpaced the growth in tenure-stream faculty hires, leaving a gap in terms of the supply of teaching. While there has undoubtedly been some restructuring of teaching work, such as increased class size and the increasing using of new technologies, many universities have also turned to other categories of academic workers to address their teaching needs.

Some universities have developed categories of academic appointment that focus primarily on teaching. While these arrangements vary by institution, the general assumption is that these teaching-stream positions involve much heavier teaching loads and little if any emphasis on research (excepting continuing professional development and pedagogical studies). These are frequently structured as full-time positions, which, following a probationary review focusing on teaching quality, involve considerable job security. Salaries for these appointments are lower than for tenure-stream faculty.

An Ontario study found that approximately 8 of the province's 20 public universities have introduced teaching-stream appointments (Vajoczki, Fenton, Menard & Pollon, 2011). A survey of teaching-stream faculty found that 87 percent were satisfied or very satisfied with their positions and 75 percent did not aspire for a more traditional tenure-stream appointment. Key informants noted that teaching-stream appointments could address the specific teaching needs of academic departments, but they also noted that there was a status differential between teaching-stream and tenure-stream faculty, given the high value placed on research.

The second category of appointment that has become important in addressing the teaching needs of universities is part-time contract appointments. The nature of these appointments varies by university, but many are contractual appointments in which individuals are employed on a per-course basis. As Rajagopal (2002) notes, it is important to recognize that individuals who are sessional lecturers can be categorized in different ways. A "classic" sessional lecturer is a professional or expert whose primary career is outside the university (e.g., as a business person, lawyer, government official, etc.) who teaches a course so that students can benefit from their special knowledge. A second category, according to Field and Jones (2016), is "precarious" appointment, which involves individuals whose contractual teaching is their primary source of income. These individuals frequently aspire to obtain full-time tenure-stream appointments, but the heavy teaching loads necessary to earn an income make it difficult to sustain the program of research that would make them competitive for these positions. In some cases, individuals take on contracts with multiple universities to support themselves.

Recent studies in Ontario provide a glimpse of the working conditions and contractual arrangements associated with these positions (Field, Jones, Karram Stephenson & Khoyetsyan, 2014; Field & Jones, 2016). As already noted, almost all of these sessional instructors are members of labor unions, and a review of these collective agreements suggests that there is considerable variation in working conditions by institution, including salary levels. Most have access to basic benefits, and some have limited forms of job security associated with seniority. Public data on sessional lecturer appointments were available at a small number of institutions, and an analysis of these data suggests that although at some institutions the growth in sessional lecturer appointments has far outpaced the growth in tenure-stream faculty, at other institutions the opposite is true, and at one university the number of sessional lecturer appointments has remained relatively stable. Several unions representing tenure-stream faculty have negotiated maximum ratios of sessional lecturer appointments, limiting the number of courses taught in the regular sessions (September to April) to a specific percentage.

Field and Jones (2016) surveyed sessional lecturers employed at 12 Ontario universities. Their findings discuss the large difference between classic and precarious sessional lecturers in how they perceive academic work. Sessional lecturers report serious concerns with working conditions, including remuneration, and suggest that they are "invisible" academic workers who are not considered part of the collegium; they frequently feel marginalized and unsupported by administrators and academic colleagues.

These recent studies of teaching-stream faculty and sessional lecturers have important limitations, including focusing on a single province, but they suggest that universities may be making quite different decisions in terms of how they address their teaching needs. Universities have developed different categories of academic workers in addition to the tenure stream, but the balance of appointments and share of teaching undertaken by these other categories appear to vary

by institution. In some cases, universities and their faculty associations have negotiated agreements that limit the utilization of these other categories of academic
worker.

It is also important to note that other categories of university teachers have also
unionized on some campuses. Teaching assistants, usually graduate students who
support the work of full-time faculty (as markers, laboratory instructors, seminar
leaders, etc.) or who, in some situations, have sole responsibility for teaching
courses, have unionized on many campuses across the country. More recently,
postdoctoral fellows, some of whom have teaching responsibilities, have also
unionized on some campuses.

Another major shift is associated with the increasing value assigned to research
within Canadian universities, given the additional resources associated with federal and provincial research funding programs. While there have always been
status differentials between faculty, the Canada Research Chairs Program has essentially institutionalized—and probably exacerbated—these status differences,
and chair appointments have frequently led to greater differences in teaching
loads. In addition to the CRCs, there has also been a growth in endowed chairs,
including a program of policy-focused endowed chairs funded by the government
of Ontario.

All of these changes are associated with the increasing horizontal and vertical
fragmentation of academic work. The horizontal fragmentation relates to the increasing growth of knowledge, and the related increasing specialization of traditional academic work. It is also associated with the growth in educational support
units that operate in parallel to academic departments, such as student affairs, educational development, and educational technology departments. The vertical
fragmentation of academic work relates to the increasingly hierarchical relationships between different categories of academic workers employed within the same
academic unit.

New Types of Universities

The expansion of degree granting to new types of public universities (such as
universities with a greater focus on teaching in British Columbia and Alberta) and
the development of new private universities have important implications for
academic work and academic career pathways. Many of these institutions are
teaching-focused; faculty workload arrangements involve higher teaching loads
than at the "traditional" universities, but the academic career pathways associated
with these new institutions tend to be only variations on a common theme. With

only a few exceptions, these private universities expect their faculty to engage in research teaching and service, and several of the academic leaders of private universities that I have interviewed have indicated that their institutions are using academic ranks as well as tenure and promotion procedures that are quite similar to those in the public universities. Average faculty salary levels at these new public and private universities seem to be lower than at the more traditional institutions.

Given the assumption that emerged in the postwar period that universities were both public and secular, the emergence of private, religious universities has raised complex issues about the relationship between religious values and freedoms, and higher education and professional values and freedoms. For example, a number of private denominational universities require faculty to sign a statement of faith or principles as a condition of employment. From the perspective of the CAUT, requiring faculty to commit to a specific set of beliefs or ideologies as a condition of employment is a contravention of academic freedom.[5] The CAUT now lists five universities that it believes are limiting academic freedom by requiring faculty to adhere to statements of faith.

At Trinity Western University, the intersection of the statement of faith for faculty and the university's decision to create professional programs in education and law has become quite controversial within professional communities. For example, the fact that the statement of faith signed by both faculty and students precludes homosexual relations, in a national environment where both homosexual relationships and gay marriages are legal, has led several provincial legal licensing bodies (bar associations) to decide that they will not recognize Trinity Western law degrees, thereby limiting the ability of graduates to practice law. This issue is now before the courts in several provinces.

The emergence of faith-based universities has therefore created a quite different working environment and different working conditions for faculty compared to their public peers, and these differences have received considerable attention by national higher education organizations, professional bodies, and the media.

Conclusion

A central feature of Canadian higher education is decentralization. There are ten quite different provincial systems of higher education, and each has assigned considerable authority and autonomy to its public universities. Academic careers are therefore largely defined at the institutional level, though networks of universities and faculty associations contributed to the development of a relatively common model that continues today. The basic structures associated with the academic profession and academic career pathways emerged by the 1970s. While many of these structures can be found much earlier at some institutions, unionization served to institutionalize rank structures and tenure and promotion processes. Unionization has been a powerful force in Canadian higher education, and one can argue that it has had a homogenizing influence on academic career pathways.

While Canadian universities have protected the central role of full-time tenure-stream faculty, other categories and classifications of academic workers have emerged, including sessional lecturers (part-time contract faculty) and teaching-stream faculty. There has therefore been a vertical fragmentation of academic work, with many of the same teaching tasks performed by individuals with very different job classifications and working conditions.

Major investments in research have created increasing status differentials between faculty, a phenomenon that was in some ways institutionalized by the CRC program. Finally, the creation of new institutional types has contributed not only to institutional diversity within provincial systems but also to diversity in terms of the relative balance between teaching and research between faculties at different institutions. The emergence of private faith-based institutions now classified as universities may have also contributed to diversity in terms of academic pathways; there is now a small faith-based sector operating parallel to the traditional secular sector.

NOTES

1. At most universities the president is appointed by the board on the recommendation of a search committee. The rectors of several Quebec universities are elected.

2. Harry Crowe was a professor at United College (later to become the University of Winnipeg). In 1958, while traveling, Crowe sent a letter to a colleague in which he was critical of the academic environment of the college. The letter mysteriously fell into the hands of the college principal and Crowe was fired on the grounds that the letter demonstrated his incompatibility with the college's mission as well as a lack of respect and loyalty to the college administration. A detailed discussion of the case is provided by Horn (1999).

3. In the province of Alberta, academic staff associations are created under the Post-Secondary Learning Act. The associations are not considered labor unions and they do not

have the right to strike. The current government is reviewing this situation and may expand the role of these associations. There were also restrictions on faculty unionization
in place in British Columbia from 1977 to 1992, but a number of universities in that province have now unionized.

4. Statistics Canada ceased collecting data on full-time faculty in 2012. In 2016, Statistics Canada announced that it would return to collecting data on university faculty, and
might move toward also collecting data on part-time and sessional faculty, though new
data were not available at the time of writing.

5. The definitions of the American Association of University Professors and the CAUT
differ in this respect. The AAUP definition of academic freedom explicitly allows for statements of faith or conduct agreed to before employment. The CAUT statement does not
make this exception.

REFERENCES

Advisory Panel for the Review of Federal Support for Fundamental Science. 2017. *Investing in Canada's Future: Strengthening the Foundations of Canadian Research.* Ottawa: Government of Canada.

Altbach, Philip G., Liz Reisberg, Maria Yukevich, Gregory Androushchak, and Iván F. Pacheco. 2012. *Paying the Professoriate: A Global Comparison of Compensation and Contracts.* New York: Routledge.

Anderson, Barbara, and Glen A. Jones. 1998. "Organizational Capacity and Political Activities of Canadian University Faculty Associations." *Interchange* 29, no. 4:439–61.

Barbaric, Diane, and Glen A. Jones. 2016. "International Faculty in Canada: Recruitment and Transition Processes." In *International Faculty in Higher Education: Comparative Perspectives on Recruitment, Integration, and Impact,* ed. M. Yudkevich, P. Altbach, and L. Rumbley, 51–75. New York: Routledge.

Bégin-Caouette, Olivier, and Glen A. Jones. 2014. "Student Organizations in Canada and Quebec's 'Maple Spring.'" *Studies in Higher Education* 39, no. 3:412–25.

Boyko, Lydia, and Glen A. Jones. 2010. "The Roles and Responsibilities of Middle Management (Chairs and Deans) in Canadian Universities." In *The Changing Dynamics of Higher Education Middle Management,* ed. V. L. Meek, L. Goedegebuure, R. Santiago, and T. Carvalho, 83–102. Dordrecht, Netherlands: Springer.

Clark, Ian D., Greg Moran, Michael L. Skolnik, and David Trick. 2009. *Academic Transformation: The Forces Reshaping Higher Education in Ontario.* Montreal and Kingston: McGill-Queen's University Press.

Dennison, John D., and Paul Gallagher. 1986. *Canada's Community Colleges: A Critical Analysis.* Vancouver: UBC Press.

Field, Cynthia C., and Glen A. Jones. 2016. *A Survey of Sessional Faculty in Ontario Publicly-Funded Universities.* Toronto: Centre for the Study of Canadian and International Higher Education, OISE-University of Toronto.

Field, Cynthia C., Glen A. Jones, Grace Karram Stephenson, and Artur Khoyetsyan. 2014. *The "Other" University Teachers: Non-Full-Time Instructors at Ontario Universities.* Toronto: Higher Education Quality Council of Ontario.

Fisher, Donald, Kjell Rubenson, Jean Bernatchez, Robert Clift, Glen Jones, Jacy Lee, Madeline MacIvor, John Meredith, Theresa Shanahan, and Claude Trottier. 2006. *Canadian Federal Policy and Post-Secondary Education*. Vancouver: Centre for Policy Studies in Higher Education and Training, University of British Columbia.

Fisher, Donald, Kjell Rubenson, Theresa Shanahan, and Claude Trottier, eds. 2014. *The Development of Postsecondary Education Systems in Canada: A Comparison between British Columbia, Ontario and Quebec*. Montreal: McGill-Queen's.

Gravestock, Pamela. 2011. *Does Teaching Matter? The Role of Teaching in the Tenure Policies of Canadian Universities*. PhD thesis, University of Toronto. https://tspace.library .utoronto.ca/bitstream/1807/31764/6/Gravestock_Pamela_S_201111_PhD_thesis .pdf. Accessed November 26, 2014.

Horn, Michiel. 1999. *Academic Freedom in Canada: A History*. Toronto: University of Toronto Press.

Jones, Glen A. 1991. "Modest Modifications and Structural Stability: Higher Education in Ontario." *Higher Education* 21:573–87.

———. 1996a. "Governments, Governance, and Canadian Universities." In *Higher Education: Handbook of Theory and Research*, vol. 11, ed. John C. Smart, 337–71. New York: Agathon Press.

———. 1996b. "Diversity within a Decentralized Higher Education System: The Case of Canada." In *The Mockers and Mocked: Comparative Perspectives on Differentiation, Convergence and Diversity in Higher Education*, ed. V. L. Meek, L. Goedegebuure, O. Kivinen, and R. Rinne, 79–94. Oxford: Pergamon.

———. 2009. "Sectors, Institutional Types, and the Challenges of Shifting Categories: A Canadian Commentary." *Higher Education Quarterly* 63, no. 4:371–83.

———. 2013. "The Horizontal and Vertical Fragmentation of Academic Work and the Challenge for Academic Governance and Leadership." *Asia Pacific Education Review* 14, no. 1:75–83.

Jones, Glen A., ed. 1997. *Higher Education in Canada: Different Systems, Different Perspectives*. New York: Garland.

Jones, Glen A., Bryan Gopaul, Julian Weinrib, Amy Scott Metcalfe, Donald Fisher, Yves Gingras, and Kjell Rubenson. 2014. "Teaching, Research and the Canadian Professoriate." In *Teaching and Research in Contemporary Higher Education: Systems, Activities and Rewards,* ed. A. Arimoto, W. K. Cummings, J. C. Shin, and U. Teichler, 335–56. Dordrecht, Netherlands: Springer.

Jones, Glen A., Theresa Shanahan, and Paul Goyan. 2001. "University Governance in Canadian Higher Education." *Tertiary Education and Management* 7, no. 2:135–48.

Jones, Glen A., and Julian Weinrib. 2012. "The Organization of Academic Work and the Remuneration of Faculty at Canadian Universities." In *Paying the Professoriate: A Global Comparison of Compensation and Contracts,* ed. P. Altbach, L. Reisberg, M. Yukevich, G. Androushchak, and I. F. Pacheco, 83–93. New York: Routledge.

Kool, Rick, ed. 2013. *Academic Governance 3.0: What Could It Be? How Could We Get There?* Vancouver: Confederation of University Faculty Associations of British Columbia.

Li, Sharon X., and Glen A. Jones. 2015. "The 'Invisible' Sector: Private Higher Education in Canada. In *Private Higher Education Across Nations*, ed. J. M. Joshi and Saeed Paivandi. Delhi: B. R. Publishing Corporation.

Marshall, Dave. 2008. "Differentiation by Degrees: System Design and the Changing Undergraduate Environment in Canada." *Canadian Journal of Higher Education* 38, no. 3:1–20.

Penner, Roland. 1994. "Unionization, Democracy and the University." *Interchange* 25, no. 1:49–53.

Rajagopal, Indhu. 2002. *Hidden Academics: Contract Faculty in Canadian Universities.* Toronto: University of Toronto Press.

Skolnik, Michael L. 1986. "Diversity in Higher Education: The Canadian Case." *Higher Education in Europe* 11, no. 2:19–32.

———. 1987. "State Control of Degree Granting: The Establishment of a Public Monopoly in Canada." In *Governments and Higher Education: The Legitimacy of Intervention,* ed. C. Watson, 56–83. Toronto: Higher Education Group, Ontario Institute for Studies in Education.

Tudiver, Neil. 1999. *Universities for Sale: Resisting Corporate Control over Canadian Higher Education.* Toronto: James Lorimer.

Vajoczki, Susan, Nancy Fenton, Karen Menard, and Dawn Pollon. 2011. "Teaching-Stream Faculty in Ontario Universities." Toronto: Higher Education Quality Council of Ontario.

Weinrib, Julian, and Glen A. Jones. 2014. "Largely a Matter of Degrees: Quality Assurance and Canadian Universities." *Policy and Society* 33, no. 3:225–36.

Weinrib, Julian, Glen A. Jones, Amy Scott Metcalfe, Donald Fisher, Yves Gingras, Kjell Rubenson, and Iain Snee. 2013. "Canada: Canadian University Academics' Perceptions of Job Satisfaction—'. . . the Future Is Not What It Used to Be.'" In *Job Satisfaction around the Academic World,* ed. P. J. Bentley, H. Coates, I. R. Dobson, L. Goedegebuure, and V. L. Meek, 83–102. Dordrecht, Netherlands: Springer.

12 | Looking across Systems

Implications for Comparative, International Studies of Academic Work

GLEN A. JONES and MARTIN J. FINKELSTEIN

The foregoing chapters have examined academic work and careers in 10 countries with a view toward illuminating their connections to national traditions and cultural context. Across these 10 stories, are there common threads? Can we identify—as we set out to do—a set of common components of academic work and careers that allow us to discuss them cross-nationally in true comparative fashion? Can we further identify the distinctive elements of national tradition and culture that shape how that work and those careers are structured—in ways that define different incarnations of what it means to be a professor? To what extent, if any, is the historic distinctiveness of those incarnations persisting? Or, to what extent has that distinctiveness been attenuated?

The Components of Academic Work in Cross-National Perspective

Perhaps the most fundamental dimension or variable of academic work that emerges across these chapters is the *relative centrality of research* to the daily academic work role. This may appear, at first blush, to be a patently obvious observation: after all, Joseph Ben-David's pioneering volume (Ben-David, 1977) first identified an emphasis on research as a key feature for distinguishing among national systems of higher education. While Germany emphasized the research mission, the UK did not; and the United States stood somewhere in between as a hybrid. National systems that have historically emphasized teaching are increasingly rebalancing the mission of higher education to include research. Thus, the universities of France, Russia, and Brazil were traditionally viewed as teaching institutions, but research became a key element of academic work by the middle of the twentieth century in French universities, and it is gradually increasing in importance within both the Russian and Brazilian public systems. While research continues to play a minor role in the academic careers of the vast majority of faculty in China, India, and even Japan, it has emerged as a major driver of academic work and arbiter of academic career success in a numerically small, albeit normatively important, elite subsystem within the university sector. These clusters or sectors of institutions are aimed at assuring national competitiveness in the global knowledge economy, and they are positioned as elite components within the broader higher education system. In Germany, Canada, and to a lesser extent the UK and the United States, the research function has for at least the past half-century been fundamental for faculty throughout the university sector—and this function increasingly penetrates into academic work life outside the university sector as the universal professional norm. For example, in the United States, perhaps the major shift in academic work and careers over the past quarter-century has been the infiltration of research imperatives even into the freestanding baccalaureate colleges. In Germany, the founding home of the modern research university, the *Fachhochschule* have now evolved to include a research function, often focusing on applied research activities tied to industry.

Closely linked to the increasing centrality of research is the global expansion—and increasing formalization—of graduate, especially doctoral and postdoctoral, education, in the university sector (Nerad & Evans, 2014; Shin, Kehm & Jones, 2018). In most of the world, doctoral students and post-doctoral students provide the human infrastructure that supports faculty in conducting research. Indeed, graduate education has grown dramatically within the university sector in the five nations that place research at the core of faculty identity: Germany, France, Canada, the UK, and the United States. In China, Japan, and Brazil, graduate education has exploded over the past decade—but largely within the elite subsystem of national research universities.

Beyond the relative importance of research and its link to the preemptiveness of graduate education, the second decisive characteristic of academic work that emerges from these chapters is the degree to which it is performed in a *competitive environment* that requires formal accountability. In Germany and Japan, for example, faculty positions routinely have carried with them per capita research funding: research funding was a "right" that accrued to the academic position. In the past decade, it has become increasingly a privilege to be won in competition.

In the United States, UK, and Canada, where research funding did not historically accrue to the position, beyond start-up funding at initial hire, faculty members have for at least a half-century needed to compete in securing external research funding—and that competition has become increasingly fierce with career (promotion) prospects hanging in the balance.

Among other things, massification has been associated with resource constraints and the increasing neoliberal assumption that precious public support needs to be competitively targeted to support the best research (let the market assure survival only to the fittest). And while pressures have increased globally to introduce competition, particularly for scientific research funding, there remain wide swaths of the global academic landscape where little competition exists, including most universities in Russia, India, and also Japan and China (where competition is largely limited to the elite subsector of the universities).

The net effect has been one of increasing vertical stratification both within national systems and more pointedly within categories of universities. Universities are increasingly ranked and judged in the marketplace by the research dollars won by their faculty as well as by the latter's production of refereed articles and scholarly citations—a great and increasingly globalized race to the top. It is difficult to overemphasize the extent to which this "new" (and ever-fiercer) competition has become a driver of academic life in some systems.

Another—and more easily measureable—aspect of competition is reflected in faculty compensation. In France, Russia, Germany, Japan, and India, faculty compensation has been, and largely remains, tied to nationally regulated pay scales where seniority is the decisive arbiter (in Germany and France it is directly tied to the civil service). Opportunities have mushroomed for "competitive" add-ons to regular compensation. At one extreme, in China's 985 and 211 universities, faculty may be paid directly—and handsomely—for each refereed journal article they produce in an English-language journal as one more jewel in the institutional crown. In France, recent reforms have placed budgetary control increasingly in the hands of campus administrations, which can now provide discretionary salary adjustments for the most productive academic staff. In Germany, while salaries may be regulated by the government, universities can offer professors a variety of work benefits, including funding for research assistants and laboratory expenses. Most Canadian faculty are unionized, and salary is largely determined by rank and seniority along a salary grid, but it is sometimes supplemented by modest merit awards and consulting activities. In the United States and UK, professors can earn supplementary salary paid by external consulting fees, and merit pay bonuses are emerging that seek to link compensation to performance metrics on an annual basis. Moreover, in these latter systems, external research funding allows for substantial supplements to the "regular" salaries of those who have successfully competed for them.

A third characteristic of academic work that emerges across these chapters is its *organizational nexus*: relative collegiality versus hierarchy. In Germany and Russia, and to large extent in China, the small number of professors at the top rule oligarchically; in Canada and the United States, academic departments typically operate on principles of collegiality through consensus (the voice of entry-level ranks equaling the voices of the most senior colleagues). The remaining five countries—France, India, Brazil, Japan, and the UK fall somewhere in between. In France, Japan, and India, civil service rules and employment legislation largely provide outside rules that circumscribe decision making around workload and the like. In the UK, governance reforms have led to increased managerialism, and academic department heads often play an influential role in decision making at the department level. Clark (1983) indeed anticipated a trend away from the chair system toward departmental forms of organization in response to the dysfunctional fragmentation that ensues from ever-differentiating academic fields and subfields— and new and emerging combinations of multidisciplinary specialties—and the associated stresses on integration and coordination.

This organizational nexus (collegiality/hierarchical) variable is largely related to a fourth variable that defines the character of academic work: the relative *degree of professional autonomy* with which it is pursued and the *academic freedom* afforded to express unpopular points of view in teaching and/or research.[1] In Germany, the UK, the United States, Canada, France, and Japan—and in India probably as well—professional autonomy for those on permanent appointments is high, as is academic freedom. In some systems, such as the UK, professional autonomy may be negatively impacted by increasing managerialism and related accountability mechanisms. In Russia and China, both professional autonomy and academic freedom are relatively lower, although individual faculty oligarchs (the chairs) may operate with considerable discretion (personal autonomy).

A fourth dimension along which academic work varies cross-nationally is its *relative uniformity or heterogeneity* across the national system—uniformity across each of the above four defining characteristics. Uniformity may be viewed *across* institutional types, but also *within* institutional types, including the university sector. So, in Canada, Germany and the "new" France, at one extreme (high research orientation) and Russia (low research orientation), on the other, the character of academic work is uniform across the university sector. In the United States, Brazil, China, and India, the character of academic work varies by location within the national university system: in China it is determined by whether it takes place in a regional university or a 985 university; in India by whether the institution is "of national importance" or a state university or private; in Brazil by whether it is a federal university or private university; and in the United States by whether it is a research-intensive university or a teaching-oriented university. What this means is that the work role of professors in some systems is invariant by type of institution or its rank within type, while in others the work role differs markedly by institutional location.

To what extent, and in what ways, are these five defining dimensions of academic work related to one another? To what extent do variations in each cohere in identifiable models of how academic work is conducted (constructed) across national settings? To what extent is each dimension independent of or substantially interrelated with the others? And to what extent do the 10 countries represented here reflect distinctive models of academic work? Conceptually, there certainly appears to be a close association between a high emphasis on research, high competitiveness, high professional autonomy, and academic freedom. Canada, the United States, Germany, and—to a lesser extent—the UK have as overall systems valorized research for decades and have promoted academic competition amid high degrees of academic freedom and professional autonomy.

Relative uniformity of academic work has characterized the Canadian and German systems, but much less so the US and UK systems. Russia, India, Japan, Brazil, and China—national systems built with a primary focus on higher education at the undergraduate level—have historically emphasized neither research nor competition in their university systems, although as we have suggested this is rapidly changing in the face of globally competitive market forces, at least for an elite cluster of institutions.[2] Among these five systems, however, there are substantial differences in overall autonomy and academic freedom.

Emerging Models of Academic Careers

Beyond the five defining variables above that we argue substantially encompass the variation in academic work across ten nations, these chapters also suggest a few key defining variables that encompass the variation in academic careers. First, of course (and most elementally), is the cross-national variation in *defining the point of entry to an academic career and the requisite qualifying credential*. The entry phase into the academic profession is dramatically different among the countries included in this study. In Germany, the majority PhD candidates are considered junior academic staff (which is also the case in some other northern European countries) and supported by research or teaching assistantships, though about 40 percent of doctoral candidates do not have a formal status with the university (other than working with a doctoral supervisor). In some countries, the PhD is a preferred but far from essential prerequisite to entering an academic career; it is possible to begin an academic career with an undergraduate degree at some state universities in Brazil, and roughly half of all professors in Russia do not have a PhD, while the doctorate is strongly preferred, but not necessary in India. In many countries (Canada, China, France, United States, United Kingdom), the PhD is regarded as the qualifying credential for almost all continuing academic appointments. Competition for tenure-stream positions in the United States and Canada frequently means that successful candidates will have a PhD but also a record of research publication and teaching experience obtained through contract (and often precarious) teaching or research positions, or through some form of postdoctoral appointment. For those entering an academic career in Germany, the completion of the doctorate is followed by a period of contract work in a university while completing the *habilitation* (which is still required in some fields), a junior professorship, or developing the roughly equivalent profile of qualifications and experience associated with being considered for a position as a professor.

In terms of the comparative analysis of academic work, these differences suggest that the level of education and experience varies dramatically for early career faculty in different countries. Individuals holding the junior academic rank in Brazil may have only an undergraduate education, while new professors in Germany will have considerable teaching and research experience. A junior academic in Russia may be hired without a PhD, then work to complete the doctorate during the first stage of an academic career, while roughly one in six will also go on to complete the second doctoral degree, Russia's version of the German habilitation. In France and India, state licensure or examinations provide further assurance that candidates have the requisite qualifications for entry into the academic career—although in India PhD holders are exempt from the national qualifying examination. In short, these differences in terms of entry-level qualifications and early-career structures and transitions must be taken into account in international comparative studies of academic work and the professoriate.

Notwithstanding the point of induction and initial qualification, perhaps the most basic defining characteristic of academic careers across national systems is *the presence or absence of a defined career pathway for new entrants*. In Canada and, to a lesser extent in the United States, Japan, and India, there is a defined pathway and timetable for career progression for those who enter the academic profession in what is variously termed a "career-ladder" or "tenure-track" position, which is nearly always a full-time position and nearly always requires the terminal PhD degree. Recruitment to entry-level positions at universities in these national systems tends to be external/broad in scope, that is, not limited to those already affiliated with the university—as, for example, doctoral students—and clearly competitive, constituting what labor economists characterize as an "external" labor market.[3] In many countries this external labor market for entry positions is primarily national (Japan, India, Brazil, China), though in some countries (United States and Canada) these searches may be international in scope.

After entering the profession, a career ladder assumes that if incumbents distinguish themselves as teachers and/or scholars (or simply, as in the case of India and France, remain on the job), they can be recognized with promotion in an orderly progression and rewarded commensurately with increased salary in predictable ways. That leads to the version of an academic career that is intimately anchored in the context of a single organization—often that of one's initial employment—which becomes a competing locus of loyalty to the academic discipline. In other words, while there is an external labor market for entry into the academic profession, the career ladder assumes an internal labor market where junior faculty move up the various ranks through internal processes within the same institution. External searches/appointments may still take place to fill specific needs, but the normal career pathway is to be promoted through the ranks within the institution. Perhaps the most extreme example of an internal market is in Russia, where universities not only frequently hire their own doctoral graduates, but the entire career, including promotion steps, commonly take place inside the same university.[4]

At the other extreme are systems where there are clearly defined academic career pathways but where promotion takes place by obtaining a new position at a higher rank. Pathways are structured but unpredictable. To the extent that it is possible to plan a career, it is one that is primarily disciplinary and national in its locus rather than institutional. Such a national/disciplinary career can be structured predictably, for example, as part of the national civil service in France or be relatively unstructured and unpredictable, such as in Germany where junior scholars often move through a series of contract positions while they complete the habilitation or obtain the profile of qualifications and experience that is needed before seeking a professorship. After the individual is appointed as a professor, promotion up through the structure of professorial ranks usually requires obtaining a more senior position at another university. Policies create an external labor market for promotion, where the most senior positions are filled by candidates from other universities. And this distinction between an institutional and a disciplinary/national career context is crucial for understanding the relationship of academics to their home institutions and to their academic field. Moreover, those nations that support a disciplinary/national career structure typically support a career pyramid, meaning that the proportion of all academic positions in the top rank (typically full professor) is decidedly small—in the case of Germany, for example, about 10 percent. In Germany and France, the room at the top of the pyramid is defined by strictly controlled and nationally budgeted vacancies, in sharp contrast to the situation in Canada, for example, where the number of full professors at a university may be far larger than the number of assistant professors.

Another critical aspect of career progression and, as it turns out, overall educational quality of the national system—whether or not there is an available ladder that specifies promotions and their timing—is the *degree of competitiveness* that is built in. Is advancement the result of marking time and checking off boxes? Or is it a recognition of superior performance in relation to one's peers—whether local or national? Are "the best" rewarded commensurately? Thus, while promotion to higher ranks in the United States and Canada depends on individual performance and not whether a relevant "high slot" already exists, it entails systematic and wide-ranging evaluations of academic work, and incumbents are assessed competitively against the highest standards of the institution and the discipline. In that sense, then, while promotion may be a function of the individual "meeting normative standards" (Musselin, 2010), it remains inherently competitive vis-à-vis a mental model of academic quality. In national settings that do not have a clear career pathway, achievement of a higher rank can be either extremely competitive, as it is in Germany or France, or markedly uncompetitive, as it is in China, Japan, and Brazil (outside the elite research universities).

A final dimension along which academic careers vary is *the relative job security they offer*, as distinguished from whether they offer a clear pathway to professional growth and upward mobility in the profession. Thus, for example, as a result of their civil service status, the entry-level *maîtres de conférences* in France have job security, but there is no certainty that the individuals will move up the clear pathway of promotion to higher ranks. They can remain in that job for their entire career—performing the identical functions at slightly increasing levels of compensation. On the other hand, the entry-level, doctoral student or research associate in the German[5] or Russian system has no such assurance—their job is subject to the whims of the professor under whom they work and the vagaries of external and/or state funding (or, in the Russian case, student enrollment in subsequent semesters!). Quite beyond the prospect of a pathway to upward mobility, the threat of basic job insecurity—or the prospect of lifetime security even in a marginally palatable position—powerfully shapes career attitudes and incentives. Job security provides a foundation for establishing long-term programs of research, sustained collaborations, and an affiliation with the academic unit and institution, positive work attributes that would be far more challenging in a precarious employment situation.

When we examine the 10 nations in our study against these dimensions of academic careers, are there definable models that emerge? Surely one obvious, if infrequent, model that characterizes systems that have focused primarily on the undergraduate education function is the academic career as *secondary* career, which is the dominant pattern in Brazil and, to a lesser extent, in Russia and India. At the other extreme is the model of the highly structured, and exclusive/primary, academic career, as found in the United States, Canada, and the UK, in which there are well-defined guideposts and schedules once entry is achieved in a pathway toward professional growth and enhancement of professional status. A variant on this is the "civil service" model, where an "external" regulated hierarchy of statuses exists, as do rules designed outside the university sector for movement within and across statuses for university staff careers. The civil service model is clearly represented by France—and, to some extent, by India. While it usually provides job security, it may not provide opportunities for upward mobility and professional growth. A third model is the largely unstructured academic career found in Germany, which Enders and Musselin (2008) refer to as the "survivor model," where the ultimate prize is enviable and rare, but a serious possibility for something less than 10 percent of those who enter doctoral education.

National Context and System Characteristics That Shape Variations in Academic Work and Careers

While many of the key ideas and concepts emerging from our analysis of the ten national cases were directly related to the structure of academic careers and career pathways, a number of key differences emerged in terms of fundamental features of the national higher education context and how these features shape or influence variations in academic work and careers. These system-level characteristics include institutional diversity, stratification, identity of the employer, level of authority over academic career structures, unionization, and other social and economic factors, including equity legislation and the broader national organization of the labor market for scientists.

Diversity and Stratification

A quarter century ago, Burton Clark observed that expansion/massification of national higher education systems is always associated with system differentiation, and indeed institutional diversity—especially in regard to the emphasis placed on research—emerged as an important analytical tool in our analysis of academic work and careers in the ten systems included in this volume

Birnbaum, in his foundational work (Birnbaum, 1983), describes seven major types of diversity, but systemic diversity—the differences in formal institutional types or categories within a higher education system—is most relevant to this study. This *horizontal diversity* between institutional types within a higher education system can have important implications for academic work because academic careers and career pathways are frequently defined by institutional categories.

The German higher education system, for example, has two very different institutional types: the universities and the *Fachhochschulen*. The universities are comprehensive institutions with both a teaching and research function, offering a range of degree programs, including doctorates. The Fachhochschulen are sometimes referred to as universities of applied science and are more specialized institutions focusing on teaching professional programs for employment (such as engineering and business) and applied research. Academic work is organized in very different ways in each of these two types of institutions because there are major differences in the missions, goals, and scope of activities among these different institutional categories. If we focus only on the university sector, however, we note that all German universities have a common mission in terms of research and teaching, and that all professors are expected to teach and conduct research. The academic role is, in short, largely homogenous within German universities.

Such horizontal diversity has frequently been viewed as a defining characteristic of higher education in the United States. There is a robust private, elite sector and less prestigious private nonprofit and for-profit universities. The public sector includes a wide range of institutional forms, including community colleges, which offer the first two years of undergraduate education (and more recently full baccalaureate degree programs in some states) as well as technical and vocational programs, four-year colleges, and research universities.

Forms of "horizontal "institutional diversity can be found in many of the countries included in this study. Higher education in Canada includes both a university sector and a college sector, and the latter includes a range of distinctive institutional types that have emerged within quite different provincial systems. There are important differences between the state and federal universities in Brazil. The *grandes écoles* comprise the more elite sector within the French higher education system, and access to these institutions is selective in contrast to the comprehensive public university sector.

The basic institutional arrangements and the existence of multiple institutional types are key to understanding academic careers from an international and comparative perspective for at least two reasons. The first, and most obvious, is that the role and career pathways of faculty can be very different according to institutional category. While they are both called "professor," the career patterns of a professor employed at a Canadian college can be quite different from a professor employed at a Canadian university. The latter has been described in the chapter on Canada in this book, but the former are primarily teaching positions (with some expectations of applied research in some provinces) and these careers generally do not have the tenure and promotions provisions associated with the university sector. In other words, academic careers can look very different and have quite different structures in different types of institutions within the same system. There may also be major differences in the terms of employment and working conditions between different institutional types. Studies of academic work in the United States have found that community colleges frequently rely much more heavily on part-time (contract) faculty, sometimes with quite precarious contract arrangements, compared with research universities, where a larger share of academic work may be done by tenured or tenure-stream professors. Understanding institutional diversity and institutional types within a higher education system becomes essential for understanding the very different ways in which academic careers may be experienced within the same system.

Our study has focused primarily on academic work within the university sector, concentrating on what may be only a subset of higher education institutions within these systems. But when we look across systems, even within this narrower frame (band), there are clearly important ways in which universities represent quite different institutional types. In the French and Russian systems, the research function was historically associated with the academies, but the importance of research within French universities increased dramatically in the second half of the twentieth century. The role of research in most Russian universities is also gradually changing, but it continues to indicate that the role of research in academic work is fundamentally different in a Russian university (or most private universities in Brazil) than it is in many of the other systems in our study.

In short, institutional diversity, both within systems of higher education and in terms of systemic differences among institutional categories across systems, especially in terms of the positioning of the research function, is a key factor in understanding academic work and academic career pathways from an international and comparative perspective. Failing to recognize these key institutional differences can lead to fundamental methodological shortcomings in comparative analysis. The "university" is not a homogeneous institutional type, and so comparing academic work taking place within two very different institutional categories can become a comparison of apples and oranges.

While institutional diversity focuses on horizontal differences between institutional types or categories, the concept of stratification can be used to look at *vertical differences in status* between institutions within the same national category, and once again research seems to be the key factor for stratification that has the most important implications for academic work. Indeed, recent studies by Cantwell, Marginson, and Smolentseva (2018) of "high participation" national systems of higher education suggest that as massification shades into universal access, such vertical stratification may eclipse horizontal differentiation tendencies. Some systems have high levels of stratification within the university sector—for example, the United States, China, and Japan—and so there are differences by institution in research productivity and prestige that have implications for academic work and careers. High status institutions select professors who demonstrate the capacity to be excellent researchers and have high expectations for research productivity. Professors benefit from the prestige associated with the institution in which they work.

The situation is quite different for those employed at universities at the lower end of the stratification continuum. These institutions may be less selective and may have quite different expectations for research activity. The German system, in contrast, seems to have little systemic diversity in the university sector, and only modest levels of stratification. Some universities have more research activities than others, but the level of difference (or stratification) is viewed as modest. Academic work and careers are less impacted by institutional stratification in Germany than in the United States or China because the system is far less stratified.

The German universities are roughly viewed as equals, compared with the United States, where there are enormous differences in academic work and careers associated with holding a full professorship at the University of California at Berkeley compared with holding the same rank at the University of North Dakota.

The concepts of horizontal institutional diversity and vertical stratification are very useful tools for looking at the characteristics of national higher education systems in relation to academic work, but the important role of research in institutional types and stratification seems to be key in the analysis of academic careers. Different systems have made quite different decisions on whether research should be regarded as an important function of all universities (such as in Germany and Canada) or whether most research takes place in a subset of institutions (such as in Brazil or the United States). One of the common themes noted in all 10 national case studies is the increasing importance that governments have placed on research. In some countries, such as China and Japan, governments are taking steps to increase both institutional diversity and stratification by providing additional funding to a limited number of institutions in order to create "world-class universities." In others, research funding is highly competitive, and increasing investments in research have led to increased institutional stratification (such as in Canada, the United Kingdom, and the United States). There are increasing pressures on faculty to pursue research within both the French and Russian university systems. The increasing emphasis placed on the role of research within higher education, undoubtedly influenced by international rankings and by assumptions about the role of research and innovation in national economic development, has significant implications for academic work and careers. It also means that these institutional arrangements are shifting and changing over time.

Employer and Level of Authority

In our introductory chapter, we discussed the potential importance of employer identity (who actually employs academic staff) *and the locus of authority* over academic career pathways within higher education systems. Both concepts proved to be useful tools for understanding important differences in academic careers. Employer identity simply refers to whether the professor is an employee of the state (national or local in federal systems), frequently holding some form of civil servant status, or an employee of the institution. Using Burton Clark's (1983) notion of "levels of authority," we note that academic career pathways are determined at different levels in different systems, and that these differences can be quite important in comparative analyses of academic work.

In several of the systems included in this study, such as France and Germany, professors have traditionally been employed by the state and have civil servant status. Faculty in other systems, such as Canada, the United States, and the United Kingdom, are employees of the university. The difference in employer identity has implications for academic work; government employees have job security and frequently conditions of employment are established by the state, while protections of job security and conditions of employment may vary from institution to institution where the university is the employer.

There are also variations among higher education systems in terms of the locus of authority over academic career pathways. In some systems academic career pathways are determined by national legislation or regulations that prescribe the appointment, rank, and promotion processes for the entire system (such as France and Germany), while in some others these frameworks emerge from institutional policy, and there can be different processes in place at different institutions.

These patterns are rapidly evolving, and there seems to be increasing hybridization in these relationships. For example, while many German professors continue to be civil servants operating under a national career framework, recent reforms have resulted in professorial appointments at foundation universities where the university is the employer, as well as new teaching-focused contract positions. Entry-level positions for individuals who have completed the doctorate and are pursuing the habilitation in preparation for an academic career have often involved university contracts for teaching or research. There has been a growth in the use of precarious university-contract academic labor in French universities. Reforms in Japan have led to a transition from civil service status for national university faculty to a situation where faculty are now employed by relatively autonomous universities where issues of job security and academic career frameworks are determined by institutions.

That many of these employment relationships and career pathways are in transition only reinforces the importance of considering the employer and the locus of authority over career pathways in studies of academic labor. Whether the employer is the university or the state makes a difference in terms of how we understand key aspects of academic careers, such as institutional loyalty, the sense of being part of a national career system, job security, and perhaps even professional autonomy and academic freedom. Transitions and reforms to employment arrangements and career patterns need to be taken into account in international and comparative studies of academic work.

Unionization

Unionization is yet another important factor associated with the national context that has important implications for our understanding of academic work. Of the 10 systems included in this study, unionization shows up most prominently in Canada, where the vast majority of Canadian university faculty are members of university-based trade unions recognized under provincial government labor legislation. In some other systems, national (as opposed to local or institution-level) trade unions play an important role in decisions related to working conditions, salary structures, and, in broad terms, representing and advocating on behalf of academic labor (such as in Germany).

Unionization is foreign to the national political culture in some countries; in others, it is legitimized under national/state labor laws or, as in the case of "right-to-work" legislation in some US states, for example, legislation establishes explicit barriers to labor union development. In some cases unionization positions faculty as members of a broader labor collective of civil servants, or educational workers.

This notion of being members of a labor collective, defined either narrowly to include peer faculty or more broadly to include other workers, has implications for the professional identity of faculty as academic labor, perhaps operating in parallel (and sometimes in tension) with their affiliation with academic disciplinary structures and their loyalty to the department and university in which they work. In some cases unionization limits managerial discretion over important decisions related to academic careers through collective bargaining or advocacy and provides another form of power or authority within institutions or systems in combination with, or in opposition to, other more traditional academic governance structures. In the United States, there has been a surge in unionization activity among both contingent academic staff (full-time term appointees and part-time sessional faculty) as well as graduate student employees.

Other Factors

Our analysis of the 10 national systems leads us to believe that there are other key national context factors that have implications for the international comparative analysis of academic work and career pathways, but more analysis is needed to explore their implications for comparative work in this field. One of these is the *role of equity legislation or social policies* that, for example, play a large role in India, where there are hiring quotas designed to promote more equity in appointments to include specific historically marginalized groups. In other countries, national legislation promotes equitable practices in hiring or seeks to prevent discrimination on the basis of gender, race, religion, disability, and so on. There is a considerable body of scholarship on equity in higher education that focuses on the academic profession, but there has been surprisingly little comparative work in this area. Our sense is that equity policies and practices within national systems could be key factors in understanding academic careers, but additional research is needed to explore these factors in a more nuanced way that could be helpful to international comparative analyses.

In addition to policies designed to promote equity (or prevent discrimination) in hiring and career progression, there are also major differences between systems in how they address issues of maternity and parenting, policies that may have major implications for issues of gender equity within academic work. The availability of maternity/parental leave, the manner in which these leaves are addressed (or not) within tenure and promotion policies, national (or institutional) initiatives related to childcare, and the like, have implications for academic careers and the participation of women as full members of the professoriate. Comparative analyses of these policies and their impact on academic work and careers could make an important contribution to scholarship in this area.

Beyond public policy approaches to equity, there is the matter of how the labor market for scientists, in particular for PhDs, is organized. National economies vary in the *"elasticity" (breadth or narrowness) of the labor market* for doctorally trained scientists and professionals. In the United States, the United Kingdom, Canada, and Germany, doctorally trained professionals have strong employment opportunities outside the university sector in business/industry and government, and the university sector must, in effect, compete with these other sectors in attracting scientific talent. That provides academics in these national settings not only with leverage to be employed in negotiating their position with their academic employer, but also alternative employment—often with more lucrative compensation and benefits. Thus, it is not unusual in the United States or Canada for an academic—particularly in the physical and biological sciences and engineering—to move in and out of academe during a career. In Russia or China, the labor market would be much more narrowly limited to the university sector, and the opportunity structure for scientific careers would be much more circumscribed.

One factor that we had anticipated would have implications for the study of academic careers was the federal (where authority is divided between two or more levels of government) versus the unitary national political structure of the jurisdiction, especially for those systems where the local government plays a major role in certain aspects of higher education policy (such as in Canada, Germany, and the United States). While there are certainly differences between federal and national systems in many areas of higher education policy (see, e.g., Watts, 1992; Goedegebuure, Kaiser, Maassen & de Weert, 1994), our reading of the 10 case studies in this volume suggests that the variations between academic career structures in different local systems within federations are relatively modest, perhaps because the academic labor market tends to be more national than local and because there are mimetic, isomorphic pressures for relatively common career structures within federal systems.

Implications

In concluding this volume, the foregoing analyses raise at least two obvious questions. First, how does the framework that we have derived inductively from the analysis of 10 national case studies square with earlier comparative inquiries concerning the academic profession? Are our insights relatively consistent with earlier work? In what ways, if any, do they diverge or provide greater clarity or focus? Second, what are the implications of this framework moving forward on strengthening the comparative study of the global academic profession? As we write, the APIKS (Academic Profession in the Knowledge Society) survey of the academic profession in some 30 countries across the globe is proceeding. Large empirical data files will be available before 2020 that enable the most comprehensive empirical analysis of the academic profession worldwide ever undertaken. To what extent, and in what ways, will our ever more sophisticated and nuanced understanding of the essential building blocks of academic work and careers allow us to press these new data reserves into service to understand both the differences and similarities between academic work in different systems and allow us to assess the extent to which we are moving to a truly "globalized" academic profession that supersedes national borders?

Congruence with Previous Studies

In many respects, our analyses echo and corroborate the early pioneering work of Joseph Ben-David (1977), Burton Clark (1983), and Christine Musselin (2010). It was, after all, Ben-David who identified the focus on research versus teaching as the primary basis for differentiating between the German, French, British, and US systems. Ben-David's analysis identified the German system as rooted in research, the French in teaching, and the British and American as hybrids; and in the intervening 40 years, as our 10 cases demonstrate (but especially in the past decade), the focus on research has grown across all systems with the emergence of the "world-class university" movement (Altbach & Salmi, 2011). Even in those systems that have historically been oriented to teaching and preparing graduates for labor market entry (e.g., Brazil, Russia, China, and Japan), elite subsectors with a strong emphasis on research that are meant to take their place in the global higher education marketplace have arisen and assumed a critical role in the re-alignment of the national system. Indeed, it is this *second-order* focus on research that we identified as the single most defining characteristic that is shaping—and reshaping—the nature of academic work. And that ascendance of research, as echoed by Burton Clark, has contributed to emerging increases in both the horizontal and vertical integration of national systems even in historically homogenous systems such as Russia, France, and the German university sector.

Looking ahead from the early 1980s, Burton Clark foresaw that the expansion of higher education globally (massification) would spawn increasing system differentiation—the establishment of new types/categories of institutions and a concomitant differentiation in the structure of knowledge as entirely new fields emerged and existing fields subdivided into ever more specialized subfields. Expansion and differentiation would be accompanied by an increasingly intrusive role of the state as higher education became too important to protect it from politics; faculty oligarchy would likely decline while the market mechanisms for attracting student consumers and negotiating institutional reputation would grow.

On most of these points, Clark was prescient: national systems with a few notable exceptions have diversified horizontally to accommodate new markets by either establishing new types of institutions or repurposing old ones. There has been explosive growth in "new" disciplinary specialties and even the organizational principles for combining fields into disciplines have shifted as multidisciplinary fields of research—for example, biophysics—proliferate. The internal mechanisms (complexities) complicating efforts to coordinate higher education have multiplied. While initially governments sought to increase their direct role in coordinating systems—as Clark predicted—what he did not foresee was the growing recognition by political leaders of the limited feasibility of ever more centralized coordination amid the full-fledged emergence of the knowledge economy and the central economic role of universities therein. National governments in all but the most "statist" systems (Russia and the former Soviet republics) have supported devolution of coordination and control to more decentralized entities, including lower levels of government, and they in turn have increasingly devolved authority to "local," institutionally based management, sometimes staffed by professional managers (rather than part-time academics elected for a specified term by their peers). This has spawned the establishment worldwide of elaborate accountability systems, so that compliance is now decentralized and not infrequently certified by peer review.

Moreover, as state influence has waned (or at least multiplied the degrees of separation from the university), the power of markets has accelerated in the new knowledge/information economy—as picked up by Clark more recently in his work on *Creating the Entrepreneurial University* (Clark, 1998). That development has transformed both the incentive structure (compliance yielding to entrepreneurship) and the arena in which institutions/universities compete: they are now directly competing in the arena of scientific research and its associated applications. This has had at least two important implications. First, it has recalibrated the role of research in national systems. National systems that once focused primarily on teaching are re-integrating the research function into their universities and, thus, re-creating the academic work role and career structure. National systems that already accommodated the research function have become increasingly driven by that function (the United Kingdom, the United States, Canada, and, more recently, France) as the primary engines of academic work and careers in some if not most institutions.

Second, this development has fundamentally altered the nature and role of "competition" in academic work. In those national systems in which faculty have historically been relatively insulated from competition (Japan, Brazil, China, Russia, and India), it has instituted an entirely new—and "disruptive"—work reality: a performance orientation largely influenced by international (largely Western) standards of scientific research.

In terms of Burton Clark's "Iron Triangle" (the three basic forces of state, academic oligarchy, and market steering of the national systems), our findings suggest that, with a few notable exceptions, the role of markets—consumer markets, academic labor markets and institutional prestige markets—has grown everywhere, even in France and China, especially as arbiters of the value of research and as incubators of a booming private sector (India, Brazil) where, for the most part, anything goes. This realignment of the steerage of national systems relates directly to our finding of the increased role of research in national systems

While Clark does identify the role of the "market" as a national coordinating strategy for higher education (in contradistinction to the state and academic oligarchy), his focus is on the broader operation of consumerism and institutional prestige-seeking in the steering of decision making in the system, rather than on the competitiveness of academic work itself. What we believe is distinctive about our analyses is the advent of competition that is clearly emerging globally across at least the elite sectors of national higher education systems. This is a relatively new development, but one that in many historically noncompetitive systems (e.g., Russia, Brazil, or China) is nonetheless reshaping the character of academic work in at least the high prestige components of the system; however, it is also promoting heightened sensitivity to increasing vertical stratification.

These factors, combined, appear to be leading to an increasing fragmentation of academic work within national systems of higher education—fragmentation based less on the proliferation of knowledge (the spawning of new disciplines and subdisciplines) than on institutional differentiation and vertical stratification. Even individuals with similar job titles working within the same national system can have very different career pathways as a function of competition and vertical stratification within the system. Perhaps more important, we are seeing a rise of new forms of academic appointments, including new forms of precarious contract positions, often operating in hierarchical relationships with traditional academic career streams. While there have always been differences in academic work associated with the disciplines (a form of horizontal fragmentation of academic work), the combination of increasing competitiveness, the valorization of research and research productivity, and vertical stratification appear to be leading to increasing vertical fragmentation within the academic profession.

If our analyses of academic work are largely congruent with and update earlier work—with the exceptions of competitiveness and diversity of appointments—our analyses of academic careers offer some distinctive highlights. Clark first identified the interplay of academic fields and institutional affiliations as shaping the dual, intersecting loyalties of academic workers. Musselin (2010) gave concrete expression to those intersecting loyalties in her comparative analysis of the careers of French, American, and German academics. French and German academics were employed by the state and the Americans were employed by their institutions, meaning that the discipline at the national level was primary in the French and German system while the institution was primary in the US system. Moreover, Musselin was attuned to the relative competitiveness in the system, distinguishing carefully between the role of competition in career entry and in subsequent opportunities for promotion. She noted that while "external" competition characterized both entry and promotion in France, it characterized only promotion in Germany and only entry in the United States, wherein academics—however fierce the competition for their initial hire—were nonetheless promoted by their institutions based on meeting basic "institutional" tenure standards (irrespective of whether positions at higher ranks were available).

In the two decades since Musselin's fieldwork in the late 1990s, the locus of control over academic careers has increasingly devolved to the institutional level, whether through new arrangements for traditional appointments (the non–civil service status professor in Germany) or the development of new kinds of appointments (as in the United States). Moreover, competition has increased either across the board (as in France) or in the elite subsector of the system (Brazil, China, Russia). Indeed, we would argue that even in the United States the standards candidates for promotion must meet are rising and increasingly reflect competitive national disciplinary standards. What emerges, then, as distinctive from our analyses of the rise of competitiveness in academic work, is the decline of job security increasingly through the establishment of new kinds of nontraditional appointments that lack a built-in career pathway.

While our discussion of national context—rooted in an appreciation of horizontal institutional diversity, vertical stratification, and employer identity—echoes our scholarly forbears, what emerges as distinctive in our analyses is the role of unions (although this can be viewed as hearkening back to Burton Clark's "guilds") and the increasing influence of national social and economic policy reflected in antidiscrimination legislation and the openness of the national labor market to PhDs.

Moving Forward

What do these results suggest for moving the comparative study of the academic profession forward? They suggest two interrelated agendas for further research. The first, or substantive, agenda focuses our attention on the megatrends we have identified across our 10 case countries and the consequences for academic work in bifurcated or increasingly vertically stratified national systems. What does the introduction of competition (marketization and commodification of knowledge) mean in historically noncompetitive systems? It certainly makes for some awkward (heavy-handed) work policies in places like China. How do national systems adopt their policies to this new order? And how do faculty adapt to these policies?

As we have noted, there are important national differences in vertical stratification. In some countries, such as Germany, the level of stratification is modest, and one might anticipate that stratification has only a modest impact on the nature of academic careers among traditional faculty. China may represent the other extreme within our national case studies, with huge differences in prestige and resources between high access institutions and the elite, highly selective research universities. It would be a mistake, however, to view stratification as bifurcation, since there are many universities that aspire to become members of the upper echelons, or to move closer to the top of international rankings. One might anticipate that senior faculty at the elite end of this stratification—those at Peking, Tsinghua, or Fudan universities—are "global" research scholars with academic work roles and careers that have much in common with their peers at American, German, or Brazilian research universities. The same might also be true at the other end of the spectrum—the high access institutions where academic work is dominated by the teaching function and where competition within academic careers may be limited. However, much more research is required to understand the implications of vertical stratification on academic careers in terms of the middle ground, the large number of institutions within the systems of China and Brazil, for example, that fall somewhere in between the two extremes.

A similar issue arises in terms of understanding the implications of the growth of private higher education, especially in Asia (China and India), Latin America (Brazil), and in the countries of the former Soviet Union (Russia and many countries within Eastern Europe) in terms of academic careers. In some countries, such as Brazil, this sector is far larger than the public system in terms of enrollment. Indeed, the emergence of a vast academic "wild west" (to use an American phrase) in places like Brazil, India, even Russia and the United States (the for-profit sector) has yielded an entirely new arena in which academic work is practiced— one that we know almost nothing about! This is certainly an arena for future research.

Another megatrend reorienting the character of academic work across the globe is the proliferation of nontraditional academic appointments, frequently referred to as contingent instructional staffing, in particular the use of part-time instructors on a course or hourly basis. The 10 countries in this volume differ in both the scope and character of such contingent appointments. In Canada and in France, continuous presumptively permanent appointments still constitute a large component of all academic appointments and thus remain the center of the instructional workforce. At the other extreme, the critical mass in the United States has shifted decidedly to contingent academic staffing, with some three-quarters of the academic workforce now off the tenure track.

What are the consequences for the functioning of universities of this increasing fragmentation and stratification of the academic workforce? What are the implications for recruitment to the academic profession and the trajectory of academic careers? A related megatrend is, of course, the increasing specialization of academic work roles, typically associated with the nontraditional appointments. There has been a growth in, for example, teaching-focused appointments in systems where academic roles were previously assumed to include both teaching and research (such as Canada and the United States), and little is known about the long-term implications of these changes on academic careers.

A second, but by no means secondary, agenda focuses on methodological issues in developing and operationalizing a framework of common metrics for the comparative analysis of cross-national data on academic work and careers. Most generally, some variation on this framework identifying the dimensions of academic work and careers as well the key features of national systems must, we would argue, inform the analysis of cross-national data comparisons in some clear ways. The most essential task—as in any comparison—is to identify a common metric across cases, and it is precisely this search for a common metric that the foregoing analysis enables.

In that quest, we might begin at the macro level to clearly identify countries whose higher education systems reflect the research, teaching, and hybrid models of Ben-David—to the extent that they persist ideal-typically—and strive to compare countries that as a whole demonstrate a basic resemblance at the level of national purpose / academic mission. Operationally, that means that comparisons between nations such as Russia and Brazil (and possibly India and Japan) may make sense at the macro level—as might comparisons between the United States, Canada, and the UK—to the extent that we are careful to take into account differences in horizontal and vertical differentiation, employer identity (civil service), and so on. But comparisons between, for example, the United States, France, Brazil, and Russia need to take into account fundamental differences in the structure of academic work and careers for the findings to be in any way meaningful. Indeed, it may be necessary to search for common metrics in comparable sectors across national systems for comparisons. Thus, for example, it may make sense to identify "elite" subsectors (e.g., leading research universities or those striving for world-class university status) across otherwise heterogeneous national systems for cross-sector, cross-national comparisons. Such comparisons are likely to be significantly more valid and illuminating than wholesale comparisons across very different nations.

Similarly, the search for a common metric may require that we identify parallel academic appointment types (insofar as these shape work roles and responsibilities)

288 Glen A. Jones and Martin J. Finkelstein

across national settings whose systems are charged with parallel missions. Thus, we might seek to compare full-time academic staff in permanent positions (whether tenured or civil service) in research-oriented national systems—perhaps even comparing those with and without defined prospects for career advancement across national settings.

Given the large differences in entry to academic careers across national settings, we may need to carefully differentiate models of career entry and undertake cross-national comparisons of newly entering faculty across countries with similar and different career entry mechanisms. Much the same may be said about later career stages—be they midcareer or career exit. Thus, for example, we might strive to examine the career exit of full-time academic staff on permanent appointments in nations with national systems focusing on research and differing in mandatory retirement policies.

In building on the conceptual work of scholars such as Ben-David, Clark, and Musselin, our case studies have allowed us to identify those aspects of national systems and academic careers that make a real difference in how academic work is performed and how academic careers are wrought. As scholars of academic work gather previous unimaginably rich empirical resources through large-scale international surveys of the academic profession, let us press these conceptual tools into service optimally to advance our comparative understanding of academic work and careers in the most meaningful ways possible.

Finally, we believe that the methodological approach that undergirds this project, the detailed analysis of academic career pathways in the context of national higher education systems, has provided an important contribution to the study of academic work and careers, but that additional research is needed to both expand and deepen analysis of national systems. An obvious limitation of this project is that it focuses on only 10 national systems, and there is a great deal that could be learned by expanding the scope of this work to include other systems. We need to develop our understanding of the academic profession in Africa, the Middle East, Central and South America, and the like. Our sense is that this project has provided a foundational starting point for what we hope will be additional projects with broader scope.

We also need additional research that will deepen this form of analysis, largely through a greater use of national and comparative empirical data to analyze national systems and academic career pathways in greater detail. As we learn more about the concepts that are central to understanding differences in academic careers, we can then engage in more detailed and nuanced analyses of these factors, then empirically study the implications of these factors for academic careers and the academic profession.

Universities are increasingly positioned as central institutions in terms of social and economic development, and in terms of national research and innovation systems. Increasing our understanding of academic work and careers is essential to the study of higher education. This project emerges from our shared interest in furthering international and comparative analyses of the academic profession to find ways of advancing the field by identifying key factors and concepts that appear to have important implications for comparative study. We believe that this project has made an important contribution to this field of scholarship, but that moving forward means applying the concepts and ideas described herein to deepen empirical analyses of academic work, as well as expanding the scope of this project to include other systems.

NOTES

1. We hasten to draw the distinction between professional autonomy to control the content and pace of work without outside pressure and the freedom to express unpopular points of view or pursue unpopular lines of inquiry without fear of retribution. While we recognize that distinction, we treat them here jointly insofar as the two tend to co-vary empirically in our sample countries.

2. In the case of Japan and China, the increasing focus on research and competition is largely specific to the elite sector within the university system and is not generalized throughout the system.

3. This has historically been less true in Japan, where the hiring to faculty positions of recent graduates from the home university (inbreeding) has been quite common. Recent reforms have sought to "open up" recruitment but at the same time have undermined stable career paths upward. Similarly, in all but the elite research universities in China, personal and family connections may still shape entry to the *danwei* (or family organization).

4. However, the presence or absence of a career path, holds very different meanings (implications) in nations such as Brazil and possibly Russia or India, in which academic careers are predominantly non-exclusive—an addition to a primary career practicing one of the professions, such as medicine, law, business. In the majority of our 10 national contexts, the academic career is the primary career—although it may allow for a secondary career in consulting or small business.

5. In Germany, the rank of junior professor was created to provide junior scholars with independence from the authority of professors. These are not permanent appointments, but individuals have the opportunity to gain experience and develop the profile of activity needed to be considered for appointment as professor.

REFERENCES

Altbach, P., and J. Salmi, eds. 2011. *The Road to Academic Excellence: The Making of World-Class Research Universities*. Washington, DC: World Bank.

Ben-David, J. 1977. *Center of Learning: Britain, France, Germany, United States*. New York: McGraw-Hill.

Birnbaum, R. 1983. *Managing Diversity in Higher Education*. San Francisco, CA: Jossey-Bass.

Cantwell, B., S. Marginson, and A. Smolentseva, eds. 2018. *High Participation Systems of Higher Education*. Oxford: Oxford University Press.

Carnegie Foundation for the Advancement of Teaching. 1994. *A Classification of Institutions of Higher Education*. Princeton, NJ: Carnegie Foundation for the Advancement of Teaching.

Clark, B. R. 1983. *The Higher Education System: Academic Organization in Cross-National Perspective*. Berkeley: University of California Press.

———. 1998. *Creating Entrepreneurial Universities: Organizational Pathways of Transformation*. Oxford: Published for the IAU Press by Pergamon Press.

Enders, J., and C. Musselin. 2008. "Back to the Future? The Academic Professions in the 21st Century." In *Higher Education to 2030*, vol. 1, Demography, 125–50. Paris: OECD Publishing.

Goedegebuure, L., F. Kaiser, P. Maassen, and E. de Weert. 1994. "Higher Education Policy in International Perspective: An Overview." In *Higher Education Policy: An International Comparative Perspective*, ed. L. Goedegebuure, F. Kaiser, P. Maassen, L. Meek, F. van Vught, and E. de Weert, 1–12. Oxford: IAU / Pergamon Press.

Musselin, C. 2010. *The Market for Academics*. New York: Routledge.

Nerad, M., and B. Evans, eds. 2014. *Globalization and Its Impacts on the Quality of PhD Education: Forces and Forms in Doctoral Education Worldwide*. Rotterdam: Sense.

Shin, J. C., B. M. Kehm, and G. A. Jones, eds. 2018. *Doctoral Education for the Knowledge Society—Convergence or Divergence in National Approaches?* Dordrecht, Netherlands: Springer.

Watts, R. 1992. "The Federal Context for Higher Education." In *Higher Education in Federal Systems: Proceedings of an International Colloquium Held at Queen's University, May 1991*, ed. D. Brown, P. Cazalis and G. Jasmin, 3–26. Ottawa: Renouf.

Contributors

Elizabeth Balbachevsky is Associate Professor in the Department of Political Science at the University of São Paulo (USP), Brazil; Director of USP's Research Center for Public Policy Studies (NUPPs/ISP); and Fellow at the Laboratory of Studies in Higher Education, State University of Campinas. From 2016 until 2017, she was Head of the International Affairs Office at the Department of Higher Education, Ministry of Education, Brazil. Since 2014 she has been a member of the Advisory Committee of the international research network "The Changing Academic Profession and the Challenges of the Knowledge Society." She is the Regional Editor for Latin America (with Andrés Bernasconi, Catholic University of Chile) for the *Encyclopedia of International Higher Education Systems and Institutions* (forthcoming). She is also a member of the editorial board of the Springer book series The Changing Academy—The Changing Academic Profession in International Comparative Perspective.

Martin J. Finkelstein is Professor of Higher Education at Seton Hall University, South Orange, New Jersey, USA. He has taught at the University of Denver and at Teacher's College, Columbia University, and he has served as a Visiting Scholar at the Claremont Graduate University, the Research Institute for Higher Education, Hiroshima University, Japan, the University of Hong Kong, and the Gumilyev Eurasian National University in Kazakhstan. He is the coauthor most recently of *The Faculty Factor* (Johns Hopkins University Press, 2016) and coeditor of *The Internationalization of the Academic Profession: Trends, Issues and Prospects* (2013, with Futao Huang and Michele Rostan).

N. Jayaram is Visiting Professor at the National Law School of India University and Visiting Research Mentor at Christ University both in Bengaluru, India. He has taught research methodology at Tata Institute of Social Sciences, Mumbai, and sociology at Bengaluru and Goa Universities. He was Visiting Professor of Indian Studies at the University of the West Indies, Trinidad, and Director, Institute for Social and Economic Change, Bengaluru. He has written widely on higher education in India. His publications include *Sociology of Education in India* and *Higher*

Education and Equality of Opportunities: Cross-National Perspectives (co-edited with Fred Lazin and Matt Evans).

Glen A. Jones is Professor of Higher Education and Dean at the Ontario Institute for Studies in Education of the University of Toronto. His research focuses on higher education systems, governance, politics, and academic work. Recent books include *Governance of Higher Education: Global Perspectives, Theories and Practices* (with Ian Austin, 2015) and *Universities and Regional Development: A Critical Assessment of Tensions and Contradictions* (with Romulo Pinheiro and Paul Benneworth, 2012). Information on his research and publications can be found at www.glenjones.ca.

Barbara M. Kehm studied German literature, history, and philosophy. In 1990 she took up a position as postdoc researcher at the International Centre for Higher Education Research (INCHER) at Kassel University (Germany) where she specialized in research on higher education. After having worked as a senior researcher at the Institute for Higher Education Research of the University Halle-Wittenberg, she returned to Kassel as a Professor and then as Director of INCHER (2003–11). Since 2013 she has been Professor of Strategic Leadership and Internationalisation in Higher Education at the University of Glasgow in Scotland. She has published more than 30 books and well over 250 journal articles and book chapters on a range of topics, in particular on internationalization, higher education governance, professionalization, and doctoral education. She was Secretary General of CHER and EAIR and is currently a member of the board of governors of two German universities.

Dan Mao is an Assistant Professor at the School of Education, Shanghai Normal University. She holds a PhD in educational economics and administration from Peking University and has been a visiting scholar at the University of Michigan. She has scholarly interests in the governance, policy, and organization of higher education, in particular in the academic profession and university funding. Her work has been published in *Chinese Education and Society, Peking University Education Review, Research in Educational Development*, and others. She recently published two studies on performance funding in Chinese in which she analyzed the policy development and policy-making process from the perspective of multiple institutional logics.

Christine Musselin is Vice-President for Research at Sciences Po and a member of the Centre de Sociologie des Organisations, a Sciences Po and CNRS research unit. She leads comparative studies on university governance, higher education public policies, and academic labor markets. Two of her books were translated and edited by Routledge: *The Long March of French Universities* (in 2004) and *The Markets for Academic: France, Germany, United States* (in 2009). She published *La grande course des universités* by the Presses de Sciences Po in 2018. She was a Fulbright and Harvard fellow in 1998–99 and co-editor of *Higher Education* from 2008 to 2013.

Peter Scott is Professor of Higher Education Studies at the UCL Institute of Education and also Scotland's first Commissioner for Fair Access. Previously he was Vice-Chancellor of Kingston University in London and a Professor at the University of Leeds. His most recent book, with Jim Gallacher and Gareth Parry, is *New Languages and Landscapes of Higher Education* (Oxford University Press, 2017). In an earlier life he was Editor of the *Times Higher Education Supplement.*

Fengqiao Yan is a professor at the Graduate School of Education, Peking University. He obtained his doctoral degree from Peking University in 1998. He serves several academic communities, such as the Beijing Higher Education Association, China Higher Education Administration Association, China Association for Education Strategic Development, and China Institutional Research Association. His main areas of research are the academic profession, private education, higher education organization, and governance. His English publications include "Commercial Civil Society: A Perspective on Private Higher Education in China"; "Organizational Diversity in Chinese Private Higher Education"; and "The Same Term but Different Connotations: Cultural and Historical Perspectives on Studying the Academic Profession in China and Other Asian Countries."

Akiyoshi Yonezawa is Professor and Director, Office of Institutional Research, Tohoku University. With a background in sociology, he mainly conducts research on comparative higher education policy—especially focusing on world-class universities, internationalization of higher education, and public-private relationships in higher education. He established his expertise in higher education policy and management through work experience at universities and public organizations such as Nagoya University, OECD, and the University of Tokyo. He is a board member at Japan Association for Higher Education Research and is a co-editor of the Higher Education in Asia: Quality, Excellence and Governance Springer book series.

Maria Yudkevich is a Vice-Rector of the National Research University Higher School of Economics in Moscow, Russia (HSE), and Associate Professor in the Economics Department of HSE. She is also head of the Center for Institutional Studies at HSE. Her research interests focus on the economics and sociology of higher education with a special emphasis on faculty contracts, university governance, and markets for higher education. She is the author of numerous papers on the economics and sociology of higher education, published in leading Russian and international journals. She has been a co-organizer of several large-scale international research projects that studied different higher education phenomena in comparative perspective.

Index

associate professors: Brazil, 126; Canada, 249; China, 178, 179, 184, 196n10; India, 156, 157, 158, 160; Russia, 103, 104; UK, 79; women, 29
Association of American Colleges, 223
Association of American Universities, 239
Association of Southeast Asian Nations (ASEAN), 8
Association of Universities and Colleges of Canada, 245, 246
audits, 73, 78
authority: over academic career pathways, 11–12, 278, 279; disciplinary, 9; institutional, 9; level, 9; national variations, 8–9; personal, 9
autonomy, institutional, 10; Brazil, 120, 125, 126, 142n5; Canada, 246–47; China, 180–81; France, 45; Germany, 24–25, 30, 35; India, 151; Japan, 200, 203–4; in strategic decision making, 6–7; UK, 68–69, 90; US, 220, 221, 224, 232
autonomy, professional, 15; Brazil, 135; Canada, 268; China, 268; encroachments, 8; France, 54, 62, 268; Germany, 268; Japan, 268; non-tenure track and, 237–38; research, 36, 135; Russia, 268; UK, 268; US, 224, 235–36, 237–39

bachelor's degree: entry-level qualification, 177–78; from two-year colleges, 221, 241n1
backdoor entry, 155, 157, 158
Balbachevsky, Elizabeth, 18
Ben-David, Joseph, 2, 5, 174, 265, 281–82, 287
binary higher education systems: Canada, 245; Germany, 21–23; UK, 68, 70, 77
birth control, 165, 232
Bologna Process, 4, 8, 28, 50
Brazil: academic career mobility, 130–34; academic degree levels, 126–30; Catholic universities, 121, 141n3; consolidation, 125; differentiation, 120, 123–24, 124–25; elite institutions, 124, 137–39; as emerging system, 119, 139–41; federal universities, 120, 121, 123, 124, 125–26; institutional diversity, 124–26; massification, 122–24; private-sector academic careers, 136–39; private-sector system, 120, 124–25; public-sector academic careers, 126–36; regional public universities, 129, 130–33; regulatory context, 122, 123–24, 125, 141n2; research involvement levels, 130–36; segmentation, 119, 123; State of São Paulo

Science Foundation, 128; State of São Paulo universities, 142n5; system expansion, 121–22, 125–26, 140, 266
Brazilian Council for Research, 133
budgets / budget management: China, 188; France, 45, 47, 48, 64n4, 65n25; Germany, 34–35; lump-sum, 48, 64n4; Russia, 101
business sector, 237, 280

Cambridge University, 68, 77
Canada, 246–50, 260–61, 270–71; binary system, 245; decentralization, 244–46, 260–61; degree-granting authority, 253–54, 259–60; differentiation, 245–46, 253–54, 259–60; federated system, 10; graduate education expansion, 266; homogeneity, 250; institutional diversity, 259–60, 261; massification, 245, 251, 256–57; trends and reforms, 250–56
Canada Excellence Chairs Program, 256
Canada Foundation for Innovation, 255–56
Canada Research Chairs Program, 255, 256, 259, 261
Canadian Association of University Teachers, 247, 248, 260, 262n5
capitalism, academic, 6
Carnegie Foundation for the Advancement of Teaching, 128, 129; International Academic Profession, 128
chairs / chair system: Brazil, 141n2; Canada, 249–50, 255–56, 259; departmental organization vs, 268; endowed, 259; Germany, 38, 40n4; Japan, 204–5, 206, 207–8, 209; Russia, 103–5
Changing Academic Profession (CAP) survey, 2, 16, 17, 142n9; Brazil, 128, 129; UK, 83, 84; US, 235–36
CHER, 18
childcare leave, 164
China: Chang Jiang Scholars Program, 191–92; Communist Party influence, 180, 192; Cultural Revolution, 181–82; *danwei* system, 175; decentralization, 185–87, 194; differentiation, 173, 174–75, 176–77, 183, 189–91, 194, 195n3, 195n5; educational reforms, 173, 174–75, 180–81, 185–86; graduate education expansion, 266; history, 172–74; internationalization, 191–94, 195; lack of academic freedom, 10; lack of competition, 267; marketization, 173–74, 175, 187, 194; massification, 181–83, 185,

massification, 1, 4; Brazil, 122–24; Canada, 245, 251, 256–57; China, 181–83, 185, 194; Japan, 203–6; resource constraints, 267; system differentiation, 274, 282; UK, 69–71, 72, 78–79, 87
massive open online courses (MOOCs), 88
master's degree, 177–78
maternity/parental leave, 164, 280
"Matthew effect," 23
Max Planck Institute, 35
Max Planck Society, 32
mega laboratories, 113
MEMO project, 94, 117n1
mentoring, 185
Mercosur, 8
mergers, 186
minority-group faculty, 81, 232–33. *See also* marginalized groups
missionary universities, 172
mission groups, 68, 72
Mitterand, François, 58
Mobility of Academic Researchers in Europe (MORE), 2
multidisciplinary fields, 268, 282
Musselin, Christine, 2, 5, 174, 281, 284–85

Nanjing University, 190
Napoleon Bonaparte, 44
national higher education systems: bureaucratic coordination, 9; combined with global subsystems, 4–5; national variations, 8–9; structural characteristics, 10; unitary vs federated, 10
National Research Council, 241n5
national social policy, 15–16
networks: academic inbreeding effects, 109–10; alumni, 123, 201, 204–6, 207; China, 190; international, 190; inter-university, 109–10; peer, 127; research funding, 134
New York University, 4
non-tenure track, US, 48, 233–35, 237–38, 240. *See also* fixed-term appointments; part-time faculty positions

OECD, 8, 22, 40n3
Open University Japan, 209–10
Organisation for Economic Co-operation and Development (OECD), 8, 22, 40n3

outsourcing, 82
overseas exchange programs, 193
Oxford University, 68, 77

paraprofessions, 77–78
part-time faculty positions: Canada, 250, 257–58, 261; elite-oriented institutions, 138; India, 154–55, 157, 159, 163, 166; supplementary employment, 166; two-year colleges, 275; UK, 80–81; unionization, 250, 258, 279; US, 221, 223, 233–34, 236, 237–38, 239, 241n2; vocational education, 221
part-time students, 97
paternalism, 102, 109
peer review, 283; Brazil, 121, 134; China, 179; external evaluations vs, 111; France, 60, 61; UK, 82, 86; US, 223
Peking University, 185, 190, 196n10, 196n17, 286
Pell Grants, 241nn6–7
Péresse, Valérie, 43
performance assessment: France, 43–44, 54–55; India, 160–61
Poland, 69
postdoctoral assistants, 28, 29, 30, 31–32
postdoctoral degrees, 126
postdoctoral fellows: Canada, 259; Japan, 212, 215; unionization, 259
postdoctoral programs, expansion, 266
prestige, academic, 13, 276–77, 283–84; Brazil, 126, 127, 134; emerging countries, 128; UK, 76–77; vertical stratification, 285–86
Princeton University, 192
private higher education, growth of, 286
privatization, 2, 6
professional associations, 224–25
professional development: Canada, 249; China, 185; India, 159–60
professional organizations: France, 48; Germany, 36
professional programs, 211; faith-based universities, 260
professional standards, 15
professions, as occupational categories, 15
professors/professorships: Brazil, 126; Canada, 249, 275; China, 178, 179, 184; France, 49, 51, 53–55, 64–65n17; Germany, 30, 33; India, 156, 160; national examination for, 53–54, 64–65n17; UK, 79; women, 29
promotion: Brazil, 128, 130, 137, 272; Canada, 247–48, 249, 272; China, 179, 180, 184, 190, 191, 272; competition, 272, 284–85;

cross-national comparison, 271–72; in
developing countries, 128; France, 54–55,
272; Germany, 272; India, 160–61, 163;
Japan, 205, 207, 209, 272; research-based,
190–91; UK, 76, 79, 85; US, 236, 272, 285
publication pressure: China, 190–91, 194, 267;
France, 60–61; India, 166; Japan, 213–14;
Russia, 114–15
publications, "invisible college" and, 127
Putin, Vladimir, 113

quality assurance, 252–53
quotas: admission, 100; hiring, 15–16, 279

recruitment and hiring, 271; academic
inbreeding effects, 109; Brazil, 123, 127;
Canada, 247–48; China, 178–79, 184, 185;
competition, 284–85; elite-oriented
institutions, 138–39; France, 44, 54, 55–56,
59, 62, 64n11; Germany, 25, 32, 39; India,
156, 157, 158, 166, 167–68; international,
111–12, 191–92, 210–11; Japan, 204–6, 213;
new doctoral graduates, 59; and research
support negotiations, 34; Russia, 105,
111–12; US, 232–34, 236
recruitment of students, 86
religious freedom, 260
research: academic inbreeding effects, 109; as
academic work component, 265–66;
collaboration with industry, 211; competition, 283; dual appointments, 226–27;
faculty autonomy in, 238; international
faculty recruitment for, 111–12; Japan,
200–201; professional autonomy in, 36; by
US government, 225–27
research and development, 1
research assistants, 27–28, 31
research associates, 212
research culture, 72–73, 90
research function: Brazil, 276, 283; Canada,
277, 283; China, 277, 283; cross-national
comparison, 275–76; France, 275–76, 283;
increased importance, 277, 282; India, 152,
283; Japan, 200–201, 277, 283; Russia,
265–66, 275–76, 283; second-order focus
on, 282; UK, 277, 283; US, 277, 283. *See also*
research performance
research funding, 277; Brazil, 122, 133, 134;
Canada, 254–56, 259; China, 186–87, 189,
192; competition for, 238, 266–67; France,
43, 46, 47, 59–62, 65n22; Germany, 33–34;

for international faculty, 192; Japan, 214;
misuse, 189; performance-based, 59–60; as
privilege, 266–67; Russia, 98, 112–16; as
salary supplementation, 268; UK, 68; US,
225–27, 238, 239, 241n12
research investments, 16
research-oriented higher education systems,
281–82
research-oriented positions: Germany, 32;
India, 166–67; Japan, 206; Russia, 98–99;
UK, 68, 79–80, 81–82, 85, 87
research performance, 7; Brazil, 120; China,
179; Japan, 213–14; promotion based on,
190–91; Russia, 106, 108; UK, 72–73
research universities: Brazil, 121, 129, 130,
131–32; China, 176, 189, 190–91, 193–94;
Humboldtian model, 32, 41n8, 44, 64n6,
235; international exchanges, 193–94;
Japan, 205–6, 212, 215; publication pressure,
190–91; Russia, 95; US, 221–22, 239, 275
resource dependency theory, 190
retired academics, employment of, 154, 155, 168
retirement/retirement age: France, 57–58; India,
154, 168; Japan, 209; Russia, 106; UK, 78; US,
233–34, 239; vacancy chain effects, 57–58
Russell Group, 68, 72
Russia, 103, 104; Academie of Science, 113, 117,
117n2; centralized nature, 99–102;
differentiation, 94–96, 98–99, 114, 116;
diversity, 94–98, 114; internationalization,
111–12, 114; lack of competition in, 267;
regulatory context, 94; Russian Research
Foundation, 115–16; specialized programs,
100; Unified State Examination, 97, 117n2;
unitary system, 10; university excellence
initiative, 112, 113–15; university model, 173

sabbaticals, 249
salary: academic outmigration and, 237; Brazil,
137, 138; Canada, 249, 257, 260, 267; China,
192, 267; competition, 267–68; discipline-
related differences, 85, 187, 189, 237, 238;
family size–based, 38, 41n10; France, 52,
64n16, 267; gender disparity, 85; Germany,
33, 37–39, 267; India, 154, 161–66;
international faculty recruitment and, 111;
part-time faculty, 258; performance-based,
78; Russia, 103, 106, 107–8, 111; supplementary sources, 38–39, 267–68; UK, 77, 78,
84–86, 267–68; unionized faculty, 231; US,
227, 230, 237–38, 267–68